Praise for *The Power of Real-Time Social Media Marketing*

This carefully researched and detailed inquiry will provide considerable insight and benefit to a truly new era of marketing.

—Roger Weir
Professor and Creator of The Learning Civilization—
a twenty-first century differential learning ecology

Smart. Insightful. A must-read for media and marketers. Everyone will benefit from their real-time perspective.

—Alan Cohen
CEO, OMD USA

What do fish tacos, data storage, and disaster relief all have in common? Each has harnessed the power of marketing that amplifies via the real-time social web. These and many other case studies are part of Beverly and Teri's engaging new book that details strategies for marketers to understand, evolve and profit in the social age.

—John Gerzema
Chief Insights Officer, Young & Rubicam
and Coauthor of *Spend Shift*

Beverly Macy is a true innovator and thought leader in the field of social media marketing. She developed a one-day workshop for UCLA Extension as early as 2007 and she has continued to help us define a full curriculum on the subject. Her students have remarked they "can't believe how much she knows about this area" and that Beverly's classes provide "everything you have to know these days to get a job in marketing." It's no wonder Beverly received our 2010 Distinguished Instructor Award. I am delighted Beverly and Teri Thompson now have published *The Power of Real-Time Social Media Marketing* to make their valuable insight and expertise available to a broader audience.

—Cathy Sandeen, Ph.D., MBA
Dean, UCLA Extension, University of California Los Angeles

Technology is changing how we communicate, how we interact, and how we market. And nowhere is that technological change more apparent and meaningful than with the applications of social media. As stated a few times in the book, it is transformational. *The Power of Real-Time Social Media Marketing* offers keen insights in conversational language. Understanding what's possible and how to use social media will be essential for every marketer and this book can help hold your hand into this brave new world.

—John Miller
CMO, NBC Universal TV Group

Like it or not, social media is here to stay, and to make an ever-increasingly significant impact *globally* on our business and on how we do business. It needs to be understood, managed, and harnessed. This book tells you how. Read it!

—Zhihang Chi, Ph.D.
Vice President and General Manager, North America
Air China Limited

THE
POWER OF
REAL-TIME
SOCIAL MEDIA
MARKETING

THE
POWER OF
REAL-TIME
SOCIAL MEDIA
MARKETING

How to Attract and Retain
Customers and Grow the
Bottom Line in the Globally
Connected World

BEVERLY MACY

TERI THOMPSON

New York   Chicago   San Francisco
Lisbon   London   Madrid   Mexico City   Milan
New Delhi   San Juan   Seoul   Singapore
Sydney   Toronto

The *McGraw·Hill* Companies

1 2 3 4 5 6 7 8 9 0 QFR/QFR 1 5 4 3 2 1 0

ISBN: 978-0-07-175263-3
MHID: 0-07-175263-3

This publication is designed to provide accurate and authoritative information in regard to the subject matter covered. It is sold with the understanding that neither the author nor the publisher is engaged in rendering legal, accounting, securities trading, or other professional service. If legal advice or other expert assistance is required, the services of a competent professional person should be sought.

> —*From a Declaration of Principles Jointly Adopted by a Committee of the American Bar Association and a Committee of Publishers and Associations*

Library of Congress Cataloging-in-Publication Data

Macy, Beverly.
  The power of real-time social media marketing / by Beverly Macy, Teri Thompson.
    p. cm.
  Includes index.
  ISBN 978-0-07-175263-3 (alk. paper)
  1. Internet marketing. 2. Social media. 3. Online social networks. 4. Marketing. I. Thompson, Teri. II. Title.
  HF5415.1265.M325 2011
  658.8'72—dc22

                                                                        2010036614

McGraw-Hill books are available at special quantity discounts to use as premiums and sales promotions or for use in corporate training programs. To contact a representative, please e-mail us at bulksales@mcgraw-hill.com.

This book is printed on acid-free paper.

CASE STORY COMPANIES

CONTENTS

contents

ACKNOWLEDGMENTS

A special thank you goes to Julia Baxter, publicity, at McGraw-Hill Professional. She attended the Gravity Summit hosted by Young & Rubicam Brands in New York City in November 2009, where we met and exchanged conversation and ideas. Her immediate, genuine openness and professionalism shone through and were the keys that led to this book. All the people at McGraw-Hill have been stellar in their thorough knowledge of the publishing business and as patient collaborators with us. We are brand enthusiasts of Tania Loghmani, Donya Dickerson, Pattie Amoroso, Mary Glenn, and Ann Pryor.

We especially wish to express our deep appreciation to all the phenomenally brilliant contributors to this work. These are some of the most far-reaching minds that are flipping the world on its head. Their willingness to walk the social media talk of openness and sharing something of value provided the inspiration we needed to meet our time-accelerated deadline for this real-time, dynamic subject. A big thanks to Rodney Rumford, cofounder of the Gravity Summit Social Media Seminars for Business and Plixi.com, for having the vision to see the latent marketing need for these outstanding Gravity Summit brain banks.

The authors are also grateful for the partnership they formed in meeting through Gravity Summit and subsequently writing this volume. The collaboration and work-life experiences we were able to contribute formed a perfect complement of skills, abilities, perspectives, education, and vision. We truly believe we came together to be of service to the business and education communities by adding our point of view to the new and compelling globally connected conversation that is taking place today.

acknowledgments

We look forward to continuing that conversation with you, our readers, students, business associates, and others about your stories, experiences, and journeys into real-time social media and beyond.

PREFACE

You need this book. You will be smarter after reading it than you were before, and all the chatter about social media will begin to make sense. For those who already have stepped into social media, the findings we present to you in a conversational tone will broaden your understanding of the global opportunities available to all businesses and organizations regardless of capitalization. Whatever your position, you will feel the call to make a life-changing decision for an initial commitment to real-time social media, make a deeper commitment, or do nothing while the parade and the world roll by.

In essence, social media is about human connections, interactions, and stories that add value and have a positive outcome. Throughout the writing of this book a common thread linked all the contributors, interviewees, and subject-matter experts. Each one eventually used the words *transformational* and *journey* to express his or her experiences with real-time social media. During our own journey compiling the fascinating material presented here, we found ourselves transformed by our subjects' compelling stories. We are confident that readers will be transformed as well by the many "wow!" moments in the pages ahead. Let us know which ones spoke to you at our site: www.powerrtm.com.

Timing is everything. As authors, our vision in writing *The Power of Real-Time Social Media Marketing* was to present profiles and describe the thought leadership of both *evolutionary* and *revolutionary* ideas and leaders who are creating new ways of looking at old problems. It is a sophisticated view of what is happening globally, why it is happening now, and what it means to individuals, businesses, and societies. Worldwide, we are in one of the toughest business climates in decades. The global financial crisis has left many in ruins, but true leaders see opportunity in chaos and take advantage of a fluid environment to find innovative ways to meet market demands. The fascinating presence of free digital platforms as alternative advertising, marketing, and promotion tools could not have arrived at a better time.

As educators, we wrote this book as an educational tool that will take your knowledge of social media for real-life applications to the next level. It is segmented into chapters and case stories rather than case "studies," being true to the human storytelling nature of sharing experiences. Chapters address and explain what "real-time social media" is through the Now Lens, why the global shift is happening at this point in history, the power of consumer conversation, social media strategies that work, tools for measuring conversation, and what the future will look like through the real-time social media Next Lens. In an academic setting, instructors will find it a valuable tool for their own education and enlightenment. It is also ideal for classrooms, in which the case studies will serve as discussion platforms for students.

Successful case stories contain insights from brave, forward-leaning thought leaders who serve as your "Success GPS" to help you navigate your own path. Their firsthand experiences will give you a comprehensive understanding of what is involved in adopting real-time technologies so that you can make an informed decision whether to implement them. From independent business owners such as Nic Adler, owner of iconic The Roxy Theatre on the Sunset Strip, to automaker Mazda of North America, each has a uniquely persuasive story about how social media revitalized business and injected dynamic ideas. Other case story subjects are described below. After reading this book, we are convinced that you will see the value of adopting these tools and will be prepared with a rationale to present your cause up or down the corporate ladder.

For marketers, this book is a window into the colossal, global, and far-reaching change in how consumers and brands interact. No one really knows what is going to happen next; that is the third most commonly shared comment made by the contributors. It is encouraging to realize that there is a vast pool of remarkably visionary minds around the world applying their best thinking to solving the toughest challenges for individuals, brands, businesses, and organizations.

Instead of isolating people, we found social media doing just the opposite for industries and causes. It has brought people together to assist those devastated by the Haitian earthquake in January 2010; one tweet helped catapult $33 million-plus in relief. Long-standing professional journalists at USA *Today* are learning new skills and are able to interact with readers as never before. The global technology giant EMC Corporation transformed itself from the inside out by using social media tools to support project collaboration and streamline processes, with a real impact on the bottom line.

Wherever we saw a thoughtful approach to integrating real-time tools, interaction increased, ideas flourished, employee morale improved, and business thrived. In a nutshell, it really works.

You will also be encouraged to know that traditional marketing and advertising are not dead. Social media is a new distribution and communication channel and should be integrated into the company and/or organizational marketing plan. Print, e-mail, digital, search engine marketing, outdoor, TV, and radio are still powerful platforms that absolutely retain their value with the advent of social media and real-time.

We applaud all those who openly shared their journeys replete with challenges and successes. We are humbled by our role in sharing those ideas with the world. The conversation continues beyond these pages online and in the ether at www.powerrtm.com, where you will find detailed information and resources from this book. You can also follow and friend us on Twitter @PowerRTM and on Facebook .com/PowerRTM. We welcome all of you to our real-time global community.

Chapter 1: Real-Time Marketing: The Now Lens

This chapter will clearly answer the question, "What is real-time?" and all the associated implications for the global marketplace. Learn about the Now Lens as we present breathtaking facts about and insights into the international phenomenon and popularity of social media platforms as well as what they mean for business.

Hear from the "digital natives" who make up a "youth bulge" that is larger than the baby boomer group and learn how their lifestyle and expectations are fueling a great deal of this technology evolution. Consumers group together and create new trends and demands that can coalesce rapidly into amazing opportunity. Real-time marketing means reacting and capitalizing on these prospects *now*.

The new anywhere/anytime engagement that consumers demand has changed the model and handed corporations that are prepared and engaged in the conversation one of the most powerful brand accelerators and business development tools in years.

Chapter 2: The Way We Communicate Has Changed Forever—Why Now?

You will be illuminated and empowered after reading Chapter 2 because the evolution of the events that have led to this point in time will all make sense. Questions that will be answered include (1) Why now? (2) What does it all mean? and (3) Why is social media suddenly *everywhere*?

A seismic shift is occurring in communications and content distribution. This chapter explores the forces that have created the perfect storm for your brand to break through the noise and rise to the top. You will realize why the use of social media is not a fad.

Chapter 3: The Power of Conversation and Engagement

Learning to listen in real-time is a powerful conversational and engagement tool. Smart listening leads to discovering where the conversations about your product or business are taking place. When those conversation clusters are uncovered, one can gather actionable intelligence to inform customer relationship management, marketing communications, and even the enterprise itself.

Sending value-added information is not enough. This chapter dives deeply into what constitutes superficial listening versus granular listening, with recommendations on interaction for authentic and successful consumer engagement.

Chapter 4: Real-Time Marketing Strategies

This chapter is a must-read for anyone charged with generating business, seeking donations, or adding heft of any kind. A company's competitive edge will depend on its level of openness to changing the way it perceives and executes real-time marketing strategies.

For the first time, businesses can stick to a strategy *and* be nimble with real-time measurement tools that can help them change course instantaneously. Old definitions, strategies, and planning methods are being redefined, such as share of voice, and when it is necessary to consider tactics *before* strategy. The strategies described here work. More detailed methodologies and rollouts are discussed in Chapter 5.

Chapter 5: Real-Time Marketing Case Stories: Lessons in Leadership

Hear the exclusive, transformational stories of real-life campaigns and best practices from top brands and rising companies. Find out what they are doing that you can implement right away. Learn some of the challenges they encountered so that you can recognize and deal with them along your own journey. Their chronicles are truly profound, and many are told here for the first time in a complete and public format.

The American Red Cross: One Tweet Turns into $33 Million for Haitian Relief

CASE STORY   Learn in real-time how the *American Red Cross* used its listening engine to mobilize Haitian earthquake disaster relief in an unprecedentedly short period and turned one tweet into $33 million in donations (and counting).

USA Today: Publishing in Real-Time

CASE STORY   Publisher *USA Today* takes on the challenges of a struggling industry by being innovative and transforming itself from the inside out, one person at a time, through social media education.

EMC Corporation: Real-Time in the Enterprise

CASE STORY   The global technology giant *EMC* uses social productivity tools in unexpected ways to achieve measurable productivity results, employee loyalty, and much more.

Orange County Transportation Authority: Transforming Government

CASE STORY   Learn how the *OCTA* demonstrated government responsiveness with public e-volvement and turned its town hall gatherings into global meetings. Its efforts show how to do more with less and build awareness with free social media platforms that empower citizens.

Wahoo's Fish Tacos: Community Building through Extreme Sports

CASE STORY   *Wahoo's Fish Tacos* builds outstanding and long-term loyalty through unique engagement strategies with powerful social media tools combined with real-world events. Learn how spotting trends can secure mutually beneficial partnerships and global awareness as Wahoo's did with extreme sports.

Mazda North American Operations: Social Media Restart

CASE STORY   Sometimes a social media strategy needs a restart. *Mazda North American Operations* fulfills its active dealer group's request for social media leadership, guidance, and presence by focusing on the passions of brand enthusiasts rather than on the brand itself.

The Roxy Theatre: Entertainment and Business Revitalization through Customer Sharing and Social Media, or "How Social Media Saved the Sunset Strip!"

CASE STORY   *Nic Adler,* owner of world-famous *The Roxy Theatre* on fabled Sunset Strip, breaks down walls and builds business as a model for his community on the Social Strip and for municipalities across the country.

DIRECTV: Customer Interaction Transforms Business

CASE STORIES   Customer relationship management and product introduction can be amplified through social media. *DIRECTV* offers a number of excellent success stories about how social media has changed the nature of its business, resulting in a quantifiable advantage over its competitors.

Chapter 6: Analytics and Measurement

Yes, it is possible to measure conversation and determine its impact on the bottom line. However, the many new social media platforms can create confusion about what to track and how to measure success. Free and fee-based measurement tools and services are available that, when pieced together, offer a very clear view of impressions, reach, sentiment, volume, and velocity.

Also, the ability to gather real-time data and adjust strategies and media buys, often in real-time, by using sound analytics can help generate substantial revenue and produce savings at the same time. Information in this chapter will provide the intelligence necessary to assess and wisely select measurement tools for your particular needs.

Chapter 7: Viewing the Future of Real-Time Social Media: The Next Lens

Now that you have acquired social media literacy and understand how fast the social stream is racing, you will want to stay ahead of the game to extend your brand reach.

The Next Lens looks at new technologies that are just starting to trend as well as what the world could look like 1, 3, 5, or even 30 years from now, fed by real-time social media data, as in face scanning, holographic interaction, and the ability to measure "truth." It is a hopeful and exciting close to the book's journey—not an end but another beginning.

THE
POWER OF
REAL-TIME
SOCIAL MEDIA
MARKETING

CHAPTER 1

Real-Time Marketing: The Now Lens

Consider the following:

o One tweet—a message with no more than 140 characters— turns into $33 million-plus in disaster aid.
o A town hall meeting on transportation systems in Orange County, California, is viewed in Russia, Western Europe, and Asia.
o Formerly struggling competitors are thriving by sharing customers.

Real-time marketing is the unlimited, boundless opportunity of *now*. This book explains why the time has come for marketers to plant a stake in the ground as thought leaders for the businesses they serve and transition their companies into this new zone. It also reveals in broad terms what is changing in the global business landscape and how businesses can adapt their strategies to maximize the power of real-time social media marketing for the present and future.

In addition, the selected case stories in Chapter 5 represent real-world stories that are just beginning to surface and illustrate the explosive power of real-time marketing. They provide exclusive insights from innovative companies and organizations that are realizing significant benefits by applying new real-time strategies. Their stories highlight specific solutions and tactics used for tackling the complex and exciting opportunities that the use of real-time and the power of social media present.

Corporate executives, small business owners, entrepreneurs, marketers, advertisers, and consumers are actively seeking education and information on exactly what is required to join the conversation and harness the potential of real-time social media marketing because the world has changed forever. There is no going back. You cannot afford to be a wallflower. Step into the conversation *now*.

People all around the world are connecting via social networks and communities with lightning speed. Every day it seems that the numbers build. The swiftness is exhilarating because real-time is what is happening in this instant, where you are or where someone else is at the exact same moment, next door or on the other side of the world. This new speed is being combined with the development of free social media platforms that create virtual water cooler spaces where people share similar interests, opinions, reviews, and conversations. These two elements—real-time and social media platforms—deliver information faster than television or radio, with a broader reach and at dizzying speeds.

The merging of real-time with social media–empowered conversations has become rocket fuel for the world of marketing. Marketers now have the ability to target consumers with laser accuracy and link them to a brand with relevant and ongoing dialogue on platforms such as blogs, Facebook, Twitter, LinkedIn, Flickr, and YouTube. The conversation chain has no limits in its capacity to sweep up every demographic and ethnicity. Facebook was started by Harvard University student Mark Zuckerberg as a proprietary way for friends to stay in touch and foster relationships, regardless of the dramatic liberties taken in the film *The Social Network*, released in fall 2010. In late 2009, Facebook's fastest growing segment was baby boomers. As of July 22, 2010, Zuckerberg announced that the number of Facebook profiles worldwide had exploded to over 500 million.[1] That number is larger than the U.S. population. To put it in perspective, if Facebook were a country, it would be the world's third largest.

According to the U.S. Census Bureau's Interactive International Data Map, 52 percent of the world's population was under age 30 in 2010. These global digital natives are mobile, socially networked, and live fluidly in real-time. The human need to connect and share is evident in the various platforms that are being embraced around the world. OhMyNews is a favorite all-digital citizen journalism community in South Korea with tens of millions of profiles, while Renren.com and its new merger partner Kaixin are a leading force in China along with Kaixin001.com and 51.com. Google's Orkut is still Brazil's top social network. Hi5 is the hub of choice in Mexico, Peru, Portugal, Romania, Thailand, and Mongolia. Maktoob is the place to be in Libyan Arab Jamahiriya, Oman, Saudi Arabia, and Yemen. V Kontakte just passed Odnoklassniki as the most popular social site in Russia, areas of Eastern Europe, and Turkey. StudiVZ is exclusively for college students in Germany. The digitally socially active in Japan are on Mixi.[2]

The map in Figure 1.1 shows social media around the world.

1.1 World Social Media Map as of June 2010

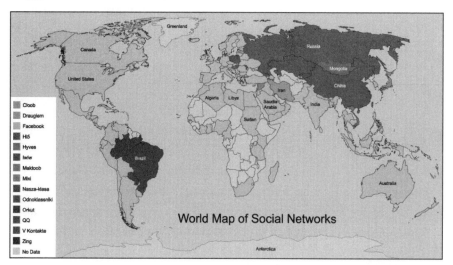

Since this human tsunami is occurring in real-time, marketers, content creators, and enterprises must view their world through the Now Lens. Consumers want directions now, search now, movie reviews now, personalized news now, sports scores now. People want it on their screen of choice—the TV, computer, smartphone, iPad, or Xbox—to share with friends, fans, and followers *now*. Consumers are creating or clamoring for content that is personalized, sharable, and available anytime, anyplace, anywhere.

Those who provide content and capabilities to these demanding consumers in real-time will capitalize seemingly overnight. Corporations that are prepared will discover that "conversations" are one of the most powerful brand accelerators and business development tools to appear in years. Conversations in real-time are shoring up customer retention and brand loyalty. More than ever, real-time marketing must be viewed as a business management function that contributes to the bottom line.

Companies that quickly learn how to master the art of attracting and retaining customers in real-time will be ready to generate sustainable, profitable growth and will end up winners in the globally connected world. Companies that don't, won't. *It's really that simple.* That is why it is imperative to take a moment to understand the following facts about and insights into these digital natives from around the planet. These are the people you will be marketing to and the companies you may be working for sooner than you think.

Global Perspectives

China

Mona is an 18-year-old Chinese native who is studying science at a community college in Southern California. Before her arrival in the United States, she had traveled extensively throughout Europe, Dubai, and Mongolia. As is typical of digital natives, borders are insignificant to her. Though she is far from her friends in China, she uses social media as a tool to stay close and see what they are doing by means of their status updates and photos. She uses the Chinese instant messaging service QQ and Renren, which is similar to Facebook. All her friends use those social platforms to avoid making expensive phone calls. Mona's goal is to continue her undergraduate and graduate work in America and then secure a job. If that does not happen because of fierce international competition for opportunities in the United States, she will return to China.

Sam Flemming is based in Shanghai and is the chairman of CIC, a company he founded in 2004 as the first and leading social media research and analytics firm in China. CIC is at the forefront of exploring Chinese digital culture, helping leading brands in that country such as L'Oreal, Pepsi, and Nike understand how social media can be leveraged across the entire organization. Sam provides this insight into the state of social media in China today:

According to the government run China Internet Network Information Center (CNNIC), which serves as the de facto source of China Internet statistics, China has over 420 million Internet users as of July 2010, making it the largest Internet market in the world. Important to note is that we are still at the relatively early stages of adoption, considering that while the United States has over 80% penetration, China has only 25%, with a total population of 1.3 billion people.

The use of social media is impressive. The most recent government standard statistics from the CNNIC show that there are 231 million bloggers, 130 million people on bulletin boards (BBS), 210 million people on social networking sites.

In China, with more people online and with more places to talk, those who are talking are more engaged than [in] any other market. Chinese consumers use native social media channels like the Xcar BBS community, Sina microblog and social networking site Kaixin to share opinions and experiences about brands by the millions.

More than just talk, consumers are even organizing themselves for group purchasing discounts and online/offline protests against poor customer service. The *phenomena* of the brand/consumer relationship that's *just beginning to happen in the* West has been happening in China for years.[3]

Africa

Gilles Bouhoyi is a Congolese-born entrepreneur who started his career at age 20 as an executive in the family business in Brazzaville, Congo. After completing his MBA, he attended the Certificate in International Trade and Commerce extension program at the University of California, Los Angeles, where he studied social media marketing. His interest in social media led him to conceive a social academic network project that got the interest of several colleges and universities, including UCLA.

Bouhoyi is also the founder and CEO of Phoenix Asset Management, a Los Angeles–based firm with a satellite office in New York that signed a partnership deal with Fidelity Investments to offer global investment products and services to private and corporate clients in Africa. Gilles contributes this insight:

Global popular sites such as Facebook, Hi5, YouTube, Daily Motion, MySpace, are mostly used for fun and to establish personal connections. Hi5 is more popular among Africans, though Facebook has recently been gaining market share. Daily Motion is way more popular than YouTube in Africa.

In the last five years, a new cast of users dominated by twentysomethings has emerged. These newcomers are entrepreneurs who use social media to advance and promote their real life businesses.

Venicia Guinot, 23, a Congolese-born student in marketing and communication in Johannesburg, South Africa, started a group on Hi5 called "Continent Noir" (Black Continent). Within

6

two years, she created an organization of the same name aimed at fighting poverty and promoting development in poor communities across Africa. Continent Noir uses its network of Africans across five continents to help choose projects to work on, organize them and look for funding.

Venicia has also launched an online magazine that she hopes will one day be the African equivalent of the Oprah Magazine: Tropics Magazine. She uses Facebook and Twitter to give awareness of the site and attract new visitors. Kwaku Chintoh is a photographer and web designer from Ghana who has launched "Moko Charlie," a bank of images of Africa to promote another view of the continent and show a face that is so often overlooked by many outside Africa. His image database is growing by leaps and bounds.

Still, much of the energy of social media in Africa is largely focused on politics. The last two years have seen the multiplication of sites like Congo World in Lingala which aims at connecting the communities of a particular Diaspora around many themes including business opportunities.[4]

India

Raj Suvarna, an MBA graduate of Baylor University who is currently based in Southern California, frequently travels back and forth to his native India. He offers this snapshot of real-time marketing and the growth of social media in India:

India is home to over 1 billion people where 18 official languages are recognized with thousands of dialects. The country is like a coin with two faces: On the one side is 42% of the population which is below the poverty line, struggling to make ends meet. On the other side is an India known for its dynamic, young, educated, multi-lingual, talented workforce ready to propel the nation's economy to new heights. India is only behind China in terms of GDP growth of 8% year over year (U.S. growth rate 3%). The middle class is expanding with rising incomes followed by an inflation rate that is not sustainable.

While MySpace was thriving in the earlier part of the decade in America, Indians were busy connecting with each other on Orkut (Google's platform for social networking) and Hi5. AIM is a popular instant messenger service, MSN was and still is the dominant platform Indians use to communicate online. Even the lack of high speed unlimited broadband and PC's in every home does not stop this generation of young Indians wanting their voice to be heard by being some of the most active profiles on Orkut, Facebook, and Twitter.

Hundreds of Indian celebrities are now tweeting and responding to their followers in an extremely informal and personalized manner bringing their fans even closer than ever before. Facebook fan pages are giving them a platform to discuss movie reviews, post pictures and even get feedback on what works and what doesn't.

The IPL (Indian Premiere League) of cricket has been a phenomenal success and its players, team owners and the governing body have done a wonderful job of connecting with the common man on player selection decisions, venues, and updates on times.

An Indian company named SMS Gup Shup has developed an easy way to communicate and share by giving the Indian consumer the ability to build a group via a regular text message, add participants and continue the conversation as a thread which all can participate in and see.[5]

Istanbul, Turkey, by Way of San Diego, California

Nahit Karaca, age 22, and his friend Onur Paskoy, age 24, attend one of the major universities in Istanbul. Nahit is entering his final year, studying urban planning; Onur is wrapping up his studies in electrical engineering. The roommates decided to spend a summer in America with jobs bicycling San Diego tourists around the restaurant district in four-seater carts. Nahit wanted to get a taste of California while trying to decide where to pursue his master's degree: Europe; the United States; or Turkey.

He, Onur, and all their friends keep in touch on Facebook or by texting on their mobile phones. While in the United States, the two young men plan to take weekend trips to Los Angeles, San Francisco, and Las Vegas. Like Mona from China, these are true digital natives who view the world as having no borders, are fluid travelers, and are always connected.

U.S. Hispanics and Latin America

Andrew Orci is the President CEO at Orci, a Los Angeles–based advertising agency that specializes in reaching the Hispanic market. He offers his insights into Hispanics' adoption of real-time social media in the United States and Latin America:

> Even before the Internet, Latinos have been intensely socially connected. For centuries, the Plaza or Zocalo was the place where people congregated to connect with their community. It's part of who we are historically. Today, Hispanics have embraced social media as a tool for expanding their connection to their social network. They have become technological leap froggers now that advanced devices are affordable and ubiquitous. They are flocking to wireless, laptops and mobile. For example: 24% of iPhones are owned by Hispanics. El Paso, Texas is the texting capital of the U.S. Hispanic use of Facebook has blown up, taking the lead over MySpace and Hi5. Hispanics are less engaged with Twitter because the platform doesn't offer the possibility of dialogue nor of more direct group interaction.
>
> Hispanics are the largest movie-going audience. They also index higher than the general market for accessing the internet through mobile (32% vs. 20%). This is mirrored in Latin America, where growth and adoption of social media is volcanic. Many

global brands fail to realize the opportunity that exists in this highly connected market. If a person in Texas buys a global brand and tells a relative in Peru, that person's relative may be the brand's next consumer. Hispanics in the United States have one trillion dollars in buying power. That is bigger than any country in Latin America. And with over 400 million Spanish speakers south of the border, the potential is enormous and their participation in real-time social media will continue to grow.

The Shared World

These youthful global voices demonstrate that static, centralized broadcast one-way messaging is a thing of the past. Now it is two-way, three-way, one-to-many, and viral for millions. The concept of "a friend tells a friend, and then that person tells another friend, and so on and so on" has truly come to pass—locally, regionally, and globally. Communication and data management are taking place in "the cloud," and the process is interactive. As a flock of migrating birds are held together by an unseen glue that tells them where to turn, dip, and fly, real-time conversations are flowing in the ether and cannot be physically contained. This is incomprehensible and counterintuitive for those in traditional business sales, marketing, and public relations practices.

In the new shared-experience world, consumers group together to create trends that can coalesce rapidly into unparalleled business opportunities. Real-time marketing will require swift reactions to take advantage of spontaneous movements, crazes, and fads as they happen. Going forward, success or failure is going to depend on how marketing and corporate communication leaders steer their companies into the dynamic world of real-time marketing.

Marketers are fast realizing that real-time is the antithesis of what they learned about journalism, marketing, advertising, and public relations:

1. Control the brand: message, position, reputation
2. Control the message: do not let it control the brand

Conversations about your brand are taking place right now regardless of whether your chief marketing officer or someone else in the company is driving the dialogue or not. The new communication shift has flipped the rules, with consumers in the position of defining both messaging and the brand. There is seemingly no control, and so companies around the world are trying to decide whether they can sit out the conversation (i.e., engage in business as usual) or should join the conversation.

A challenge for companies looking to adapt this new conversational marketing to old models is that they run the risk of wearing out their welcome in their eagerness to join the conversation and be relevant. They forget that conversation is a *dialogue* and tend to get shrill by trying too hard, selling too much, and speaking too loudly and too fast. On Broadway, this is known as "flop sweat." You are not sweating because of the bright, hot klieg lights. You're sweating because you're losing the audience. You know it, and they know it.

What is the downside to all this real-time communication? In a word, differentiation. Because everything is coming so fast—the digital fire hose is on full blast—brands' messaging runs the risk of becoming blurred in the minds of consumers. Today's global consumer is experiencing a head-spinning deluge of brand messaging. "I've seen something just like this but can't remember where" is the consumer statement advertisers and marketers all around the world dread.

The bottom line is that no industry is immune. For example, studies show that women make most health-care decisions for the family. If your business is health care, meet the mommy bloggers who are talking directly to the "power moms": women age 25 to 54 with at least one child who represent nearly 20 percent of the active online population in the United States, according to Nielsen Online. This demographic wields more influence than ever. "Consumer Empowerment" is one of the shingles hanging over the door of mommy, daddy, and parent bloggers, with more categories and demographics finding their voice every day. The effect of social media and real-time marketing on business makes it more important than ever to understand and strategize how your brand will engage in these newly formed communities.

Restaurants? Cruise ships? Meet Yelp, message boards, and Facebook wall posts. Government, disaster management, retail, manufacturing, financial services, advertising, entertainment—the list goes on, and all are affected by active consumers who are more than happy to tell the brand what they think and share what their experience has been in real-time. Power is in the hands of the consumers. They have discovered their latent clout with corporations and other organizations as well as the influence they have on their peers.

For example, it is well known that candidates in the United States from both political parties began to discover the power of online communities and fund-raising during the 2008 presidential election. In fact, Barack Obama raised more campaign funds through modest donations in that election than any other candidate in U.S. history.

However, it was not a matter of disconnected individuals acting alone and mailing their checks to raise $650 million. What was significant was the amount raised by first-time campaign supporters who reached out to peers online. Newly engaged donors offered to match the contributions of other first-time donors with an additional $25. For example, a person in Philadelphia would encourage a person in Denver who had never made a political donation to do so by matching that person's $25 contribution; then the new donor solicited a peer. This created an exponential donation chain of uncalculated proportions that has completely changed the model for political fund-raising.

The same horizontal escalation can apply to any business, cause, or industry. Engage customers in real-time with something of value that they can share, and then watch the magic happen in the horizontal conversation when that conversation is shared, passed along, and shared again.

Potential customers are out there asking questions, seeking advice, and gathering recommendations, ready to distribute information about every topic imaginable. Real-time social media platforms are handing companies a gift by enabling them to become part of the conversation. Once your organization realizes this, you are on the road to monetizing this new reality.

Real-time marketing is the execution of a thoughtful and strategic plan specifically designed to engage consumers on their terms via digital social technologies. *Digital* has become synonymous with *immediate* and the expectation of instantaneous content delivery. Add to that location-based social platforms and every type of information fed through the real-time broadband ether, and one can see how consumers know what is going on, where, by whom, and right now. Real-time *marketing* is distinct from actual social media *platform tools* such as Twitter, Facebook, and Foursquare. They are separate and different entities. A telephone is not the same as the conversation taking place on that phone. The telephone is a communication tool.

The phenomenon called latent market demand is also relevant to real-time content and marketing solutions. A latent market is basically an undiscovered segment. We have reached the point where real-time marketing and digital technology are feeding each other in a continuous cycle. Think of iPhone apps. Who knew that consumers would flock to and purchase iPhone apps in the billions *until* the apps were created? This is a classic example of a market that was born when the appropriate products became available to meet a need. This latent market is two sides of a coin coming together: (1) those who are on the lookout for something new and (2) those who are creating in real-time.

To reap opportunities, use the "fish where the fish are" approach. Is your company or organization developing real-time marketing and branding strategies, from products to promotions, to satisfy this latent demand for next-generation social media marketing solutions? Be in the space where there is vibrant activity, listen for a need, and then muster the corporate courage to step into real-time.

Dell figured this out by adopting social media in its early stages. It realized that its customers were talking *about* Dell, so why wasn't Dell talking *to* customers? The company made headlines by announcing that it was successfully selling used equipment via Twitter, reportedly up to $20 million-plus via Dell Direct. The sum, though impressive, is actually a fraction of Dell's total revenue but an excellent example of fulfilling a latent market demand. It was unclear if people would buy computer equipment via Twitter, but they did and continue to do so. One hundred to 200 employees push news feeds but also connect with customers on the platform. Because Dell is a direct marketer, feedback from its customers is all trackable and measurable. The next step was to expand the company's social media win into customer relationship management and product development. Dell successfully figured out that learning more about customers can move the revenue needle.

Another interesting outgrowth of real-time interaction is the rise of peer-to-peer recommendations, opinions, and reviews. *Reviews are the new advertising.* In the past, customer relationship marketing (CRM) evaluation forms were filled out (or not) by customers and then dropped into a suggestion box. The use of this method was accompanied by great doubt that the comments would ever be read by someone who cared. The mystery box has been replaced by the "I Like," "5 Star," and "My Comments" options embedded into social media platforms that are immediately reread, responded to, and passed along. People respond to thoughts from those who are "just like me." There is an inherent trust factor in receiving seemingly honest advice or firsthand experience and recommendations from people who are "just like me" instead of from a disembodied advertisement. The sheer mass of opinions leads to daily, hourly, now reviews of limitless topics, producing a veritable waterfall of information. Choice overload created the need to access millions of other consumers online or by mobile who serve as both filter and aggregator about subjects of mutual interest.

Here is what Larry Page, cofounder of Google, said at ZeitGeist Europe 2009 about the necessity of understanding real-time:

> I have been telling our search team that they need to search on a per second basis. They laughed at me and said it's ok it's just a few minutes old. I said no, it needs to be every second. . . . An advanced, integrated solution is required to be able to "listen" to a collective voice and to "respond" in a relevant and engaging way. As more web service APIs become available, the possibilities to effectively exploit real-time demand scenarios become very interesting.

Real-time streaming video is not just for sharing your child's music recital. The U.S. military and the Pentagon have adapted consumer-driven technology such as satellite television and digital video to give pilots, combat troops, and commanders at headquarters a real-time look at the enemy on computer screens. For the first time in warfare, troops on the ground can see the enemy miles away on live video feeds from Afghanistan. Predator drones in the Middle East are being controlled by pilots at Creech Air Force Base near Las Vegas, Nevada.

Even the Vatican has a branded YouTube channel. If two of the most historically traditional and private institutions in the world see the value of social media, there must be a reason. Whether your brand is new or established and whether it involves cancer medicines, commercial real estate properties, legal services, or sunglasses, you should realize that social media and real-time marketing are becoming a must.

Smart real-time marketers are embracing and enabling the sharing and instant opinion/reviewing process and converting it into brand loyalty, brand retention, and increased sales. With real-time and screen of choice offering mobile interconnectivity, new tools are required to craft messages that result in a continuing conversation between consumer and brand.

15

Twitter has established itself as *the* real-time snapshot for users of the new global database, propelling what people are thinking, feeling, and experiencing around the world. There are portal review sites mirroring every industry to share and receive opinions. This is complemented by geolocation or location-based platforms such as Foursquare and Gowalla that have early adopters shifting their habits to know what is happening where in their immediate footprint.

At the 2010 South by Southwest Conference (SXSW) in Austin, Texas, some attendees reported a shift from Twitter to Foursquare and Gowalla to receive real-time information about events taking place at any particular moment at the conference. Some reported that the ability to speak to friends at different venues almost at will by sharing their location information was making more sense because it gave them the ability to make decisions about what to do or where not to go on the basis of that knowledge. Also of note is that in spring 2010, Bravo TV announced that it was teaming up with Foursquare to try out social interaction and location awareness for key reality shows in real-time.

As a connected global society, people are sharing opinions, reviews, thoughts, and movements with one another all day, every day. That in itself is remarkable. We call it the real-time global brain. It represents a new form of openness that transcends media, politics, and boundaries and can serve as a powerful search engine, a breaking-news blaster, and an early-warning system. It is our collective intelligence. Every tweet, wall post, blog comment, and review is indexed by Google, Bing, and other search engines. A whole crop of technology companies are emerging to help marketers and companies make sense of this metadata in terms of influence and sentiment. Real-time conversations and posts may seem random, unreliable, or unmeasurable when in fact they can be quantified and analyzed.

As the body of metadata continues to grow, it becomes even more meaningful and intelligent, giving life to this dynamic global brain. There is a reason why, in early 2010, the Library of Congress of the United States announced it was going to archive all tweets back to

2006 and into the future. We are creating real-time data and historical data simultaneously. That is the Now Lens.

People and organizations are making practical use of real-time marketing data for promotion, communication, business development, awareness, lead generation, government services, and education. There is also a larger, more expansive view of how bits of information that are seemingly unconnected become an ecosystem with local, regional, and global implications for the individual, the corporation, institutions, and society. Is it possible that our flock of birds—random bits of information streaming in real-time—might actually be responding to predictable laws of nature?

Consider *chaos theory*: "the theory of apparent randomness . . . whereby complex natural systems obey rules but are so sensitive that small initial changes can cause unexpected final results, thus giving an impression of randomness." Chaos theory was born from studies in the 1960s by Edward Lorenz, who discovered it accidentally while investigating weather predictions. This biological-atmospheric sensitivity is popularly referred to as the "butterfly effect" to describe how a butterfly fluttering its wings in the Amazon can cause a typhoon in Asia. "Large output from small input" is the phrase most often used.

The supposed influence exerted on a dynamic system by a small change in initial conditions certainly can be applied to what's happening in the collection of data and the real-time global brain. The three key elements of chaos theory are (1) nonlinearity, (2) system states, and (3) how things are ordered when they emerge from chaos. In real-time social media, a small bit (140 characters) that was dispersed in a nonlinear fashion (Twitter) appeared random but emerged as an organized $33 million-plus American Red Cross fund for Haitian earthquake victims. That is stunning.

Just as chaos theory states that little changes can have big impacts, the same holds true in real-time marketing. Simply stated, little things can mean a lot. Here is another example. Imagine a drop of rain falling on the peak of a mountain in the Continental Divide. If the raindrop falls just a fraction of an inch on the west side of the peak, it will end up flowing out to the Pacific Ocean. If it falls on the east of the peak, it will end up in the Gulf of Mexico. A very slight change in initial position can have a drastic change on the final outcome and a thus produce a potentially major impact.

We are living chaos theory in real-time with the presence of social communities and digital platforms that deliver communication in its multitude of forms almost as fast as thought. Real-time marketing is tasked with being an explorer, searching for innovation, market niches, diversity, alliances, acquisitions, and long-term forecasting in an unknown future. This requires disrupting traditional methods of planning, media buys, and customer relations. Standard marketing strategies and tactics are inadequate in this changing time. In complex, turbulent environments, speed in recognizing opportunities and responding is essential. At times, this will require flipping the model, such as starting with a new tactic and working backward to devise a strategy. The global business environment requires stakeholders to co-create the new real-time marketing blueprint at nano speed.

The case stories in Chapter 5 offer insightful, detailed examples of how uncontrolled bits of data are being measured and utilized to affect sales, brand awareness, and bottom-line success. This type of predictive modeling is not new. Many industries have been using some form of predictive modeling to set actuarial tables for decades. However, real-time marketing in tandem with social media platforms have taken this to a new level, with unimaginable outcomes that already are affecting us all. The seemingly random collective intelligence we are building is identical to our flock of birds and has powerful functions and meanings.

We find ourselves at a pivotal moment in marketing and business history in which real-time sentiment and conversation are the new currency, and the ground is shifting beneath our feet. Yes, the basics of advertising, branding, and communicating still apply, but finding a way to integrate this newly surfaced component requires participants to take a different view of the world.

This new element, the Now Lens, calls for the ability to see the coming of age of conversational marketing in tandem with social technology platforms. It is the immediacy with which brands have to act and react to market conditions. It is consumers searching for trust in advertising by turning to their friends and peers for recommendations and reviews. It is listening and reacting to an explosion of user generated content.

More important than a pair of three-dimensional glasses, the real-time Now Lens with social media in its crosshairs has the attention of the most sophisticated companies on the planet, which want to harness collective intelligence for real-time competitive advantage.

Let us look at how the emergence of the Now Lens is laying the foundation for examining the fundamental shift in the way we communicate and why all of this is happening now.

To help you grasp its impact and what it means to marketers, Chapter 2 will provide insights and compelling information to give you a clearer understanding of all the social media chatter out there and how to use the Now Lens successfully.

CHAPTER 2

The Way We Communicate Has Changed Forever—Why Now?

A seismic shift of global proportions has occurred that will forever alter the way people communicate. It is a radical reinvention that encompasses the creation, distribution, consumption, and sharing of communications content. The change we are witnessing is potentially the most significant since the invention of the printing press for the widespread distribution of information and knowledge among populations and will have an enormous impact in terms of encouraging discussion and debate, building philosophies, and starting movements.

As this reconfigured business ecosystem unfolds, it is thrilling to some and daunting to others. Do we dare take a united lockstep into a truly global, technological, changing, and connected future in which everyone can hear, talk to, and/or see one another in real-time free of location restrictions? What about the downside? What about privacy, security, control?

One thing is certain: Throughout history, when information becomes accessible to major segments of society that previously did not have it within their reach, extraordinary events occur. This is no different.

But why right now? Why is social media suddenly everywhere? Even local newscasters are encouraging audiences to follow them on Twitter after giving the traffic report. Facebook currently has nearly twice as many profiles as the population of the entire United States, and human resources departments are using LinkedIn as a recruiting and due diligence tool in making hiring decisions.

New social marketing platforms are cropping up daily, specifically designed to enable communities of like mind and location. Conversations are playing out on video, photos, text, and audio file platforms and are being shared and then shared again via blogs, podcasts, Twitter, wikis, and social networks galore. The dynamic changes unfolding before our eyes constitute a wake-up call for businesses to realize that the elevated consumer voice literally has the power to make or break a company and its brand promise overnight.

Marketers have always been required to keep a finger on the pulse of consumer behavior. Now real-time marketers are being tasked with the role of sociologist-psychologist-technologist to track emerging consumer communication patterns in addition to their ongoing responsibility for keeping the brand authentic and transparent. What forces have created this perfect storm that is allowing real-time marketing to influence all aspects of communication, customer service, information, education, and government at this particular point in time?

To grasp what has led to real-time as a way of life and understand how it affects marketing, it is necessary to look at the evolution of communication in the world today. Take a step back to review the trends, patterns, and history in which we partake as both observers and contributors and how they play out in our everyday business and personal lives.

When the Internet arrived as a new information portal in the mid-1990s, it required specialized skill to program and design Web sites. In 2001, companies such as Yahoo!, eBay, and Adobe developed WYSIWYG (what you see is what you get) Web site templates that were easy to build and consumer-friendly. Hotmail was revolutionary at that time because it provided e-mail access away from the office on the Web. Until then, e-mail was company or Internet service provider (ISP)–based. Hotmail, founded by Jack Smith and Sabeer Bhatia and launched in July 1996, set everyone free in terms of customizing communications channels to suit personal and professional needs.

In 2003, MySpace took the Web template to a granular level with the launch of engaging personal profiles, which were essentially simple Web site templates filled with whatever information one was willing to reveal. For Millennials, openness to display private information online with current or new friends fed the astounding growth of MySpace and other communities to follow. When MySpace first arrived, a mainstream comment was, "Why would anyone want to put all his or her personal information out there for the world to see?" The explanation was then and is now people's need to connect.

Much has been learned since those initial MySpace days about privacy controls and safety, however, MySpace showed us the internal desire for human conversation even if it takes place in a virtual community. Technology provided a platform for open communication by way of personal Web sites in real-time, and Millennials embraced it.

The fascination with Facebook is another example. College campuses are still appreciated as keepers of intelligence and harbingers of "the next cool thing." When it was no longer necessary to have an .edu e-mail extension to be part of Facebook, the general public and future-thinking businesses stormed the gates of that previously exclusive, key-demo walled garden. Facebook had more privacy controls than MySpace, which also made it attractive to adults who were previously reluctant to join a community. Until mid-2010, overall user experience had been positive and had altered millions of opinions about what it means to be in a digital community. Then Facebook adjusted its privacy controls and saw a drop in users. The nascent platform is still making changes that are being played out as of this writing. In addition, a competitor is in the wings. Josh Weinstein, Princeton '09, is launching "College Only" in fall 2010 exclusively for college students with an .edu e-mail. He had 25,000 sign-ups in one month . . . before it even launched.

Twitter appears to be the Hotmail of this decade in terms of creating a new paradigm. It is also one of the rare digital platforms that initially was introduced to a young tech demo, dropped by it, picked up and catapulted by an older demo, and then reintroduced to younger users. The sharing of conversations, photos, opinions, and news in virtual communities such as Twitter continues to move in an upward trajectory with no signs of diminishing.

A large factor in the skyrocketing adoption of social platforms is that they are free. The Great Recession of 2007–2010 has rocked almost every household and business in some form and has caused a hunt for ways to economize. The ability to send a direct message (DM) to a friend and receive an immediate response for free instead of paying phone or text charges is appealing. Existing fees that consumers pay for the Internet or phone service are largely ignored because the platforms come at no cost. This makes the give-and-take of communication accessible as consumers and businesses search for ways to do more with less.

Digital Natives, Technology, and Economics

A unique alchemy of technology and global economics is blending into a powerful, fluid throng called digital natives. This new global demographic has arrived en masse and has grown up with digital technology. Dr. Urs Gasser of Harvard's Berkman Center refers to digital natives as Millennials "who have spent their entire lives using the Internet as an extension of themselves." Millennials have also been tagged as Generation Y or, more accurately, by Don Tapscott as the "Net Generation" in his work *Grown Up Digital: How the Net Generation Is Changing Your World*. More than 81 million people in the United States were born between 1977 and 1997, and they now make up 27 percent of the population. By comparison, the baby boomers, born from 1946 to 1964, were 77 million strong and are now only 23 percent of the population.

Just as boomers grew up with television and influenced music and politics, the Net Generation grew up with the Internet, computers, cell phones, and video games. They download movies, music, and information on mobile devices, choosing not to buy the hard version. They are comfortable with their role as the center of their own networks of friends and content. As 21-year-old Californian Francisco Calderon succinctly explained while simultaneously operating a laptop, PC, iPod, cell phone, CD player, and HDTV, "I am the network." They converse and share and create content, which then transforms them into programmers or independent broadcasters.

Boomers have held the position as the most highly educated and wealthiest generation in America up to this time. They also have a reputation for indulging their offspring and grandchildren with technology for privilege, competitive advantage, or both. Technology in multiple forms (computers, video and digital cameras, MP3 players, laptops, cell phones) is part of their children's everyday wardrobe. Millennials have also enjoyed more discretionary parent-provided income than earlier teen/young adult generations, money that is spent on clothes, music, and electronic accessories. Since Millennials are often the early adopters in a household, adults are consequently pulled into gadgetry. This is fueled by the parents' own curiosity as they try to keep up with their teens as well as their own attempts to be identified as early adopters. Digital natives also propelled the adoption of text messaging among adults. Countless parents, grandparents, aunts, and uncles have been forced to learn how to text in order to communicate with their own children, and this has created a technology tipping point.[1] The September 11 World Trade Center attacks, youth violence, and an unfortunate rise in campus sniper terrorism placed phones in children's hands because their concerned parents wanted to reach them quickly in an emergency.

According to Tapscott, the Net Generation's key values and behaviors are as follows:

○ They prize freedom.
○ They want to customize things.

25

○ They enjoy collaboration.
○ They scrutinize everything.
○ They insist on integrity in institutions and corporations.
○ They want to have fun even at school or work.
○ They believe that speed in technology and everything else is normal.
○ They regard constant innovation as a fact of life.

The Western obsession with youth culture continues to shine a spotlight on all the latest gizmos that end up with Millennials. For the most part, they are driving the wide-scale adoption and use of the real-time technologies that are spilling into culture on all levels. Therefore, marketers must keep an eye on what digital natives value and how they use technology to communicate differently.

If this is a world economy—and it is—and if everyone is a potential customer, take a moment to appreciate these global demographic realities. Although the United States is home to a large Net Generation, it is but a subset of the "youth bulge" in the world's population. The growth of the youth bulge is immense and is taking place in emerging countries: Latin America, sub-Saharan Africa, the Asia/Pacific region, and the Middle East. India has more than 650 million citizens under age 30, many of whom speak English. That is just about double the entire population of the entire United States. It is not a coincidence that the regions currently experiencing the most positive global economic growth are India, South America, and China. The population is aging in Japan, North America, Europe, and Russia, where intrinsic financial recovery in those areas is sluggish.

The worldwide youth bulge is composed of its own twenty-something digital natives who are just as active on broadband Internet and mobile as their American digital native counterparts. Their preference is to develop communities based on lifestyle and taste rather than national affiliation. Borderless global brands have created the "Sex in the City" female consumer who lives in Sydney, Paris, or

São Paulo. There is also the "American Idol" consumer (Philippines Idol, Czech Idol, Danish Idol, Indian Idol), who is the new face of the global citizen. The youth bulge individual is a person who studies or lives abroad and works in foreign countries more than was the case for any prior generation. This nomadic lifestyle has great appeal to socially curious, adventurous youths who are not confined by geographic boundaries. They are consuming and sharing information in real-time as they go. One of the ways savvy brands and their agencies are maximizing reach to this group is with a matrix of lifestyle and entertainment content. Businesses are hungry for untried, engaging methods to communicate with this international demographic on a macro and micro level.

Social platforms that deliver real-time information have therefore surfaced at the perfect time and at the right price for these legions of people with their diverse application requirements. This is a major reason these platforms are now everywhere. Individuals, companies, and marketers have been handed the gift of real-time marketing tools at a fraction of the cost of traditional paid media. Expensive research, focus groups, and awareness campaigns can be replaced with online surveys, blog comments, and tweets by anyone or any business. For years, marketing professionals have been talking about creating a relationship between brands and consumers. The missing link has been realized in the rise of new free social marketing and social technology platforms that enable dialogue among consumers, peers, and brands on a global scale.

Traditional definitions are being flipped. "Share of voice" is no longer something that can be bought by outspending the competition to be heard the loudest on TV, on radio, or in print. It has been redefined as the activity and volume of *conversations* by people taking place in social media about one's service, product, or brand. It is the voice of consumers empowered on free, connected soapboxes to share opinions, reviews, and evaluations. Technology, openness, and economics have been dropped upon a generation that has chosen to pick up the ball and run with it.

The present adoption curve of real-time social media is extremely similar to the growth of Web sites in 1999. At first, companies were suspicious of Web sites and their value as a new channel for information distribution. After all, they had brochures. Web sites were considered a novelty, and it took years before companies accepted them as standard business tools. Now corporations around the world are stunned by the speed at which both good and bad news travels on the real-time Web. Soon communicating on social platforms will become standard practice too.

What Does It All Mean?

The next few years will see disruption in social, business, organizational, and cultural systems. We are at a global threshold that can tip either way: toward a chaotic free-for-all or through the Now Lens that provides a vision for the future. The demand for instant messaging, everywhere presence, and always-on real-time communication capabilities has been building for years. Why is it important to understand the progression of real-time technologies and their adoption and meaning? Their significance lies in the reality that companies will prosper or fail because buying decisions have shifted to this powerful consumer peer-to-peer arena. It also means that businesses are evolving from the inside out, and this is why the shift can be uncomfortable. New communication tools have been born and are making a lot of noise, filled with comments about one's brand. Going forward, leaders will need to embrace the opportunities of shared assets because traditional leadership will not sustain business.

Seen through the Now Lens, we are composing and transmitting thousands of written messages destined for far-off places thousands of times a day, similar to the invention of the telegraph over 150 years ago. Short-form microblogging and text messages could be the evolution of Samuel Morse's creation approximately 160 years ago, as illustrated by the instructions on the telegram form: "Message goes here. Be brief."

According to Retro-Gram, back when telegrams started, if simple poetic brevity was not good enough, some people resorted to the use of code to make their telegrams as short and cheap as possible. As early as 1845, independent entrepreneurs were publishing books of codes for use in telegrams. You can see it in old black-and-white movies: "Just arrived in Paris STOP Wish you were here STOP."

Before long-distance telephone services were readily available or affordable, telegraph services were very popular. Telegrams often were used to confirm business dealings and, like e-mail, were commonly used to create binding legal documents for business transactions. The height of the telegraphic age was the 1920s and 1930s, when Western Union maintained a fleet of 14,000 uniformed messenger boys, on foot and on bicycle, and many thousands more operators, clerks, and copyists. Then came the famous singing telegram, popularized by Western Union.

In 1998, Tom Standage wrote a book called *The Victorian Internet*, which explored the historical development of the telegraph and the social ramifications associated with the development of this technology. He confirmed that the development of the telegraph essentially mirrored the development of the Internet. Both technologies can be seen to have had a powerful effect on the speed and transmission of information. The process is being repeated with real-time platforms.

Internal business operations processes are also being transformed by new collaborative communications platforms. Companies are making the best use of employee collective intelligence and crowd-sourcing to help departments achieve better business results through collaborative real-time solutions. The latest developments in enterprise collaboration software include social networking technologies behind the company's firewall, with platforms such as Yammer that are similar to Twitter but are designed specifically for use within a company or work group. "White-label" social networking platforms such as Mzinga and KickApps allow for a private enterprisewide social network. These platforms are excellent for quick updates on projects, finding out what everyone is working on, and information gathering. Major companies report that social technology platforms are broader than e-mail and enable immediate collaboration among employees, management, partners, customers, and other stakeholders. "Presence-driven" communication can facilitate spontaneous, highly productive interactions. Team members and outside stakeholders are able to get answers and reach shared understanding quickly, in real-time, without interrupting the flow of work. Teams that do not share time zones or geography can contribute and stay informed of progress.

We are also witnessing the rise of behavioral data models that are being used to serve relevant ads and purchase opportunities that are based on a consumer's recent behavior. Though controversial, behavioral targeting has been used by veteran marketers to determine relevance for years through the collection of data regarding Web pages viewed, search terms used, and products purchased. Think of the Amazon.com feature introduced over a decade ago that sent a message saying, "Other people who purchased this book also purchased the following . . ." The evolution of behavioral targeting has led to contextual targeting, in which specific behavior on many sites is tracked and aggregated, based on an interrelated series of discoveries of user-inputted information and habits. This is what helps the ads on sites like Google Search and Facebook appear relevant and specific to a consumer. This is the ultimate in one-to-one marketing to be sure.

Placing all of this targeting in real-time is a new development. Serving relevant content to consumers on social sites is fresh territory to mine to maximize customer engagement, boost loyalty, and increase transaction conversion. Marrying behavioral targeting with virtual currency and virtual goods is also an element of this evolution. Virtual economic exchange integrates (1) currency, (2) goods available through direct payments, and (3) consumer behavior. This data is analyzed to determine which of the three to deliver and when. Unless you are one of the millions playing FarmVille or Texas Hold'em, you may be unfamiliar with the rapidly rising real-time economy that exists totally in the virtual world. Suffice it to say that this new economy has emerged out of necessity as social network sites investigate creative ways of monetizing their traffic. The discovery that virtual currency and virtual goods are the most effective way to do so is slated to produce a multi-billion-dollar market.

Real-time marketers are learning how to understand dynamic influencing factors that may not be as simple as the models used in the past. Product ratings and reviews attempt to alter perceptions. As of April 2010, to "like" something or someone became even more powerful because Facebook changed product and business "fan" options and pages to "like." E-commerce leaders will have to adjust their algorithms to factor in unexpected influences like this when they surface in realtime. Companies tend to be fearful of the multiple changes that real-time brings to business processes. So, in addition to being fearful of hearing what brand critics say ("like" or "do not like"), they are afraid of what it means as to how they have conducted business in the past. This is why social media literacy and corporate education are critical success factors.

Depending on one's perspective, the main downside for brands amid all this new real-time communication and transparency is that everyone now has a voice. This sounds like an oxymoron. Didn't brands always want to hear from the customer? Didn't a brand want open access to its biggest fans? Yes, but it turns out that branding is ever more important and harder to achieve. Consumers are being inundated by a digital waterfall, and the risk is obscurity from oversaturation of choice. Brand equity can and does influence consumers' buying decisions, but getting there is not so easy and is not packing the punch it might have in the past.

Conversely, more companies view listening to the consumer and community voice as an opportunity with a great upside. They are brave enough to audit their own brand portfolios' current reach and the extent of their networks. They are willing to make an honest assessment of their ability to start a conversation, join a conversation, and ultimately respond to the information.

This begets questions: Does this mean that every brand and every company should be in social media? What about highly regulated industries such as pharmaceuticals and government? When will the tools make sense for business-to-business companies? How does real-time marketing play in these arenas? What proof is out there that social media—Twitter, LinkedIn, Facebook, blogging—will affect the bottom line? The answers to all these questions are "yes" and "now." There are endless opportunities for organizations in real-time social media. Social media, when connected to search marketing, content marketing, and public relations strategies, can help an organization boost search engine rankings, build relationships, convert leads to sales, reduce costs, and manage and strengthen the brand. When these factors are set into motion, they also enhance attempts to position oneself as a thought leader and innovator.

However, without a strategy, a halfhearted social media marketing attempt can do more harm than good. Some companies have tossed up a Facebook page or a Twitter account and handed the task off to an intern. This is not only foolish but potentially dangerous. First, consider the years, the money, and the resources put into building a company's brand. In some cases, this amounts to billions of dollars. The misguided rationale is, "If they are on Facebook (or YouTube), they must know what they're doing." Shockingly, this is being done by companies of all sizes. Second, posting unapproved or unmonitored status updates and comments could cause jeopardy for a firm. Tweets, wall posts, and LinkedIn updates that refer to a company, particularly a publicly held company, may come off as unprofessional or even be a liability to the company.

Real power lies in knowing how to build and engage in real-time conversations for the long term and secure "customer for life" relationships via the new dialogue that is now available. This includes a reinvention of integrated marketing that leverages traditional, online, and real-time social media. Most companies already have integrated marketing strategies in place that govern reputation management, brand positioning, and public relations positioning. Those who grasp the value of integrating social media with existing strategies and smart tactics will increase consumer and stakeholder interaction to great benefit. They will connect by creating relationships and communities of engaged and connected users who share conversations. This applies to small and large businesses regardless of industry.

Brands will ask internal and external suppliers to help solve problems. Collaborative technologies, mobile devices, unified communications, and social technologies and platforms will have to overlay customer relationship management, marketing, product development, information technology (IT), and all the different divisions within the enterprise. If a company selects one of these areas and infuses it with real-time marketing, a sizable bounce to the next level will occur if this is executed strategically. Keep in mind that the increased workload of responding to real-time marketing opportunities that become available is not about doing it *all* but is about deciding on the *right* combination for a business and doing it *well*.

The good news is that stakeholders now have the tools to communicate directly with their audience without multiple middle layers affecting the message. Global organizations are given the ability to communicate and compete 24 hours a day, and they need tools that enable seamless communication.

Here are some of the common misconceptions about real-time social media:

- I can see how social media applies to products, but I do not think it applies to services.
- I don't have time to be on Facebook (Twitter, LinkedIn, YouTube, etc.) all day.
- My company is too highly regulated. We will *never* be on social media.
- This is just for kids.

If one of these statements sounds familiar, it is time to revisit those notions, whatever your product or service is. The digital stars have aligned to cause these changes now. What at first seemed a fad for teenagers has fundamentally altered the marketing and sales landscape.

If you are a new brand ready to race out of the gate or an established brand that is not sure which way to turn, take comfort in knowing that you are not alone. Although there are advantages to being on the leading edge, it is also a good thing to be a fast follower. Unfortunately, most businesses tend to procrastinate. Events and time are increasing at an accelerated rate.[2] Do not wait. That is why real-time social media use is rising so fast.

Individual brands and corporations are scrambling to stay afloat, restructuring, and renegotiating traditional media contracts. Reportedly, 55 to 75 percent of media and advertising agencies turned over CEOs in the period 2008–2010 to bring in marketers who have digital awareness. No more handing off reputation challenges to the public relations department and hoping detractors will miraculously disappear. Be a Boy Scout: Always be prepared. It is wiser to develop a well-thought-out social media strategy over a targeted period of time than to be forced into the position of an early adopter because of an emergency.

Such was the case with JetBlue back in 2007 when an ice storm hit the eastern United States. JetBlue thought the weather would break and it would be able to fly; however, the weather conditions did not abate. At the peak of the problem, nine airplanes full of angry passengers sat for six hours or more on the tarmac at John F. Kennedy International Airport in New York. JetBlue had been a brand darling until then, yet one heavy snowstorm tarnished a hard-earned stellar reputation. Jet Blue founder and chief executive David Neeleman apologized for the horrific delays and customer inconvenience in an unprecedented mea culpa on YouTube. This became a corporate communications milestone: a CEO speaking directly to the customers on a digital platform relevant to them.

It bears repeating that if a brand refuses to listen or communicate with customers or clients, you can bet its competitors will. That is why brands need to be where conversations are taking place now and then have a follow-up plan to maximize this intelligence. Education and information are your greatest weapons and will reduce mistakes and alleviate fear. Learn from those who have gone before by reading the case stories in Chapter 5. You will discover that social platforms are manageable and that it is greatly rewarding to see the fruits of your labor in this new field. Yes, communication has been changed forever, and we are just at the beginning of a brilliant new era.

> *In the future, everyone will get 15 minutes of privacy.*
> —Scott Monty, chief marketing officer, Ford Motor Company

The privacy ecosystem is undergoing a seismic shift as well. We are now in the age of "find and be found" as opposed to the early Internet period of "protect my identity at all costs." Online companies have been collecting vast amounts of data from and about consumers since the early days of the Internet. During this time, consumer confidence has been constantly challenged to expand and adapt as technology capabilities increase. The contradiction is that social media users enjoy the personalization aspects of social technology platforms while at the same time wanting to preserve privacy.

We are seeing a sort of generational shift. The youth bulge demographic has a very different attitude about online privacy. Indeed, the future of anonymous activity online is a subject of deep debate and discussion around the world. It is generally thought that future advances in online security will offset the privacy concerns that are emerging today. As the use of real-time platforms continues to grow and expand into areas of government, learning, and commerce, robust and foolproof identification systems will be expected and required. As individuals interact on digital platforms, the line between their online/offline identities becomes blurred. People are making à la carte privacy choices based on what is important to them. However, there is a correlation between open identity adoption and a rise to protect anonymity. For example, privacy concerns are being addressed in a beta community called "Strings." Strings.com mirrors Facebook with the exception that all updates, reviews, and postings are entirely anonymous. No one can see who is generating the content, which addresses the need for privacy while participating in a community.

Think back to the beginning of e-commerce, when many consumers were appalled at the idea of entering their credit card numbers into a site such as Amazon or eBay. That has changed, of course, but it required an evolution of trust and security. The system is still not without frailty or problems resulting from breaches of privacy in the online world. The double-edged sword of social media is that everyone is entering tons of personal data into dating sites, social networking sites, professional networking sites, and the like. Making data and content sociable, ratable, and sharable is part of the new real-time ecosystem. This openness is part of the connectedness and the dynamic that are intriguing to most participants.

The tricky part occurs when that data is used to target users in ways they do not want or are not expecting. Mark Zuckerberg, CEO of Facebook, has noted that with the rise of social media online, people no longer have an expectation of privacy. He has said that privacy is no longer a "social norm." Then, in May 2010, Facebook continued its series of shocking privacy-loosening moves and is still attempting to clarify what privacy means in the Facebook universe (see http://www .facebook.com/privacy/explanation.php).

For digital natives, the essence of social media is to promote sharing and new connections. This is a space where meeting strangers is actually preferred. The Internet is viewed as a tool, connecting everyone through his or her favorite movies, foods, political views, photographs, music, and ideas. However, many would argue that even the Wild West was tamed with laws, schools, and societal norms. The debate will rage on.

The key for marketers will be to see how and where this all goes. New location-based apps are entering the lexicon and complicating this subject even more. It is important to remember that we are at the very beginning of a shift that will continue to change and evolve. Will the concept of "everyone will get 15 minutes of privacy" prevail? We will either descend into the muck of identity theft and stalking or rise to a higher standard that is both realistic and accommodating. One thing is certain: The cultural norm of privacy has changed forever.

All this is happening in the dynamic conversation space. In Chapter 3, we will explore the nature of digital conversation itself and the rules of engagement to keep the dialogue going.

CHAPTER 3

The Power of Conversation and Engagement

There is a conversation taking place about your brand, your industry, and your competitors in real-time with or without you. It is happening on the Internet and on mobile platforms around the world right now. You have less control over what people are saying than you used to, but there is good news: Social media-empowered conversations about brands are redefining the art of conversation, and business professionals are learning to master the new world of friend-driven marketing.

True conversation is a circular flow of thoughts and opinions between two parties with mutual respect. Both contributors fill a need in each other and are engaged by what the other has to offer. That hook, or engagement, has them coming back for more. This is true whether the dialogue is in person or in digital bytes. Active and engaged consumers have found a new voice and are defining what a brand signifies, what it is worth, where it can be found, and if and when it should be purchased.

The implications of conversational marketing and real-time are dawning on product and brand managers as well as their advertising and public relations partners. The chaos that anytime, anywhere social media created in 2008 and 2009 grabbed the attention of companies and caused them to rethink the value of conversation through their integrated marketing and communications strategies.

The focus for most of 2009 was on exploring how to create an online presence in social media that would expand the brand's audience and increase awareness of events involving the brand and also improve traffic/transactions on a hub Web site. Brands realized that their customers increasingly were turning to those sites as their primary source of news and to share information with others. Customers want content where they regularly live online versus seeking it out on a Web site. Clearly, the volcanic numbers alone demonstrate the necessity of engaging on social media platforms.

"Social customers" want a brand to pay closer attention to what is being said, where it is being said, why it is being said, and strive to anticipate where the conversation is going. What matters most is engagement and collaboration on their terms. Authenticity and transparency are even more important than consistency of the brand message.

Paradoxically, seeking the "voice of the customer" has been a priority for some time. There is a long history of VOC initiatives in the annals of corporations all across the globe that are designed to gain a detailed understanding of customer requirements and receive key input for new products or services. But most of those initiatives were controlled and one-way. Companies invested in expensive focus groups, interviews, and surveys that were based on customer experiences with products and services. This data ultimately fed customer satisfaction programs that built sophisticated algorithms designed to develop customer loyalty and customer retention rewards programs. One of the first manifestations of this was the frequent-flier miles program. Those little rewards cards hanging on your key chain from a variety of businesses are also a result of such initiatives.

Thus, an entire industry was born in the customer relationship management (CRM) industry. It focused primarily on three key elements of building and maintaining the customer relationship: (1) customer satisfaction, (2) customer loyalty, and (3) customer retention. It was revolutionary at the time and helped make customer satisfaction and loyalty part of the company's stated mission. CRM also facilitated the development of efficient supply chain management systems that drove prices down because stores could provide "just in time" merchandise that, theoretically at least, met the customers' stated requirements. This was the best in class at the time and continues to fuel many brand strategies around the world. The CRM industry boomed and proved highly profitable. No one doubted that the voice of the customer was being heard. The enormous amounts of data the CRM systems contained were proof that customers' needs were being met.

Imagine the surprise of the industry when in the early 2000s consumers began to harness the power of the Internet and their new online environment, where they discussed their true brand experiences among themselves. Suddenly, with the advent of blogging and podcasting in 2003 and 2004, consumers found a voice, and what they had to say was not always a reflection of the rosy picture painted by CRM systems. In fact, often that voice was, and still is, venting or even ranting. Brands and companies began to whisper privately, "Maybe we don't really want to hear what the customer has to say. It seems so negative." But the genie was out of the bottle.

Brands and companies need not worry. There is a substantial number of thoughtful consumers out there who want to be brand advocates ready to voice support. When a brand disappoints them, they want to express how it can serve them better. Some are even big cheerleaders and love the brand no matter what transpires, to the point of self-policing fan sites. Customers are made up of critics, "prove-it-to-me"s, and advocates. All these consumers are clamoring for brand transparency and authenticity.

This brings us to the rise of the social CRM Now Lens and the new voice of the community. The current conversation evolution is happening *among* customers, users, partners, affiliates, fans, detractors, and other stakeholders. Social media tools support conversations that are open, frank, and public. The voice of the customer and the voice of the community are getting louder as stakeholders share everything under the sun because they can. Real-time marketers need to lend an ear because they should.

The shift in communication has been captured by what Markyr Media principals Kyra Reed and Marjorie Kase refer to as "the cult of conversation." Markyr Media is a social media agency in Los Angeles, California. While working with clients, they observed a shift from the cult of personality to the cult of conversation powered by real-time, open social media.

"'The cult of personality' had a wall that separated fans and consumers from accessing information about brands or celebrities," Reed said. "People were mysterious and inaccessible. But now, the wall is gone and has given way to the 'Cult of Conversation.' It isn't about chasing after an image someone else is pushing on you or says you have to *be* in order to be happy. Instead, the 'Cult of Conversation' is about access and openness. It is looking to one's friends to see what they think about something. They look at Facebook news feeds to find out what's important. It's not about image, it's about conversation."

Reed and Kase further break down the cult of conversation to identify *semisocial* versus *social* media personae. The cult of conversation is based on a three-C's pyramid: (1) conversation, (2) connection, (3) community (see Figure 3.1). As with a three-legged bench, if one of the C's is weak or eliminated, social media efforts will totter or fail.

1. The entry point to social media is Conversation:
   a. What are you going to say?
   b. How are you going to say it?
   c. Are you a *semisocial* personality? (This persona talks about the brand and gives only information relevant to the *brand*.)
   d. Are you a *social* personality? (This persona talks about what is relevant to the people who follow the brand. Only gives information relevant to *personality*.)

3.1 The Cult of Conversation

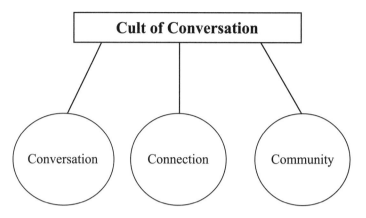

2. Connection
   a. Conversation style will determine the type of connections that will take place on social platforms. (This can lead to crowdsourcing, business development, leads, and associations.)
3. Community
   a. Arises out of meaningful conversation and connection.
   b. Becomes the place where these two elements flourish and continue to grow.
   c. Must be fed with new, meaningful conversations.
   d. These conversations generate stronger connections that make the community an engaging environment for participants.

What is astute about their observation is that it distinguishes between brands that enter social media to serve themselves (semi-social) and brands that truly want to get to know customers, learn what is important to them, and become part of their world (social). Their findings have shown that the most effective social media campaigns, and the most memorable, are social. As an observation, Reed cites Pepsi as a brand that has moved from the cult of personality to a fully social cult of conversation. Pepsi's brand evolution over the years began as a patio cola that evolved to moms, then youth appeal, followed by celebrity that was aspirational and image-driven. Now, the Pepsi "Refresh" campaign is a crowdsourcing charity undertaking. It engages communities to select a deserving nonprofit in their towns or neighborhoods where customers can see direct benefits tied to the Pepsi brand. Its campaign is all about inclusivity and accessibility. It remains to be seen if Pepsi made the right choice in shifting dollars from paying for its 2010 Super Bowl commercial to supporting the Refresh program. Only time will tell if it will experience success as measured by goodwill, sales, or both. However, the significant point is that Pepsi, a global company, is willing to take a risk in real-time.

Listening

Show me a good conversationalist and I'll show you a good listener.
—Anonymous

One of the first things a social media marketer or consultant must tell a new client is to set up a "listening strategy" using social technology platforms such as Twitter, Facebook, and LinkedIn. It does not mean hastily erecting a Facebook page to "get friends" and "post something on the wall."

Companies that already are conducting reputation monitoring and competitive strategy initiatives know that both require listening and scouring the media for brand mentions, articles, and so on. If the information is accurate and favorable, it provides a positive base on which to build. If it is not, reputation management departments correct negative information in the appropriate way. Companies are learning to set up Google Alerts on their products, brands, and services as well as those of the competition to track them and keep them up to date on competitors' activities. If they have not done so yet, they need to.

The extension of reputation management to social media means that the listening platforms have changed. The traditional reputation management resources included clippings from the press around the world and then evolved to the use of tools such as Google Alerts. Today dashboard systems monitor brand mentions on Twitter, Facebook, blogs, YouTube, or all of them. In some cases, individuals are assigned to monitor the social layer "in real-time." The main point is to find out where the conversation is taking place and migrate there.

Beginning in 2008, the terms *sentiment* and *influence* were introduced into the real-time ecosystem to describe how to begin measuring the different aspects of listening. In addition to listening to mentions, companies and brands started to realize that they needed to listen to "influencers," the leading voices whom others listen to, or the "just like me" and word-of-mouth consumers. Social media platforms allow users to express themselves in a multitude of positive, negative, mixed, and neutral sentiments.

However, a real conversation is about listening *and* talking. When do brands and companies get a chance to speak up in this new paradigm? The answer is that most of them need to take a step back and reflect on the essence of conversation and determine the purpose of the conversation. The purpose could be to build brand awareness or provide customer support. It might be executive communication or information relevant to a product launch. Whatever the reasons are for stepping into the conversation, the contributions of the brand had better add value to the dialogue or the conversation will be ignored or shut down.

Conversational marketing was a term that became famous with *The Cluetrain Manifesto*, which was written in 1999 by Rick Levine, Christopher Locke, Doc Searls, and David Weinberger. A printed publication that elaborated on the manifesto was published in 2000 by Perseus Books under the same name. The first thesis in the manifesto was that "markets are conversations." At that time, the Internet was revolutionizing the way people could connect with one another, and Cluetrain helped highlight opportunities for companies to connect directly with their customers online.

Before that time, advertisers relied on mass communication to reach large consumer audiences. Mass marketing worked. (It still does in many cases, by the way.) Newspapers may be going through an agonizing transition period, but television still reaches a broad audience in one swoop. It aggregates the most eyeballs at any one time (over 1 billion people tuned into Super Bowl 2010) and commands the most advertising dollars (over $70 billion per year).

Mass marketing originated in the 1920s with radio and evolved in the later part of the twentieth century with television. For the first time, advertisers were able to reach a broad section of an audience— literally *broad*cast—with each advertising message. Products that most people needed or wanted could be advertised to a large general market through these media with extensive reach. For example, products advertised during national television programs reach consumers in the entire country. As long as the products were available nationwide, advertising reach to a huge demographic was and still is considered a successful marketing strategy. Traditionally, consumers seeing products advertised in television commercials are more likely to choose them over similar store products that are not promoted. Showing television viewers the actual product and communicating benefits such as getting sparkling white teeth by using Brand X toothpaste increases sales of advertised products. As the commercials are repeated, the frequency creates brand awareness by reaching eyeballs or ears listening or tuning in at different times. Reach and frequency delivered the message that led to action or a purchase. Brand recognition occurred as consumers began to identify a product through its packaging, name, and promoted benefits. Mass marketing also inspired brand loyalty by reminding consumers of the benefits of a product over competing goods. Through a mass marketing strategy, brand managers created wide appeal for their products to match the broad scope of their audience.

However, mass marketing by nature is undifferentiated marketing. Mass marketing targets everyone at once. Differentiated marketing focuses on at least two different market segments. Each segment is reached through unique promotional strategies, and the results are analyzed to determine future outreach. This type of market concentration can be extremely effective in creating product sales but is more expensive than mass marketing. Real-time social media provides direct paths to segmented, untapped markets that can differentiate a brand from the pack if you get there first.

Joining the Conversation

There is power in consumer-generated conversations. They have meaning and relevance to the consumers who brands eagerly want to access. Social media sites are listening fields with individuals who describe their preferences voluntarily.

The new approach to real-time marketing means that the brand has to be invited into the conversation, and the ticket is *adding value*. The brand message on its own does not constitute adding value. Offering helpful suggestions, intervening if there is a problem, and sparking new ideas about how to use the brand qualify as value. The brand will find out what to contribute by listening.

If it sounds like a continuous circle, it is. Think about your own life and relationships. There is a natural give-and-take. You listen, and then you add to the conversation. You do not enter a cocktail party shouting your news or message: "Hey, everyone! We just bought a new car! You need to know this!" Instead, you walk up to a group of two or three people and listen to the tone and direction of the conversation. Then you add comments that are relevant and meaningful to the conversation and the group. Someone builds on your comments, you build on his or hers, and friends are made. This is the power of conversation. Real-time is about being social, remembering that conversations are a dialogue, not a monologue. Once the brand successfully joins the conversation, people can't stop listening.

Customer Engagement Planning

Companies large and small are defining what constitutes engagement on the basis of their objectives. Once a social footprint is established, the next step is to determine how the brand will engage in the two-way conversation in the long term.

Authentic engagement involves entering the conversation where your customers are active and where identified influencers are spending their time. By first listening carefully, you discover what people are saying about your brand and what they want. Then you will be better prepared to join their conversations in a natural way and offer solutions and ideas to help enrich their experiences.

Now that your community has been built—people "like" your brand and service and share your content—you should consider ways to keep brand fans coming back to your sites. You should build your engagement plan and consider ways your team can add value in the form of useful and/or entertaining links, content, information, and resources.

Relationship management is being redefined. Companies need to look at their business holistically, not in terms of silos or roles. Marketing and sales, service and support, customer experience, employee experience, innovation, collaboration—all have engagement touch points internally and externally. However, most companies cannot move fast enough to get in front of what customers and stakeholders are going to say and do. Tools are being created to help manage engagement points and responses. As was mentioned before, we are seeing the birth of social CRM as a way to help operationalize engagement. Simply gathering X number of "followers" or fishing for "likes" is not a strategy. Building a base through effective engagement is a strategy.

There is evidence that companies are picking up the pace on developing social media customer engagement strategies and tactics. The *Customer Engagement Report 2010* (http://econsultancy.com/

reports/customer-engagement-report) by Econsultancy highlights the following:

- ○ The proportion of company respondents that regards customer engagement as "essential" has increased to 55 percent, up from 52 percent in 2008 and 50 percent in 2007.
- ○ The tactics that have come to the forefront for driving customer engagement are social networking and Twitter activity. Presence on social networks has almost doubled, and micro-blogging has gone up fivefold.

People are using online channels as their primary source of information and communication. We are looking at an entire world that will be connected one way or another very soon. New generations of business workers are now able and will be able to collaborate and communicate in real-time. Entire economies will go mobile as emerging markets and countries go directly to an unwired infrastructure. Clearly, it is time to think about how your brand will engage with these new consumers, stakeholders, and businesses.

What is new is that customer engagement is not just a brand's connection with the customer. It is also the customers' engagement with one another in the horizontal, viral aspect. This is the true measure of success in real-time marketing and is what creates the long tail of engagement.

Tactically, brands must begin writing and publishing content with embedded links to other content, pictures, and videos to meet the expectations of the online audience. This encourages engagement and facilitates sharing. Conversely, lack of engagement limits brand leadership effectiveness and ultimately defeats the purpose of the medium.

A smart combination of listening to the online conversation already taking place, learning what people want, and then providing what they are open to receive from the brand constitutes the winning ticket. The goal of customer engagement is to establish the right message at a connection touch point that is based on understanding and defining customer needs. Evaluating social platforms to achieve customer engagement goals should include those that will best support retention and business objectives.

Engagement can mean video, polls, games, photo sharing, e-mail, blogging, and podcasting. Engagement strategies present an opportunity for brands to align content creation for social media with a company's priorities and involve cross-functional interaction and collaboration. Social media engagement can also be used for frontend campaigns and appearances to help guide the conversation and generate buzz.

Being friendly helps. Here is a fun exercise to do while thinking about your engagement strategy. Read *Building Wonderful Friendships* by Hyacinth Fraser, who also writes for Answerlife UK. It may seem a bit corny at first, but try to think differently. Especially in this age of blurred brands, stand out by getting back to basics.

How to Build Wonderful Friendships According to Hyacinth Fraser

- Keep your friends in mind and ask them how you can help them.
- Check with them on a regular basis; find out how they are doing.
- Surprise them.
- Be really grateful you have the friends you have.
- Give without expecting anything in return.

It is not that much of a stretch to apply these simple rules to your business. Arriving at a "high-touch" relationship with your customers is a form of competitive advantage. Markets are made up of people, and the basic tenet of treating people the way you want to be treated still works.

Marketing Communications in Real-Time

First of all, what is MarCom? *MarCom* is an abbreviation for "marketing communications." Some think of it as public relations, and in many companies it is. Public relations as a discipline is also undergoing change. MarCom is targeted interaction with customers and prospects using one or more media, such as direct mail or e-mail, online and offline newspapers and magazines, television, radio, billboards, telemarketing, the Internet, newswires, and more.

MarCom in real-time is undergoing the same seismic shift that is shaking all of marketing and communications. Strong marketing communications strategies have served corporations and organizations fairly well over the years. Now brand managers need to think about how they communicate in real-time as well as with whom, because each message requires a thoughtful, targeted approach. One size does not fit all. Companies have to shift marketing communications away from reactive reputation management and adopt the new social technologies that make communication immediate. The two-way nature of interaction is certainly defining the parameters of how quickly we communicate today.

Embracing real-time communications requires a global outlook. It also requires the ability to understand and directly interact with constituencies/influencers and give a portion of editorial and conversation control to the customers. Give them channels where they can get involved with your content. Listening and monitoring should be standard practice. For those in MarCom, listening is an excellent way to dip a toe into the social water, develop an understanding of what is going on, and get input from your community on the best way to pursue further engagement. Asking questions is an excellent way to gather valuable, pertinent information. It is amazing how much activity can result from posting a video or picture on a Facebook page with a question: "What do you think?" or, "Who's your favorite?" People love to participate, and they do it! Just follow the number of comments of the Facebook pages of Levi's, Coke, or Nike. You will find hundreds of people talking about the brand, unprompted and unscripted. That is a marketer's dream!

Every big company is fearful that the conversation is going to veer negatively, and sometimes it does that. This is where a strategy pays off. If the company thinks this through, it can develop a strategy for the negative sentiment that may arise, just as it does for any crisis.

The discipline of public relations is even more important in real-time. Public companies will continue to use the press release as a primary means of positioning news. Press releases for public companies are actually legal documents. They are vetted multiple times to check what they say and make sure they accomplish certain goals. Putting news out on the wire is not going away any time soon.

Justin Goldsborough, digital strategist at the global public relations firm Fleishman-Hillard, commented on the benefits his profession can bring to clients regarding social media: "Education is really important, so we provide a type of Social Media 101 to our clients, on trends we are seeing and how it relates to them. Companies are looking for leadership in this area." In addition to education, Justin made the following recommendations: "Be a valuable part of the community and be completely transparent when talking about your business. Use social media to engage as a person or as a brand. Brands can take on a persona that can be trusted so they may engage with the community as a person. This is new for some companies. After seeing different tweets from your brand name, people will know you are a business but are acting in your community like a person. It requires a different way of interacting with the public."

When asked about moving companies to consider adopting social media, Justin observed, "Corporate cultures are hard to change. That's why social media education is so important. If they are locked internally and scared, it makes the process of change difficult. Trying to operate one way externally and differently internally doesn't work."

To create a receptive atmosphere and encourage learning, Fleishman-Hillard has developed a social media game along the lines of Trivial Pursuit™. Justin explains, "When it comes to something as critical as how employees use social media, which can have a significant impact on brand reputation, companies can't afford for training not to stick. Unfortunately, employees are not going to throw a social media policy party or get out of bed early to rush to the office and review the new company digital do's and don'ts. One solution we are strongly pursuing is using social media to teach social media.

"The approach we are testing is two-pronged. The first piece is to turn real-life social media case studies involving our clients' employees into an IRL[1] learning experience. We create a Trivial Pursuit-type game customized for our clients with questions relating to social media policies, answering customer service questions via social networks, handling inquiries from bloggers, and more. In most cases, the questions come from real situations. At the training, employees divide into teams, play the game, and then discuss the questions with a panel including PR, Marketing, HR, and Legal reps. The second piece is to continue the education conversation after the social media training session ends. Brands can facilitate this by giving the governance board the opportunity to blog about social media policy internally. It also allows employees to ask questions in real-time as they emerge." Fleishman-Hillard is a stellar example of a traditional profession reformulating its services to enrich clients in an engaging way in real-time.

The staple of public relations, the press release, has become easier in the last decade with services such as PR Newswire and PRWeb. Now PR professionals need to make a commitment to learn about the new digital social media release for public relations and how to use it. The digital release contains all the text of a regular news release plus multimedia photos, graphics, video, and links to important documents and files, all of which give even more background information about the subject to readers. Corporate content can be repurposed for video and audio podcasts as well. This makes a press release more interesting and engaging and, quite literally, makes it come alive.

Most important, a social media release allows the community—your audience—to have a conversation about your release via comments. Share buttons then make it easy for users to distribute the release on all the different social networks. It is not a replacement for the standard press release but rather an add-on. Social press release platforms such as PitchEngine, along with several others, are available for one's company or organization to adopt.

Approach the discipline of communications as a process, a dialogue. Do not be afraid of the market talking back. Embrace user comment and content and then put mechanisms in place that encourage response. It is far cheaper than a focus group. Finally, investigate Web site stats and learn how to track campaigns more effectively.

Real-time communications will be a central part of every brand and marketing department in the near future. A real-time manager will sit alongside established disciplines such as media relations, internal communications, brand management, and analyst relations. His or her role will be to integrate real-time social data into every aspect of corporate communications as a fundamental part of the department's thinking. Keeping up on all the latest trends and being fluent in the language of real-time conversations will give this new function a seat at the table for all brand-related decisions. We are all living in a real-time world, and the sooner we can professionalize this role, the better.

The good news is that unlike marketing disciplines of the past, the role of a real-time marketing department and what it tracks are infinitely more measurable than a press clipping report. The new communications practices outlined above can be analyzed in seemingly endless ways [the number of blog comments, the number of Really Simple Syndication (RSS) subscribers, etc.]. Long-distance communication today is essentially free for both work and social activities. Groups of people no longer need to be geographically close to get a sense of closeness and shared experience. The way this shift is applied to business, teaching, learning, creativity, and so forth is still being defined in an evolutionary process that is being sped up exponentially by occurring in real-time.

Public relations and advertising have been the primary vehicles for communicating brand messaging. Typically, what traditional ad agencies have done brilliantly is create commercials. The process was to develop a product and a message and then send it out one-way to millions via TV, print, outdoor, radio, trade shows, and so on. A crisis plan was tucked away just in case. Finely tune the message, spread the word, and increase sales—it was all clear-cut. Advertising worked—the golden days when Hollywood and Madison Avenue ruled the world. Most CEOs and business owners believe that the only purpose of advertising is to increase sales. That may be true today, but actually advertising is a relatively new thing in the history of the world.

The first known paid advertisement in America was an announcement seeking a buyer for an Oyster Bay, Long Island, estate that was published in the *Boston News-Letter* in 1704 (http://adage .com/century/timeline/index.html). In 1742, after purchasing the *Philadelphia Gazette*, Benjamin Franklin's *General Magazine* printed the first American advertisements. Thus began mass communication supported by advertising.

Advertising also was a way to underwrite the free exchange of ideas and information in the marketplace and help grow the economy. The expense of producing the paper was covered by advertisers, and so the cost to readers was virtually eliminated, increasing the number of people who would see the advertising and thus grow the market. The upside for advertisers was that they controlled the message and that advertisements helped boost sales. The trade-off was friendly: the opportunity to create a free exchange of ideas and brand control. For the most part, the paid advertisement model has remained the same until now.

But to be successful in this new real-time arena, a different skill set is required that starts by understanding that it is not about spamming 30-second one-way commercials. Forward-leaning companies see these trends and implications for business and are creating cross-department task forces composed of legal, public relations, customer relationship management, reputation monitoring, corporate communications, human resources, and marketing. The discussion is about whether they should enter this confounding new world and, if so, how to communicate their brand message and image. We will also see interchanges between customer relations, marketing, and product development like never before. Internal engagement and escalation procedures will be recalibrated to reflect the real-time nature of communications. The mission will be to spread messages to new audiences through emerging social technology channels and participate in various user communities.

The tables have been turned. Companies that are able to both listen and engage for the long term will be successful. Those that do not master this art will not attract the attention or gain the loyalty of the market that is bestowed on others. Real-time communication may seem daunting, but no more so than entering any new conversation among unfamiliar guests. Listen. Have something valuable to say. Be a friend to get a friend. Your market will reward you by sharing their satisfaction with one another. All these gems are most effective when funneled into a powerful real-time marketing strategy; this will be explored in Chapter 4.

CHAPTER 4

Real-Time Marketing Strategies

T raditionally, *strategy* is defined as the direction and approach an organization takes over the long term to meet the needs of the market and fulfill business expectations.

A *marketing strategy* is the road map that enables an organization to concentrate specific resources on the greatest opportunities to increase sales and ratings, achieve a sustainable competitive advantage, or deliver value to its customers and other stakeholders. After all, a business that does not generate revenue is not a business but a hobby. Even not-for-profit organizations have goals around fund-raising to grow and sustain the good things they provide.

As we have seen, the skyrocketing growth of real-time social media has radically changed the way organizations communicate with their customers. Determining how traditional marketing and real-time social media work together and complement each other requires a recalibration of current integrated marketing strategies that layers in these new tools and tactics.

For years, marketing professionals have been talking about creating a relationship between brands and consumers. The missing link has now been realized in the form of new free social marketing and social

Web platforms that enable dialogue among consumers, peers, and brands on a global scale. Traditional definitions are being flipped. Share of voice is no longer something that can be gained by outspending the competition to be heard the loudest on TV, on radio, or in print. It has been redefined as the activity and volume of *conversations* with people taking place in social media about one's service, product, or brand. It is the voice of consumers empowered on free, connected soapboxes to share opinions, reviews, and evaluations. Expensive research, focus groups, and awareness campaigns can be replaced, or at least enhanced, by online surveys, blog comments, and tweets.

Social media is exactly what the name implies: media that is social. What happens in the online social space mirrors what happens offline. People interact, discuss, share interests, find trust and respect, and make judgments—all in the moment or in real-time.

When marketers approach social media as a viable business intelligence platform, they often get unexpected insights into consumer opinions and shared experiences. Conversation and engagements occur, for example, via comments, posts, blogs, photos, videos, forums, and location-based platforms. Companies should consider this an open window to what consumers, competitors, partners, and other stakeholders are thinking and saying, anytime and anywhere. Imagine being able to respond immediately on the same platform. Nic Adler, owner of the world-famous Roxy Theatre on the Sunset Strip in Los Angeles, was monitoring Twitter one night when he read a tweet from a customer saying that her drink was weak. He saw her profile picture, had the bartender mix a stronger drink, found her in the club, and delivered it to her. The next tweet she sent raved about The Roxy. Nic's objective is to create loyal customers. He uses social media strategically, and in this case Twitter was the forum that delivered real-time results. Read more about how social media transformed The Roxy Theatre as well as business along the Sunset Strip in Chapter 5.

Social media does *not* replace traditional marketing. Print, online, TV, outdoor advertising, and radio still have a place in the promotional mix. Traditional media can be a useful tool to ignite a conversation before it takes on a life of its own. At this time, most advertising and media spends will remain in the traditional channels; however, watch for companies to realign budgets and move more dollars to social media as they experience the power of real-time marketing. The most successful marketing strategies are those that fully integrate a social component with traditional media in a targeted effort. This can be done only by having a seat at the table during the earliest stage in the media planning/advertising process.

Current social media watchwords are *transparency, authenticity, engagement, conversation, community, sentiment,* and *influence.* To veteran marketers, these words are familiar; to the new marketer, they are the lifeblood of successful real-time strategies. Consumers use these criteria to measure brand promise. If a brand does not deliver, the company will definitely hear about it. Real-time strategies self-monitor to ensure that these watchwords are adhered to and reduce any potential friction.

Real-time marketing strategies are contingent on objectives. Objectives could range from building awareness, to recruiting top talent, to increasing sales. Thus, strategies vary with the objective and the target demo. Strategies to deliver on an objective then have to reflect the overarching brand strategy in order to be successful. Kelly Sheehan, a social media consultant and strategist for global auto and beverage clients, explains, "This is a topic of great discussion among social media planners when asked by a client to deliver a 'social media strategy.' What is that exactly? Ideally, the social media strategy should reflect the overarching brand strategy that trickles downward. Then how to approach the social media aspect becomes tactical. The social media strategy still has to be 'on brand' and come from the brand core. It's not rogue but covers all parts of advertising and marketing efforts." Sheehan goes on to describe common brand missteps: "A number of brands come into social but they don't know what they want to achieve. How are they going to treat conversation and loyalty? This is critical for determining KPI's [key performance indicators] in order to determine success metrics: Is it purely video views, volume, and value? The best results strike a balance between quantitative and qualitative."

Conversation as Strategy

Everyone is talking about the importance of finding the conversations that are taking place about the brand and determining what these consumers *like* by *listening*. This seems paradoxical. How can real-time be about *now* but still require listening and patience? Simple. The process is just like offline conversations. After listening, one enters the conversation by adding something of value, a piece of information about a topic that is favorable. The *like* may not even be about the product. In other words, it is not all about *you* but about the friends you keep and the friends *they* keep. Perhaps they make comments about travel or fedoras. What positive comments can you add on either subject?

That "something" or "conversation currency" will be different for everyone based on the objective. It starts to become clear that this new ecosystem presents a fundamental change in marketing planning and execution because opinions and conversations change in real-time. Strategies must be fine-tuned to allow for quick adjustments that are based on evolving conversation sentiment and activity. Observe the trends of how companies and brands are responding to customers or handling reputation management to get a sense of which social media tactics or technologies they use in their strategies.

Remember that conversations are connecting people around the world in real-time. Because various cultures and ethnic groups use social media in slightly different ways, listening and execution strategies also need to be adjusted according to the conversation target. Andrew Orci, President CEO of the Los Angeles–based Hispanic advertising agency Orci, whom we met in Chapter 1, explains:

Hispanics use Facebook more than Twitter because they are not limited by the number of characters in their conversations. In addition, the Facebook platform makes it easier for more people within the user's network to interact at the same time. This is important to Hispanics because it facilitates and expands their ability to interact with others in their community. And it more closely replicates the real-world, face-to-face interaction that has always taken place in the Latino culture.

Every Latino is at the center of a complex social network on which he relies for information, interpretation, and validation in making decisions on products and services available to him. This network consists of family, friends, coworkers, neighbors, acquaintances, and professional advisors. The network is multilingual and multigenerational, and it spans all levels of acculturation, and is geographically dispersed within the U.S. and throughout Latin America.

Through the strategic use of real-time media, brands can effectively and efficiently leverage the power of individual consumers and their extended social networks—online and offline.

According to Quantcast April 2010 data, Hispanics overindex on MySpace compared to Facebook. Hispanic culture is highly music driven. Since MySpace has evolved into an entertainment community, Hispanics overindex on this hub. This is a clear example of why brands must take into account cultural behaviors and interests to find conversation hubs.

Regardless of who is driving the conversation, real-time marketing strategies require a degree of nimbleness since the brands or businesses they serve run the gamut from conservative/traditional to newly launched. Consider Mark Zuckerberg, CEO of Facebook, who discussed privacy with the famed blogger and social media maven Robert Scoble in June 2010 and said, "We are learning in real-time." Skeptics complained that the type of course correction indicated by Zuckerberg was "winging it" and that companies should have everything thought out before the launch. Indeed, that is the tried and true model that has been followed over the last 50 years.

Companies traditionally do the following:

1. Set overall strategy
2. Conduct massive market research
3. Build "end-to-end" go-to-market strategies
4. Create brand positioning and messaging
5. Launch
6. Repeat steps 1 through 5

The new business model of working it out in real-time, crowd-sourcing, transparency, and forward momentum is both breathtaking and confounding, depending on one's capacity for stress. Mark is in his mid-twenties (26 at the time of this writing) and potentially represents the new real-time CEO "normal." This leads one to ponder if current and future CEOs will choose to develop their businesses' strategies with full transparency, in public, in real-time. Is this what consumers and stakeholders want? Since Zuckerberg created and leads one the largest social communities in the world, future CEOs most likely will emulate his style. Logic dictates that we probably will see more of these real-time, work-it-out-as-we-go entrepreneurs in the very near future.

Zuckerberg's comment that they are working it out in real-time appears to be a blatant contradiction to set planning and traditional business models. However, if you look below the surface, his business displays several attributes of real-time marketing strategy.

Competitive Strategy in Real-Time

Most people believe that in the competitive global market it is critical to have a strategy that ensures a consistent approach to offering products or services in a way that will outsell the competition. That, combined with a well-defined tactical methodology for the day-to-day process of implementation, is what makes for a winning combination.

Veteran master strategist Phil Cannon of Xerox Corporation refers to it this way:

> I play scenarios out for best- and worst-case options, and when deciding next steps in the selling process always consider landscape, influence, and variables. I want the customer to feel comfortable that I am operating in their best interest . . . that I am a consultant. I play devil's advocate to every next step idea. . . . I play worst-case scenarios to figure what to do in those eventualities. Ultimately we want to beat the competition and help the customer win.

Successful real-time marketing strategies include the following:

o Listening
o Responding
o Staying nimble
o Engaging in reputation management
o Thinking counterintuitively

One of the most definitive books ever published on strategy— Harvard Business School's Michael E. Porter's *Competitive Strategy: Techniques for Analyzing Industries and Competitors*—was written back in 1980, before the PC, the Internet, or social media.

Porter's Five Forces identified competitive influences that shape every single industry and market. It set the benchmark for how the companies that constitute those industries should view the competitive landscape. These forces help marketers analyze everything from the intensity of competition to the profitability and attractiveness of an industry. The Five Forces framework is still applicable and is used in today's business environment (see Figure 4.1).

Porter notes, "Competitive strategy is about being different. It means deliberately choosing a different set of activities to deliver a unique mix of value. The essence of strategy is in the activities—choosing

4.1 The Five Forces Framework for Developing Competitive Strategy Still Applies in the Real-Time World

Five Forces Analysis

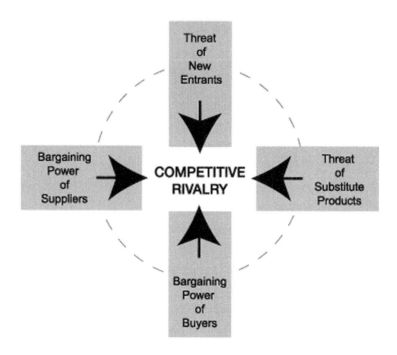

to perform activities differently or to perform different activities than rivals. Otherwise, a strategy is nothing more than a marketing slogan that will not withstand competition."

Another approach prevalent today is the Blue Ocean Strategy contained in a 2005 business book by that name written by W. Chan Kim and Renée Mauborgne. Those authors convey the high growth and profits an organization can generate by creating new demand in an uncontested market space, or a "Blue Ocean." Success is more likely to happen this way than when a company is competing head to head with other suppliers for the same customers in an existing industry. Social gaming is a good example of Blue Ocean, as FarmVille and Texas Hold'em appear to exist in an uncontested market space—at least for now. One could argue that the entire real-time social media space is classic Blue Ocean as it careens onto the radar of more and more companies, brands, and organizations.

Even further back than Blue Ocean or Porter is the master strategist Sun Tzu, author of *The Art of War*, which remains a classic strategy guideline to this day. The iPhone's disruptive introduction into the marketplace is well documented. Sun Tzu emphasized the element of surprise (disruption) by advising that one not divulge the formation of one's forces and tactics beforehand and then attack when the competitor is unprepared:

- Be extremely subtle, even to the point of formlessness. Be extremely mysterious, even to the point of soundlessness. Thereby you can be the director of the opponent's fate.
- The formation and procedure used by the military should not be divulged beforehand.
- Attack when they are unprepared; make your move when they do not expect it.

In fact, most of the market was not ready for the surprise of the last decade: social media and real-time communication. A handful saw it coming, but the fact is that most businesses are just waking up to the realization that something has shifted. Their companies and employees are requiring new online skills to keep up or stay ahead of the competition, engage customers, and respond appropriately. The business community has a long way to go. Starting at the beginning, let us look at brand basics and real-time social media strategies in the big picture.

Branding in Real-Time

All companies seem to know that they need a brand or that they have a brand, but people still have difficulty defining what a brand is. Here are some definitions:

- ○ "A brand is a promise."—Ian Ryder, vice president for brand and communications for Unisys Corporation
- ○ "A brand is a conversation."—Steve Rappaport, director of knowledge solutions for Advertising Research Foundation
- ○ "A brand is a set of expectations."—Nicholas Ind, author of *Living the Brand*

Branding in real-time creates a center of gravity, a locus of intention and action that draws in fans, advocates, partners, and power. This requires superior skills from real-time marketing and branding executives if the companies they guide hope to compete in the global marketplace. Branding in real-time is a challenge to differentiate your product or company from the others through the gravitational pull of your brand, 24/7, anytime, anywhere. Consumer engagement can help carry the marketing load by implementing a strategy that gets people to talk about your brand around the clock in ways that sets you apart from the rest of the pack.

Global firms spend billions of dollars a year to build and maintain strong brands. They know that a prominent, recognizable brand can drive revenue growth and mitigate competitive risk. Even in recessionary times, smart marketing executives pitch for and get additional media dollars to continue developing brand awareness so that they can take advantage of the reduced voice of cash-strapped competition in the marketplace.

Free real-time social platforms layered with mainstream media are the new recession-friendly tactics for brand building both domestically and internationally. The effect that globalization has had on real-time marketing and brands has been spectacularly fast. Some new brands are seemingly born global or at the very least experience a quick rollout from home or lead countries into foreign markets. Long-established brands aggressively enhance their dominant positions across the globe, threatening less marketing-savvy local or regional brands. We see this in Chinese businesses in particular, both mainland and foreign. It has nothing to do with the ability to run the actual business. China was state-supported for decades, resulting in a general lack of under-standing and knowledge of marketing to build brand awareness and revenue.

It is also alarming how many companies do not understand the basics of competitive differentiation, much less how to maximize it via real-time marketing. In 2009, McKinsey published the results of a survey of nearly 1,700 executives from around the world that paints a highly positive picture of the business returns that result from what were called at the time Web 2.0 deployments.

Close to seven out of ten respondents (69 percent) reported that their companies "have gained measurable business benefits including more innovative products and services, more effective marketing, better access to knowledge, lower cost of doing business, and higher revenues."

In the survey, half the respondents reported that Web 2.0 tech-nologies have fostered in-company interactions across geographic borders, 45 percent cite interactions across functions, and 39 percent cite interactions across business units.

The measurable benefits cited span both knowledge management and simple cost cutting:

○ Increasing speed of access to knowledge: 68 percent
○ Reducing communication costs: 54 percent
○ Increasing effectiveness of marketing: 52 percent
○ Increasing speed of access to internal experts: 43 percent
○ Increasing customer satisfaction: 43 percent
○ Decreasing travel costs: 40 percent
○ Increasing employee satisfaction: 35 percent

The top-rated technologies in terms of internal use were the following:

o   Video sharing: 48 percent
o   Blogs: 47 percent
o   RSS: 42 percent
o   Social networking: 42 percent

For external use, such as connecting with partners and suppliers, the following technologies delivered the most benefits:

o   Blogs: 51 percent
o   Video sharing: 50 percent
o   Social networking: 49 percent
o   RSS: 45 percent

The survey revealed that the more technologies used, the more benefits the company accrued. As McKinsey put it:

Web 2.0 delivers benefits by multiplying the opportunities for collaboration and by allowing knowledge to spread more effectively. . . . Among respondents who report seeing benefits within their companies, many cite blogs, RSS, and social networks as important means of exchanging knowledge. These networks often help companies coalesce affinity groups internally. Finally, respondents report using Web videos more frequently since the previous survey; technology improvements have made videos easier to produce and disseminate within organizations.

New Strategic Considerations

We can conclude that strategy remains critical and that the element of real-time needs to be added posthaste. Following is a brief discussion of strategic areas every company needs to consider.

Real-Time Market Leadership

As we have seen, social media and real-time require companies to establish a different culture of communication to be effective. Because social technologies are having a direct impact on the way businesses operate, companies are trying to understand the challenges and find the best strategies. Bringing openness to what previously was considered proprietary material is disconcerting at first; however, companies such as Cisco and Kodak openly share their social media strategies on their Web sites for any and all to see. Sharing and transparency are two key elements of social media. To be true to the social media call, industry players are communicating, networking, and learning together to develop strategies and policies for the long-term success of their organizations.

The entire enterprise ecosystem is being affected by social and real-time technologies. In fact, because opening up social channels potentially affects multiple enterprise functions, companies are enlisting change management professionals to help them transform into real-time organizations. It necessitates answering questions such as: What is the scope of this new process? How many departments will be impacted? How many people will we need to hire? What is the time frame for the change? Additional considerations in a change management process are the organizational attributes, impacted groups, risk analysis, and so on.

The operational function that *owns* social media will utilize the various listening tools that are available and respond to conversations, help solve problems, and engage with customers and prospects. In some cases, this may mean that a big brand is mentioned literally 10,000 times a day. This brings up a key decision that has to be reached early on: Where do social media and real-time *live* in the organization? Is this a marketing function? Or is it an extension of customer relationship management, corporate communications, investor relations, or public relations? Once that is determined, the issue of who trains the organization on the value of the tools or sets policy will arise.

69

The short answer to where social media lives in a company is yes to all of the above. It can start in any one of the divisions, depending on which one is the ripest point of entry. However, the genesis of introducing social media to a company depends on (1) the culture of the company, (2) commitment from the highest executive levels to reeducate the workforce, and (3) the staff's commitment to change. These three elements will determine whether the internal transformation begins as an overall rebirth of the entire enterprise or starts one person, one department at a time.

The long answer is that deciding where social media lives will be a pivotal point in the evolution of the enterprise. Multiple points of entry are possible. The dirty little secret in most companies, large and small, is the continued "silo-ization" of departmental functions. There is a turf war out there in corporations, with each division protecting its ground. This fear and defensiveness is the antithesis of the open leadership required to survive and thrive in real-time. The real issue here is finding a way to close the gap between operational silos with cooperative bridges.

This much is clear: Because social media require authenticity and transparency, the primary social functions cannot be outsourced. It really requires the core voice from within the company. If no one on the inside is comfortable with taking on the task, consultants are needed to educate, advise, and guide campaigns as well as analyze and measure results. Ultimately, learning needs to be absorbed internally so that the voice comes from within the enterprise regardless of who creates the messages. Once real-time social media has been placed within a company with positive results, the process tends to spread to other divisions naturally. The best scenario is to fold social media into an enterprise across all divisions at once instead of parceling it out over time. That was the case with EMC Corporation, which made a commitment to assimilate social media into the enterprise with successful results directly connected to a higher stock price. The corporate journey is featured as a case story in Chapter 5.

Companies also need to decide if the voice in social media is that of the *brand* or a *personality*. Will the "brand" maintain a Twitter presence, or will a group of employees tweet on behalf of the brand? It turns out that either strategy can work as long as the company discloses its approach. A brand voice is reminiscent of the traditional spokesperson strategy. Most marketers know that Coke has always maintained a brand or company voice. The cola company has never had an official spokesperson. This is not an accident but a strategy. Pepsi, in contrast, has enlisted spokespersons including Britney Spears, David Hasselhoff, Enrique Iglesias, and Beyoncé Knowles. It should be noted that Pepsi made social media news when the company announced it was pulling out of advertising in Super Bowl XLIV in 2010 in favor of its new Refresh project. It is a completely social, crowdsourced, sharable, and ratable endeavor.

On the customer service front, consumers are having accelerated conversations among themselves about a brand, product, or service, and they are often able to solve problems and share information, eliminating the need for intervention from the customer service department or product marketing group. Forums have been around for a while, but the real-time nature of the new channels encourage interaction where questions are answered.

The market leaders will be those who operationalize social media functionalities to help achieve business results. Most companies go straight to asking, "Where's the ROI?" As in any new business process, the ROI (return on investment) is not always going to come in a traditional, straightforward manner. But as businesses have operationalized CRM and supply chain management over the last 30 years, social media and real-time have and will have a great effect on the way business is conducted.

The Collaborative Enterprise

Creating an enterprise that is collaborative and finding internal communication platforms for project and team work has been an expressed priority for most businesses. How well they do these things is another story. Companies have realized that there is advantage in providing collaborative software in the workplace that supports people in both their individual and cooperative work for at least the last decade. There are numerous tools to create virtual desktops, storage, and sharing in the cloud. Social technology platforms are accelerating the way people work together from the traditional proximity or geographic co-location paradigm to a virtual co-location paradigm. Again, it started with Web 2.0 tools such as wikis. Now internal portals and community platforms, Google Groups, and Google Buzz all provide types of virtual collaborative space. The social enterprise is truly an exciting frontier.

Sean Moffitt and Mike Dover are the authors of *Wikibrands*, which is part call to action and part action plan for businesses. They outline how to use the power of customer collaboration to drive businesses forward. Mike explains, "Crowdsourcing can be described as encouraging a 'contest economy,' but it can work. It allows those who were not able to participate in the past a chance to do so." Mike and Sean present the FLIRT model as a collaboration guide (*F*ocus, *L*anguage, *I*ncentives and Motivation, *R*ules, *T*ools and Platforms).

Social media and real-time tools that enable content consisting of text, maps, video, photos, files, and more are making their way into enterprises and are affecting employee effectiveness and efficiency as well as transforming the face of the enterprise. Yammer, Present. ly, Laconi.ca, and other real-time communication platforms for companies, groups, and organizations are gaining traction. Interestingly, Yammer was created for the employees of Geni, a family tree Web site, and is often referred to as Twitter for the corporation. Unlike Twitter, which limits users to 140 characters, Yammer users can type as much as needed and reply to specific messages. Proponents of enterprise microblogging platforms note that e-mail is no longer as efficient as it used to be. It is a communication tool but does not support real-time collaboration. However, detractors say that employees are reluctant to sign up for fear of being monitored by the employer and other employees.

Real-Time Search

Search engine optimization is both an art and a science. Millions of dollars have been spent by companies seeking to maximize their brands in search results. Real-time search just may change the find and be found game. The ability to search real-time status updates is already changing search behavior for early adopters. Search results become both more dynamic and more personalized, which means that search engine marketing will begin to look more like social media marketing. Key words will matter less, and freshness will matter more.

Think back to the plane that went down on the Hudson River in New York in 2009. The Now Lens presented that information *first* on Twitter. Newscasters were heard reporting, "This just in from Twitter. . . ." In fact, the Twitter search engine is proving to be very powerful as it tracks real-time events.

Here is a stunning example of the new world we are living in: The U.S. Library of Congress operates the National Digital Information Infrastructure and Preservation Program. According to its Web site, the LOC is pursuing a national strategy to collect, preserve, and make available significant digital content, especially information that is created in digital form only, for current and future generations. In April 2010 it was announced that Twitter messages will be archived permanently by the Library of Congress—all public tweets, starting from their inception in March 2006. This newfound zeal for real-time search is filling a latent market demand to know what has happened in the last one or two minutes. Everyone's looking for information in the moment, through the Now Lens. Paul Yiu, principal program manager of Microsoft's Bing, offers these insights:

Users have always been demanding about knowing the latest information, from knowing the medal count during Olympic season to updated weather information. Looking at the query logs, it is clear users expect major search engines such as Bing to access this type of information to answer their questions and help them make decisions.

While the nature of the information is different from traditional Web search, the concept of relevance stays true. Quality, trust, popularity, and timelines are the keys to rising above the noise, just as they are in traditional Web search. In addition to ranking documents, Bing now ranks the people behind the documents.

Some signs we see as signals of quality and social authority:

○ **Quality**: sharing links in Tweets and Facebook updates
○ **Trust:** other trustworthy people are sharing the same content. Not being part of spammy-looking communities
○ **Popularity**: Number of people retweeting or liking what you said/shared in the last minute, hour, day, or week
○ **Timeliness:** freshness and uniqueness of content

A brief history of search engines discloses that the very first tool used for searching on the Internet was called Archie (the name stands for *archives* without the *v*, not the red-haired teenager of comic book fame). It was created in 1990 by Alan Emtage, a student at McGill University in Montreal. The program downloaded the directory listings of all the files located on public anonymous FTP (File Transfer Protocol) sites, creating a searchable database of file names. Whereas Archie indexed computer files, "Gopher" indexed plain text documents. Gopher was created in 1991 by Mark McCahill at the University of Minnesota. (The program was named after the school's mascot.) Because these were text files, most of the Gopher sites became Web sites after the creation of the World Wide Web. In the early 1990s, the venture capital community in Silicon Valley started paying attention to the search market. Excite was introduced in 1993 by six Stanford University students. It used statistical analysis of word relationships to aid in the search process. Within a year,

Excite was incorporated, and it went online in December 1995. Jerry Yang and David Filo created Yahoo! in 1994. It started out as a listing of their favorite Web sites. What made it different was that each entry, in addition to the URL, also had a description of the page. Within a year the two received funding and Yahoo!, the corporation, was created.

This was followed by Lycos in 1994 and Infoseek and AltaVista in 1995. Google was launched in 1997 by Sergey Brin and Larry Page as part of a research project at Stanford University. Its genius at the time was to use inbound links to rank sites.

In February 1998, Jeffrey Brewer of Goto.com, a 25-employee start-up company (later Overture, now part of Yahoo!), presented a pay-per-click search engine proof-of-concept to the TED conference in California. This presentation and the events that followed created the pay-per-click (PPC) advertising system that is used today. Google then started search engine advertising in December 1999. The rest is history. Paid search is a multibillion-dollar business. Understanding SEO (search engine optimization) and SEM (search engine marketing) became critical in maximizing revenue for both online and offline companies.

Now *Google* is a noun and a verb. Googling something is part of our lexicon, like Xeroxing. However, until recently, these search results displayed only what the engines collected and stored in their databases. That information was historical. In this case, "historical" can be a day or two old or several years old.

Enter real-time search engines that index and deliver social media content and activity within minutes or even seconds. Headline news, natural calamities, rescue efforts, current events, and programs are all examples of what real-time search tracks. It also means doing superfast indexing of sites such as Twitter. Twitter operates in real-time and also offers real-time search tools that are getting more sophisticated every day. In December 2009 Google launched a real-time search feature that now appears on the search results pad. There are links to articles and tweets ranging from 5 to 60 minutes ago.

This tiny section of the social media and real-time market is exploding with innovations because real-time search can be used to leverage branding and advertising efforts by looking through the Now Lens. Real-time search is emerging as the best new listening tool to learn what consumers are saying about a brand or product right now. It's also imperative that brands be in the social media mix to be indexed in real-time by the search engines.

With real-time information, consumers will demand that companies react more quickly and be more responsive to them and their needs and requests. If they are not doing so already, companies will have to monitor hot topics, plan new promotion activities, and ensure that content is coordinated across Web sites, blogs, press releases, Twitter, Facebook, and LinkedIn to guarantee that all the pieces of the marketing puzzle work together.

The implications of social media and real-time search delivering all types of information for business are profound. Behavior pattern recognition is available almost instantly, allowing companies to capitalize on just-in-time marketing and social customer relationship management opportunities as never before around the world. This is already happening in Japan and China, where Baidu is used for real-time search.

Social Technologies for Learning Platforms and Education

Schools and corporate training environments have struggled to keep pace with mainstream digital and computer technologies because of high program costs, dated texts and materials, and general lack of interest. At the same time, students and employees are demanding Web-based tools in classroom and training environments that reflect the way they want to learn. Seok claims that "e-learning" is the pedagogy for new learning in the twenty-first century.[1] Today, most academic students at all levels get their information from the Internet. Students and employees want to watch, research, learn, and share information with one another. Some current social learning platforms offer distance education options that add course flexibility, decrease costs, and build general enrollment.

Companies such as the Nibi Software Group in Stillwater, Minnesota, have leveraged real-time and social platforms to configure YouTube, wikis, and Facebook Connect in a learning platform. This allows educators and students to interact anytime, anywhere, and learn or teach a variety of subjects. In addition, stakeholder communities composed of students, teachers, and administrators can collaborate to evolve the subject.

Troy A. Peterson, CEO and cofounder of the company, explains that there are a growing number of video educational resources on the Web, and this overwhelming growth of available information demands editors to identify, collect, and curate that content. The Nibi Software Group provides that curation and recently announced its new mobile application on Nibipedia.com.

Employee education within the enterprise using social technologies is also a new frontier. Corporate training has seen budget cuts over the years as a way to reduce expenditures. Internal education can be enhanced with free social tools to provide videos for product training and executive communication. LinkedIn is being used for lead generation in the sales department and for talent search in human resources.

It is clear that it is imperative for all organizations—commercial, nonprofit, government agencies, small business—to provide education and training to employees and senior staff on social media so that they can gain proficiency on the platforms and awareness of how tools will affect business positively.

It is also critical to make sure that all associates understand the company's social media policy. If a company does not have one, it needs to get one fast. Most likely, a number of employees already have Facebook pages, blogs, and Twitter and Flickr accounts. Clear guidelines on what can be shared as an employee versus what is personal will protect staff from potentially tarnished images or liability. Employees should be encouraged to ask themselves, Who am I representing here? Who else is likely to see this? Ultimately, employees are potentially the most powerful brand ambassadors, so they should be aware of the social media policy and the implications of that policy.

Privacy and security concerns have become more prominent and will remain a significant issue, specifically as they relate to social sites. Reminding employees to check and regularly monitor their social media profile privacy settings is imperative. Many companies ban social sites from use during regular office hours.

There are mixed opinions about this open versus closed policy. A major U.S. technology company on the East Coast allows employees to access their own social sites because that is where they get real-time information that could serve clients. Other companies claim that access is distracting and squanders company time. At the very least, human resources and marketing/media relations should be given direct access. It is hard to believe, but there are major corporations and institutions that will not allow this.

Getting Started

In addition to presenting the broader overview of real-time marketing strategies, this section answers ever-present questions about the how and what of real-time marketing strategy. What do we do first? How do we do it? These questions come up so frequently that they need to be answered immediately. Nothing beats a well-planned strategy flaw-lessly executed with successful results. Here are some proven tactics that work.

Get Educated

The first step is to get educated and informed on the subject of social media and real-time marketing. Learn what is a myth and what is here to stay. Attend seminars and Webinars and schedule executive training for your senior teams. We are at the beginning of a shift that will have far-reaching implications. Seek the experience of experts and your peers. Find consultants who can help take your company into this new world with solid business practices and procedures.

Get Practical

The next step is to get practical. To develop an effective real-time marketing strategy, start with listening as research. Put aside what you think you know about your potential target consumer and your preconceived notions about the brand. This is a journey of discovery. Set up profiles on social media for the purpose of listening to what is being said about your business, by whom, and how often as well as determining sentiment. Carefully review the profiles of the biggest fans and critics. Gauge and track like interests and media choices. Then compare the cost of hiring an outside research firm and doing time-consuming focus groups to that of free audience and consumer real-time research. The information gleaned will be priceless.

In addition to researching outside your company, look inside. Conduct your internal technology and brand audit. Understand your internal and external technology habits and proficiency. Information gathered from this exercise will reveal who in the company may be familiar with social platforms and be available to contribute insights to the overall real-time strategy or spearhead an internal social media task force.

When possible, get employees together in an informal atmosphere for the technology and brand survey. People typically enjoy sharing their favorite choices about entertainment, sports, or news and how they consume media. At the outset, employees often think they do not participate in social media only to learn that they engage more frequently than they thought. If in-person gatherings are prohibitive because of company scale, try videoconferencing on Skype or Webex, for example. Post the findings so that employees can see the results and how they compare to one another. Assign someone to tally answers and track those who are the most savvy about social media.

The employee survey should include the following, at a minimum:

1. Do you use the Internet to search for information?
2. Have you ever commented on an article or blog?
3. Do you have a blog?
4. Do you have a social media profile on LinkedIn, Facebook, or Twitter?
5. Have you ever watched a video on YouTube?
6. Do you watch video on your phone?
7. Do you play online video games with multiple users?
8. Have you ever commented on a forum or chat room?
9. Have you ever posted any photos to Flickr?

Set Objectives

After assembling the real-time social marketing team and your target consumer's social profile, determine the company's overall objective. Is it to build brand awareness, start having a voice in social media, or sell products or services? Listen to what interests your customers and then consider what kind of events or topics they would like that could generate conversation about your business. Because conversation is organic, it gives life to every other element of a campaign, so look at real-time platforms that will support buzz.

Starting with tactics has been known to cause great frustration among traditional media types because it is counterintuitive thinking. Nevertheless, it is an excellent exercise to free the media team from the traditional advertising process. Unfortunately, too many brands, regardless of industry, will craft an expensive, traditional advertising and media campaign and then try to plug in a social media component as an afterthought. This leaves everyone annoyed if the social media portion does not deliver on expectations.

Effective real-time strategies can and do exist without a traditional ad buy component. Kogi BBQ trucks and Zappos are making social media history by having launched and maintained significant financial growth supported entirely by social media brand awareness. Kogi is now famous for tweeting where it will park in Southern California to its foodie fans, who line up around the block, and Zappos was recently bought by Amazon.

Traditional and Social Media Layering

It is worth repeating that the best real-time marketing strategies are those that include traditional and social media layering. When possible, premiere TV commercials on the company Facebook page and branded YouTube channel. This helps subscribers feel that they are getting special treatment, buys social currency, and often increases organic buzz. Make sure the real-time portion is in cadence with the overall rollout of the entire marketing campaign. Cadence is the rhythm, beat, and phased implementation of a marketing campaign. The real-time marketing layer is the organic portion of cadence.

Also, make all social profiles brand-specific and not one-offs for separate short-lived promotions. The goal is to accumulate likes, followers, and subscribers for remarketing purposes. Many companies squander millions of potential customer relationships by not implementing an engagement strategy to mobilize fans as brand advocates for future engagement. Successful real-time marketing strategies have the specific core elements called out here. Keep in mind that commitment to social media will last longer than most marriages.

Successful Real-Time Marketing Strategy Elements

- Deep listening
- Responsiveness: engaging and respectful dialogue with consumers
- Free research
- Planned cadence
- Integration with traditional and digital platforms
- Generating, participating in, facilitating conversation
- Sticking to a plan while nimble
- Having a reputation response plan

○ Thinking counterintuitively
○ Making a long-term commitment

The social media press release is a powerful tool in the real-time arsenal. In addition to being indexed by search engines, it can be posted on the company Web site, blog, or Facebook page and tweeted. This is one of the easiest and fastest ways to drive awareness of one's company, yet not all businesses have discovered this. There are many free or low-cost services that will report open rates and pick up data. PitchEngine is becoming a favorite. This is an affordable, viable alternative to online press release distribution companies that charge high monthly fees. Level of service, price, and features vary among online wire services. A social press strategy should always be included as one of the marketing layers.

Twitter, according to technology beta tester and app developer Rodney Rumford, is a particle accelerator. Regular users have strong voices even though approximately 60 percent of new users drop out in the first 30 days. Retention is about 40 percent. That is very acceptable compared with a successful e-mail campaign with an open rate of 1.5 to 2 percent. Twitter messaging is managed with an editorial calendar that looks like an Excel chart where specific tweets can be scheduled and released via automation, thus reducing labor time. Do not let the fact that one can use only 140 characters limit your imagination. Tweets can contain links to free video downloads, a vacation giveaway, or a chance for a test drive. Tweets serve as a path to Web site videos or wherever one wants it to go.

Avoid the mandate of setting hard numbers for Twitter followers or Facebook likes. Businesses misunderstand the relationship process when they demand "5,000 Twitter followers" or "20,000 friends on Facebook for my brand." This is flawed and misdirected thinking because in real-time marketing it is not about the *quantity*; it is about the *quality*. Be real. Give consumers information that is useful or entertaining, preferably both.

No one knows if or when Facebook will burn out, but one can expect that it or its unknown cousin will remain. An effective use of Facebook in business is to create custom tabs or pages for a business or brand for promotions. Facebook provides template tabs, but it is advisable to hire a company that specializes in custom tab or app development. Also be advised that the Facebook back end can have technical difficulties that might lead to custom tabs being deleted. Facebook keeps the glitches to a minimum, but it is wise to be aware of snags at the outset. These potential problems should not exclude Facebook from a real-time marketing mix.

YouTube is one of many video-sharing sites and has a comments feed that can be public or private. People can become subscribers of a YouTube channel and get updates if any content changes. Monitoring the site is left up to the company or agency that oversees the video. A critical piece of information for companies that set video view benchmarks is that from the moment a commercial or video is uploaded to YouTube, the rating clock starts ticking. Viewership must reach 250,000 within the first 48 hours for a video to get "ranked" as one of the "most viewed." Reaching this position generates more curiosity, which then increases viewership. Administrators for YouTube and Facebook should not delete all negative comments. It is advisable to delete profanity or offensive language, but criticisms encourage dialogue and commentary. It will become evident to viewers if the channel has only glowing reviews. "Remove" and "delete" have different functions as well. "Remove" blocks the negative message but still counts it in the overall view tally. "Delete" gets rid of the comment forever and is not tallied. If the goal is to increase viewership numbers, remove but do not delete.

Placing video on YouTube will reach a global audience. Kevin Yen, director of strategic partnerships at YouTube, recently said, "Anyone can record a video, add complex and sophisticated special effects, and share it . . . with translatable subtitles to the world. And as this market matures, the rewards for these original content creators and distributors will increase." Video is the most sought after content on the Internet and mobile. Comedy is the number one viewer draw on YouTube. Celebrities and news are leaders as well. There are over 300 video-sharing sites on the Internet. The world is definitely watching user-generated content.

Streaming video or live video is another engagement tool in a real-time marketing strategy. Oddly, this is an underused platform with a tremendous upside for businesses if executed correctly. Delivering streaming video is relatively simple. Instead of distributing video that sits on a site for playback on YouTube or Hulu, video is streamed live on the Internet either by hard wire or wirelessly. Conferences, concerts, government meetings, and classes can be streamed live from different parts of the world in different languages. Shoppers can become models by showing off their outfits on a live stream delivered throughout the store and online. Ustream and Justin.TV are only two of the many streaming companies that provide this service.

The Altamira cave paintings in Spain might be thought of as the precursor to photo sharing. Viewing pictures fills a primal need and continues with the popularity of photo-sharing sites such as Flickr and Photobucket. Facebook is the world's largest photo album for its 500 million-plus users. Create conversation and generate free publicity by asking friends and followers to submit photos of themselves interacting with your brand. Ask them to vote or comment on their favorite and then let them see the favorites. Setting up a Flickr account for a business increases exposure for the company because the titles or tags are searched. That is why photos should be posted with titles whenever possible.

Interactive two-dimensional and three-dimensional screens can serve as conversation starters. Technology exists that will let a shopper change an outfit on an avatar to a different color. Layering 3-D with alternative reality and gaming is the most successful way to earn product recognition. When all these activities are led by a solid real-time marketing strategy, conversation and buzz can explode like a volcano.

LinkedIn often is overlooked as a relevant social platform for business. It is not just a job search site. Take another look. Over 65 million profiles reflect an upscale, highly educated marketplace. It is like a virtual trade show: Everyone is there, and you can connect and talk with those you know and those you would like to know. In addition to its function as a job recruitment site, groups and discussions present the opportunity to build brand trust and showcase expertise.

Lessons Learned: Fail Fast and Fail Forward

Maybe what Mark Zuckerberg meant in his quote earlier in this chapter was that "working it out in real-time" enables a company to fail fast and move forward quickly. The idea is to move forward and move on. Social technology resources are so inexpensive that companies can take more risks, fail fast, and recuperate even faster. Real-time social technology functions are now commonplace so that *not* having sharable, ratable, location-based platforms will make a company or organization the odd man out.

New revenue streams will be enabled in almost every industry as real-time feeds and applications allow companies to change in mid-stream to make user-customized and personalized shopping available. Companies can tweak features, ads, and marketing campaigns in a shorter time frame. If something is not delivering expected results, it can be changed in real-time. If it does work, it can be easily replicated, augmented, and repeated faster across more platforms. Real-time marketing strategies will move in concert with these business shifts as well.

Even if a business is not Internet-based or does not work in real-time, its current customers and other stakeholders are weighing in on the brand in real-time among themselves. Companies should be thinking about analytics tools that measure these positive and negative sentiments as part of their overall research to help create more revenue-enhancing responses.

The bottom line here is to do something, even if it fails at first. Do not be a poser talking a good social media game but not really being engaged. Get your team educated and figure out how to jump in regardless of the form it takes, even if it is an extension of current reputation management or competitive intelligence. Fail fast and keep going. Do not sit this out too long or you will wake up one day and realize that everyone is speaking a new language you don't understand.

Learn from Your Peers

The power of real-time marketing lies in its immediacy to listen and respond. It is also the most granular and cost-efficient way to reach customers. This chapter has shed light on overall strategic thought and tactics as well as inspired creative ideas.

The case stories in Chapter 5 illustrate the transformational power of real-time marketing when a commitment is made to learn, strategize, and execute with the tools outlined here. We continue our journey with you and others who are opening their own new real-time chapter.

CHAPTER 5

Real-Time Marketing Case Stories: Lessons in Leadership

Once people grasp the potential power of real-time marketing strategies and social technologies, they tend to ask: Would my business benefit from social media? What do we do? How do we get started? How do we know if we should be on Facebook or Twitter or LinkedIn—or all of them?

All those questions confronted the businesses and organizations featured in this chapter. The success stories we have gathered are from top brands and rising companies with real-life campaigns that illustrate best practices and provide clear answers to the most frequently asked questions about social media. These documented journeys are helping to accelerate world-changing ideas and spotlight the positive impact we can all have individually and collectively on local and global communities created by social technologies. Their innovation, solid work, brilliant thought, and courage will astound and motivate you to think and communicate differently through the Now Lens.

Whether their stories directly reflect your industry is immaterial; the vitally important part is the similarities among organizations confronted with change. Their journeys will provide real solutions that will light your path. Some speak about foundations and strategies that led to success. Others give detailed information about platform selection and use. A common theme is the belief in social media education and information as a critical starting point. Every subject acknowledged the essential need for internal social media training and proficiency. They all found that education helped them navigate obstacles to success. Another thread was internal resistance to change. Whether moving from a closed, proprietary culture to an open one or adapting to new collaborative tools, these thought leaders met pushback with wisdom and tenacity. They and their stories challenged existing boundaries to shine a light on the possible. Yet another common thread emerged during the interviews: Every subject described his or her step into real-time social media as a journey. Without exception, each one knew this was only the beginning, and these organizations will continue to evolve over time, discovering new communicating tools and methods as they arise.

The use of case stories as a learning tool is well established. Harvard, Stanford, Wharton, and many other business schools use the case study method in their curricula. It is well documented that lessons in leadership can and do emerge from studying business conflicts others have faced and conquered. Since these case stories are about social media and conversation, we decided that the term *case story* better exemplified the transformational engagement experiences within and outside the enterprise.

Rigorous selection criteria were exercised to identify the case stories included here. There were many worthy candidates we wished we could have included. Representatives from some of the world's biggest companies and organizations contacted us to submit their best practices and lessons learned for this book. The following collection made the cut because they showcase ideas, trends, challenges, and opportunities that define not only the Now Lens but the Next Lens as well. Their stories convey granular executions that also have global applications. We believe they truly exhibit the power of harnessing these new real-time tools and applying them to today's challenges.

Although our focus is on real-time social media marketing cases, what you will read goes beyond branding and marketing. It will be evident that globally and collectively we are standing on the verge of significant market evolution. Our contributors realized this along the way as well.

Doing the background work on these case stories, interviewing key people, and following the trail from the beginning to end was a transformative experience for the authors as well. We are in awe at how innovative and inspiring these people were and how their hard work and vision produced and continue to generate tangible, measurable results. We are pleased and delighted to introduce you to the dedicated people quietly architecting transformations across a variety of industries; their stories contain lessons in leadership for everyone.

The American Red Cross
One Tweet Turns into $33 Million for Haitian Relief

CASE STORY   People can be enormously generous in times of disaster. This story takes that generosity to soaring heights and details how the Now Lens of real-time communication is very immediate, something that is critical in emergency situations. We describe a quantum leap for all marketing—not just cause marketing—because it showcases the best in technology, people, innovation, giving, and trust relationships.

Mobile giving was placed on center stage by real-time social media and leveraged immediate, unprecedented donations for the American Red Cross Haitian relief efforts in response to the devastating 7.0 earthquake that occurred in January 2010. Text donations were coordinated by mGive in a joint effort with the U.S. State Department and the American Red Cross. Anyone with a mobile phone and an account with a major wireless carrier could text "Haiti" to the number 90999 and donate $10 to the Red Cross. That amount was charged to the donor's cell phone bill.

According to our friends at the Red Cross, it is important to note that most donations in a disaster are raised in the first few days. Real-time donations for Haiti broke all records, topping $33 million. It is truly a profound story on multiple levels that will have long-lasting effects on the nature of fund-raising.

ORGANIZATION   The American Red Cross

INDUSTRY   Nonprofit

OBJECTIVE   Quickly deliver relief to victims of the Haitian earthquake catastrophe

STRATEGY   Give people who want to help a means of doing so immediately

INTERVIEWEES
Susan Murray, Senior Officer, the American Red Cross
Wendy Harman, Director Social Media, the American Red Cross
James Eberhard, CEO, Mobile Accord
Katie Dowd, Digital Technology, U.S. Department of State

OTHER KEY CONTRIBUTORS
David Diggs, *Chairman, CTIA*
Katie Stanton, *Special Advisor, U.S. Department of State*
Brad Blanken, *Mobile Accord, formerly with CTIA*

real-time marketing case stories: lessons in leadership

Peggy Dyer, *Chief Marketing Officer, the American Red Cross*
Susan Watson, *Former Director of Marketing and Visibility, the American Red Cross*
Josh Kittner, *Senior Marketing Consultant, the American Red Cross*
Doug Gardner, *Jump Market Strategies, Consultant to the American Red Cross*

Why This Is Important to You

Forget everything you thought you knew about fund-raising. Organizations and people around the world are realizing that they can participate in fund-raising efforts quickly and easily wherever they are "in the moment" via their mobile devices. This is a game-changer. Because total charitable giving will soar in the future, understanding how this happened is extremely significant for nongovernmental organizations (NGOs), fund-raising organizations, and their businesses partners. This case story illustrates how cause marketing benefits can be realized across the board in terms of aid giving and co-branding awareness building.

Combining Twitter, Facebook, YouTube, and mobile texting gave stakeholders in the American Red Cross Haitian relief case story the ability to update, solicit donations, and post on-the-ground eyewitness reports in real-time. It also spread the word faster and farther than anyone expected. The butterfly effect was triggered—small, seemingly random actions by people created great and lasting change. The same basic processes can be duplicated for local, regional, national, and international fund-raising efforts. Not all nonprofits have the name recognition of the American Red Cross. However, if they look to this stellar brand and the new path it has carved for effortless giving, smaller or lesser known organizations will want to follow in its footsteps.

Rapid deployment of text Haiti to 90999 in the United States helped raise millions through a "Text Haiti" appeal that let mobile phone users make a $10 donation to the American Red Cross via a text message. In addition to the value of merging mobile and real-time social media, businesses can learn the importance of building relationships and sampling technology ahead of time so that when a significant opportunity presents itself, systems will be in place, and everyone will rise together.

- Relationships are the key, and foundations are critical. The interactions of the three stakeholders—mGive, the State Department, and the Red Cross—were in place.
- Small amounts, ease of use, and more people equals a much greater gain for the cause.
- Smart phones in the hands of users serve as touch points for businesses and brands with clients or consumers.

Mobile minicomputer capabilities are driving financial transactions of all types, not just purchasing goods but making donations, which was their purpose in this

91

case story. The same mobile functionality can be applied to a variety of uses across industries on a local or a global scale with unforeseen benefits.

Events that led to the American Red Cross Haitian relief donation cascade can be told best through the eyes of those who made it happen. Every decision maker was thoughtful, focused, and committed to the end goal. These skills are essential in crisis situations, whether corporate or altruistic.

Introduction: The American Red Cross

Headquartered in Washington, DC, the American Red Cross was founded on May 21, 1881, by Clara Barton, who first heard about the international aid network while on a trip to Europe after the American Civil War. Originally designed to protect individuals injured by war, the American Red Cross has evolved into the single largest supplier of blood in the United States and is synonymous with emergency relief, education, and training.

The American Red Cross played a pivotal role in helping the U.S. government create the Federal Emergency Management Agency (FEMA) and serves as the principal supplier of mass care in federally declared disasters. Though it has very strong ties with the national government (the President of the United States is its honorary chairman), the Red Cross operates as an entirely volunteer-led organization supported by donations from the public. It also works very closely with the International Committee of the Red Cross in addressing the effects of international conflict as well as delivering assistance to victims of natural disasters around the world.

In addition to evolving the scope of its services, the Red Cross has transformed its outreach. Wendy Harman was hired as the director social media and has ushered the organization into social media by developing and overseeing the brand's presence on Facebook, Twitter, YouTube, and Flickr. Wendy Harman and Susan Murray were at the center of Red Cross Haiti earthquake relief awareness building through real-time social media.

The Situation

DATE January 12, 2010

LOCATION Port-au-Prince, Haiti

TIME 4:53 p.m. ET [1653 local time (2153 GMT)]

OVERVIEW A 7.0 magnitude earthquake that lasted approximately 35 seconds hit 10 miles west of the capital city, Port-au-Prince, at a depth of 6.2 miles. It was the most powerful temblor to hit the island country in 200 years. Within the first 48 hours, an estimated 30 aftershocks continued to strike the area, ranging in magnitude from 4.2 to 5.9. In addition to the city, with a population of roughly 2 million people, the quake left 3 million in need of emergency care. As of June 30, 2010, there were 230,000 earthquake-related deaths in addition to 300,000 injuries.

Considering that 90 percent of Port-au-Prince was destroyed and victims' remains continued to be discovered in the rubble, fatalities are expected to rise.

The Challenge

As soon as the massive earthquake struck Haiti, it was clear that it was of catastrophic proportions. Communications with the island were cut off almost entirely, virtually isolating the country. Reports started to trickle in that the presidential palace and government buildings had been destroyed. The world community would be summoned to help this stricken neighbor.

Timing and Sense of Urgency

Susan Murray's Perspective: The American Red Cross

The majority of the funds raised for our Haiti relief efforts were raised over the course of the first few weeks. In the case of our specific mobile fund-raising efforts, the vast majority was raised in the first two weeks. Our experience with disasters has shown us that immediacy is key. It is important that people have a safe and easy way to give quickly. People are ready and willing to give when a disaster strikes, and it's important that we have a way for people to get involved in helping quickly. Mobile giving allows everyone a fast, easy way to turn compassion into action and allows the Red Cross to help more people.

Katie Dowd's Perspective: U.S. Department of State

We didn't understand the extent of the damage and we didn't understand what the needs were going to be, but we knew that money was the easiest and fastest way that people could give.

Background

The first 12 hours in the Haitian relief effort brought together relationships with key people that stretched from the United States to the Middle East and ranged in duration from one week to decades. Their communications played out in real-time and resulted in action that was catapulted by mobile, social, and traditional media.

It is vital to grasp the importance and power of relationships as well as tested systems as a foundation to communicate with and mobilize millions of people toward a common goal swiftly. All our contributors confirmed that if those relationships and systems had not been in place, the alacrity and success of the undertaking described here would not have occurred.

Key Point: These relationships mirrored fundamental social media elements of openness, authenticity, and transparency in real-time.

Building the Initial Community: Relationships
The American Red Cross
CTIA (International Association for the Wireless Telecommunications Industry)
Mobile Accord
The State Department

Susan Murray—Background
Senior Officer, the American Red Cross

I had been working with the Red Cross off and on for eight years total and served as director of corporate partnerships from 2001 to 2006. I was interested in mobile, and wanted to manage our partnership with CTIA because I saw a lot of potential for the mission of the Red Cross. I got to know David Diggs, head of CTIA's Wireless Foundation. We started talking in 2002 on how to use mobile for emergency preparedness and blood drive recruitment. David began working with us on mobile fund-raising at that time as well. We started with the 2004 Indian Ocean tsunami and fund-raised around Hurricane Katrina. Those efforts raised around $120,000 and $150,000, respectively. They were spearheaded by David, CTIA, and his member carriers who were part of the "Text 2 Help" campaign. It was back when a short vanity code was used for texting, so we picked 24357 as our short code because it spelled "2HELP." We were pleased with our efforts and deemed them successful for their time. We were amazed that so many people were willing to give $5 through their phone bills.

Our agreement with CTIA allowed us to implement Text 2 Help any time there was a highly visible regional or national disaster. As with our online channel, we understood that local media coverage would be necessary to build awareness for the need and explain ways to give. Since donating via cell phone was so new, it was even more important that we build awareness for the channel through local media promoting the short code.

Over time, we discovered several shortcomings with the code 24357 given to us by CTIA—the $5 donation limit and our inability to collect donor information (which prevented us from contacting these supporters again). David and I remember talking when Katrina happened; we decided to pick $5 as the amount to donate. We thought that since text and mobile giving were so new, people might be reluctant to give more than $5 initially, and we decided to move forward with a $5 campaign for the Disaster Relief Fund. We now know that people are willing to give $10. The other shortcoming of 24357 was that we were not collecting all the donor data, like cell phone numbers, because we didn't have an ASP [application service provider] involved. We were not allowed to create opt-in messages or send outbound messages to the donor group. We recognized that this inability to capture and cultivate these new donors was an issue we wanted to rectify. At the time, our Text 2 Help partners (who were providing this service to the Red Cross and the public for free) were not willing to act as an ASP for the Red Cross. Around the same time, I left the Red Cross for two years to have my two children and work with other nonprofits. When I came back to help the Red Cross on different projects, including mobile giving, I was thrilled to be able to work again with CTIA and David Diggs.

In 2009, the Red Cross began to develop a more proactive and longer-term approach to the organization's mobile strategy. We were willing to invest in an ASP so we could start collecting donor data and see what we could do with mobile giving. We issued a request for information to some of the top mobile ASPs and conducted preliminary interviews. We were poised to hire an ASP to run our own program related to 24357 or secure another short code. One of the ASP finalists was Mobile Accord out of Denver, Colorado. We were in the final stages of interviewing companies when the earthquake struck Haiti.

Wendy Harman: Background
Director Social Media, the American Red Cross

I love the social Web more than most people do, but the week before the earthquake, I was frustrated. While I felt confident about the Red Cross's presence—we're great at listening, engaging, providing valuable content, and generally inciting meaningful discussion—we weren't getting great results in driving mission-related behavior. For instance, during Typhoon Ondoy (September–October, 2009), "Red Cross" was a trending topic on Twitter for over 24 hours with thousands of people retweeting a call for donations, but we didn't receive an increase in donations at all.

On January 12, 2010, I had packed up my office and was preparing to leave at five o'clock when I heard the report that a major earthquake had just hit Haiti. I remember turning around and walking back to my desk. This time, the public was ready not only to spread the word, but to actually take action too.

James Eberhard: Background
CEO, Mobile Accord

In 2001, I started up a company called 9squared. It was the first ringtone distributor company in the United States. The billing mechanism to charge ringtones on the cell phone bill is the same mechanism to charge donations. I sold 9squared in 2004 to a company in the UK [United Kingdom] and moved to London, where I ran our global office. During that time, I got the perfect exposure to mobile giving in the UK. There was a campaign for LIVE AID going on at the time, and in six days it raised £2.2 million. I was amazed at the power of mobile giving. I was coming from a place where I was selling ringtones to the youth market. They were buying ringtones as 30-second song clips for $3 each. I never really felt like I was giving back so seeing the power of mobile giving, I thought to myself, this is what I'm going to do. I'm going to enable this and put together a mechanism that will help drive social media, social awareness, and be able to help a lot of people around the world.

95

^That's when I moved back to Denver in 2005 and set up Mobile Accord for the mission of enabling mobile giving. It took three years for us to launch our first donation campaign because we had to get the carriers to embrace the channel and get them to waive their fee. The United Way Campaign was the first day-to-day mobile donation campaign launched in the United States. I met Richard Holbrooke a few years ago and told him about what we were doing with mobile phones and text donations. As soon as he entered the administration as the special representative for Afghanistan and Pakistan, a member of his team, Ashley Bommer, reached out to me and started talking about how to use mobile phones to help distribute information, help empower people through real-time knowledge information, and build a social network. We started working with the U.S. State Department on that and launched Humari Awaz, which is a social network in Pakistan. Secretary Clinton announced it at the end of October last year. We anticipated 24 million messages delivered in the first year. Within the last seven months, we've delivered 300 million messages. We've been able to bring a million people in Pakistan together.

We have an amazingly robust platform that is able to do location-based billing transactions, social media, and MMS [multimedia messaging service]. It provides the ability for Pakistan to raise money for donations. So we are out there with Ambassador Holbrooke's team in discussion with the carriers and telco regulators. Advancing social change through the distribution of information is the core mission of what we are doing.

Katie Dowd: Background
New Media Director, the State Department

I was in the campaign environment for my whole life before I joined the State Department. I ran Senator Clinton's Internet team when she ran for president. We used digital tools to follow her travels, convey her mission, and share information on a bilateral meeting. We also use the tools to solve problems; for example, the State Department used Twitter to dispel rumors of a coup in Madagascar.

We were just beginning to break into the potential for mobile during the presidential campaign. Certainly mobile reached a tipping point with Obama and his text message initiative about who his vice president nominee was going to be. Even then, they had not been able to truly mobilize the channel into a fund-raising tool. At that point, we hadn't been able to either and struggled similarly for Senator Clinton.

We talk about this a lot. We just had not been able to help people make that switch to feel comfortable making a transaction through social media and seeing it as a mode of donating. It will be very interesting to see the real change happen when people no longer have any hesitancy to hit a button and pass money through their phones, especially as mobile banking and remittances get bigger around the world.

Tuesday, January 12, 2010
TIME 4:53 p.m. E.T (2153 GMT)
7.0 earthquake hits Port-au-Prince, Haiti
THE FIRST TWO HOURS

Katie's Perspective: U.S. Department of State

From the SD side, this is what happened right after the earthquake. There was little information about the extent of the damage and lives lost. We knew basic communication channels were down. Our chief of staff and counselor Mills reached out and asked for ways that we could get information from Haiti and provide support.

There are three of us in our department: Katie Stanton, me, and Caitlin Klevorick. We got on the phone and came up with the idea to use mobile to encourage people through their cell phone to donate and to get this up and running right away. In order to make things happen quickly, we decided to divide and conquer. Stanton contacted James at four o'clock in the morning in Pakistan so we could get Mobile Accord on board. Understanding the need, he mobilized quickly.

I contacted legal to make sure we could work with the Red Cross, that there were no concerns. We vetted with our chief of staff and counselor to be ready to go all out and promote the effort once we had clearance. We quickly mobilized to get approval here and set up. We came to an agreement that we would all work together and established "text Haiti to 90999" within hours after the earthquake hit. By 7:30 or 8 p.m., we were live with this.

It was at that moment that our team here at the State Department really mobilized to help promote and get the word out about this being the main avenue through which people could have the biggest impact in helping right away.

James's Perspective: Mobile Accord

4:30 a.m. Islamabad, Pakistan

It was about 4:30 in the morning. My phone starts ringing off the hook. It was a call from Katie Stanton at the State Department. I just met Katie for the first time a week prior at a dinner with Secretary Clinton discussing foreign policies. The relationship with Katie was developed right there at that dinner. So she called and woke me up. Told me the earthquake in Haiti had just happened and could we turn on a donation campaign for it. Katie and I were looking at who should we have as a partner and agreed on the Red Cross.

At that point, I called my guys back in Denver. I let them know that the earthquake just happened in Haiti and that we needed to do a donation campaign. My team reached out to the Red Cross. We turned on a campaign in an hour. We let the State Department know it was live.

Susan's Perspective: The American Red Cross

That night at about seven o'clock, I checked my e-mail and received a message from David at CTIA introducing me by e-mail to Brad Blanken at Mobile Accord. Brad had worked at CTIA with David on their short code program and remembered that CTIA had done a program for the American Red Cross in the past. He contacted David and asked who to contact at the Red Cross to get a mobile fund-raising program up and running.

I was already familiar with the company because we had just received responses to our RFI from them saying that they really wanted to do a mobile program, had the support of the State Department, and had a code they wanted to use and the keyword *Haiti*. I do not know if Brad was aware the Red Cross was already talking to Mobile Accord, but the timing was right and we went into handling the details and securing a mobile agreement within minutes of getting that e-mail from David Diggs. We decided $10 was the right amount, and I'm glad we did that because it was affordable and impactful. I'm convinced that if we stuck with $5 as our giving option—as we did with our prior mobile fund-raising efforts—we would have raised half as much. A relatively small percentage of donors opted to give more than once (and I don't think $5 donors would have gone to the trouble of giving multiple times).

Wendy's Perspective: The American Red Cross

It quickly became very clear this was a major event. We immediately placed our director for international response operations between a Flip camera and a map of Haiti to acknowledge the disaster and inform the public, "We know the earthquake in Haiti has happened. We do not have a lot of information yet, but we will keep you informed about our response efforts and staff on the ground as soon as we know." This was the first video about the event to be uploaded to YouTube and was placed on their home page for several days. Within one hour of the earthquake we similarly updated Twitter, Facebook, and our blog and continued to update an information-hungry public with every piece of news we had for many weeks.

Building Awareness in Real-Time
THE NEXT 12 HOURS

James's Perspective

It must have been six or seven o'clock Denver time when we turned on the campaign. From there it started going viral with Twitter and other mechanisms. The next morning about 9 a.m. Denver time the campaign had done $170,000 to $180,000, all driving off of social media. Close of first day $3 million, the next day was over $5 million dollars, and it continued from there.

We noticed primarily Twitter, and to some extent Facebook, really accelerated media's interest in writing the story about mobile donations and about Haiti.

98

Susan's Perspective: The American Red Cross

The fact that the media were reporting the disaster immediately made it clear that the earthquake was big. MSNBC and CNN were actually reporting the short code, which gave it legitimacy. It was also on Twitter. Twitter may have even been first. It all happened so quickly. Cable news outlets such as MSNBC and CNN were also continuously reporting the code.

There were some nerve-wracking moments when people well-regarded in social media were saying the text code wasn't legitimate. Some well-meaning people were familiar with our 24357 code and thought that 90999 was not legitimate. The Red Cross and the State Department aggressively corrected these misperceptions by using our social media channels. We would not have had the same outcome had we not been so forceful about refuting that rumor.

Wendy's Perspective: The American Red Cross

As soon as we received the text code from Mobile Accord, we tweeted, "You can text "HAITI" to 90999 to give $10 to relief efforts." The White House and State Department tweeted at about the same time. That was about 9:30 p.m. By the next afternoon we had raised $3 million. That has never been done before. By January 14, there were 2.3 million tweets about the mobile giving campaign. It completely restored my faith in the ability to drive real action with social media.

Katie's Perspective: U.S. Department of State

Right when we convened with our team here and were ready to go, we activated a number of social network communities that we specifically work on for the State Department. We have our Twitter feed @StateDept, State.Gov; we have an active Facebook profile, YouTube Channel, and Flicker; and we also have a number of properties throughout all our embassies, including Haiti. The whole western hemisphere region has a very robust social networking presence. Several of our ambassadors have their own Twitter feeds and FB pages. Our Public Diplomacy Office also has a series of properties through what is America.gov. Once this was turned on, we used all of those networks and communities to get out information.

We immediately reached out to my counterparts at the White House and the other agencies: the Department of Justice, Department of Energy, Department of Commerce. We reached out to all of them to let them know we set up this effort and asked if they would help in any way they could. They were all willing to promote this through their channels.

It was all over the news. Celebrities really took to it. Ben Stiller has over a million followers on Twitter. He retweeted us @StateDepartment, which took the text Haiti campaign to all of his networks and communities. We had a lot of communication with Jimmy Buffett about texting 90999, Whoopi Goldberg, Robert DeNiro. We saw various celebrities do short clips on TV. We were also using those to help reinforce the message.

99

THE NEXT 7 DAYS
Susan's Perspective: The American Red Cross
The first few days are critical. I've seen people who don't understand that all hands are on deck when you are in crisis mode. You can't work a normal day because people desperately need your help, and others desperately want to help them. You work around the clock because things can go wrong. Some things did go wrong, but we were there to fix them. We had to be there to respond to mobile ad aggregators who wanted to do campaigns for us and create mobile ads. We had to figure out how to code them so they could be tracked. How do we get permission so we can track the ads and figure out what this information means so we can learn from it? We were doing this sleep-deprived and stressed while at the same time actually getting the information about what the Red Cross was doing on the ground in Haiti.

We had our own Red Cross SWAT team supporting our Text Haiti efforts. Peggy Dyer, the chief marketing officer, led strategy and oversight. Our social media director, Wendy Harman, oversaw all our pivotal social platforms. Susan Watson managed external promotional partners like the NFL, Josh Kittner managed external outreach to our mobile donors, and consultant Doug Gardner helped me liaison with carrier partners. All the carrier people were really going out of their way, around the clock too, to make everything work. So we're feeding people the important, impactful information about what we're doing on the ground while managing the social media too. It's a lot more work than it seems. There is so much groundwork laid before and so much work done the first two weeks so snags don't become huge problems.

There are companies we work with closely, and they are good examples of creatively finding ways to promote 90999. An Xbox game included "Text Haiti to 90999" on an in-game advertisement, which can be altered anytime.

Employees were giving in different ways, and they were also helping their customers to give. DIRECTV and Comcast tested banners for the first time, so while viewers were looking at the channel directory, a banner was added at the end to "Text Haiti 90999." They had never done this before.

I was working every weekend, but I was grateful to do it. I would get rejuvenated when I was able to hear directly about the people being fed and sheltered with funding facilitated by us. It's an honor to be a part of something so powerful.

Katie's Perspective: U.S. Department of State
It was over that next week that we did all we could to help promote the donation code. The secretary gave briefings throughout that whole week on the situation in Haiti and was constantly mentioning the short code. We were using all of our convening and connecting abilities to get the word out through our offices here at the State Department. Several people at the State Department—Alec Ross, Jared Cohen—have large followings on their own personal social networks, so we also leveraged them.

The Secretary did a short video piece that we used to help get the message out. We tried packaging it for all the different media to get information out about the opportunity to give as fast as possible. First Lady Michelle Obama promoted it.

We could never have imagined how successful it ever would have been. There was no benchmark that we were trying to get to, but we certainly could never have anticipated how fast the numbers would grow. From the secretary down to everyone around here, reaching $30 million within a week took our breath away to see how everyone used their mobile phones to contribute.

James's Perspective: Mobile Accord
The unique thing about this is that what started as a little snowball was quickly picked up by news media. Within hours you have thousands of people talking about it becoming a Trending Topic on Twitter. Then the news media started integrating the message, saying, "This is what's going on in Haiti. If you want to help, go to the RedCross.com or text Haiti to 90999." Everyone within a matter of a day had that message integrated into their stories. It became the connection point between here's a problem and global travesty to here's a way you can help right now. Regardless, the mobile phone is the one item people keep with them all the time. So it's a connection point that helps close the loop for people to give back.

THE NEXT 30 DAYS
Susan's Perspective: The American Red Cross
The established relationships that were in place made this happen. If we didn't have the relationship with CTIA, we would not have jumped on it the way we did. We were ready for it. We were also ready with a proactive program to communicate to these valuable new supporters. And we sent four messages within four or five weeks so that we could start building relationships with our new donors. It wouldn't have happened if we weren't ready for it.

If we didn't have really good people like Wendy, it wouldn't have happened either. She was established in the social media community and knew how to communicate with this audience.

The Red Cross is going to have a long-term plan, and we'll be in Haiti for a very long time—until every last dollar is spent. There will be dollars allocated to long-term assistance and rebuilding Haiti better. I think the hope of everyone is that Haiti will be better than it's ever been.

Wendy's Perspective: The American Red Cross
I can't remember what life was like before the earthquake. The way I have been affected by it has changed who I am. Each disaster is different. Social media was not new when the Haitian quake happened, but we saw for the first time how powerful social media really is, and for the public to have a voice and a role in the response from all over the world.

The way the American public came together to participate in this initiative was an amazing bright spot in the midst of an inexplicable tragedy. I am really proud of the impact social media had and of our organization.

101

James's Perspective: Mobile Accord

The reasons we were able to do this is because we were prepared and we were quick. Making sure procedures are in place can let you effectively handle activity and turn up additional capacity within a moment's notice. We had the capacity and infrastructure in place because we were two years into mobile giving. The first mobile giving campaign was launched in February 2008. The small cases helped us become more organized and be more prepared for traffic.

Alicia Keys did a call on *American Idol* in 2009 for her Keep a Child Alive Campaign (ALIVE to 90999). The one call to action on *AI* raised $450,000 with a $5 text donation. We planned for that moment, to put the capacity on the system and were able to handle it. We ramped the infrastructure. Having that event on *AI* live put us in the position of being able to support the level of traffic for the Haitian relief effort. We've never seen a campaign that has driven this volume. Being quick and responsive is extremely important in a situation like this.

Katie's Perspective: U.S. Department of State

If the foundation had not been there, it would have taken longer. Thankfully, the State Department developed a great relationship with Mobile Accord and has been doing some very interesting things with them on mobile in various countries, and the State Department has a great relationship with the Red Cross. It was so easy.

Three million Americans contributing $10 through their phones made this the single largest mobile donation program that I think we've seen in the United States. This is probably the highest percent of households you've ever seen give a donation through mobile versus the Internet, a traditional telephone call, or through the mail.

Execution of Internal Strategies

Susan Murray, the American Red Cross
- Improve mobile outreach effort for fund-raising
- Establish real-time social media platforms
- Forge key partnerships

James Eberhard, Mobile Accord
- Be prepared
- Have scalable systems
- Test capacity
- Forge key partnerships
- Execute social change

Katie Stanton, The U.S. Department of State
- Establish real-time social media platforms
- Develop mobile platform for information and fund-raising
- Forge key partnerships

Strategy Elements

The overall strategies can be distilled to these key elements:
- Built internal social media proficiency internally over time
- Invested in new mobile technologies
- Listened to stakeholders and donors
- Made strategic adjustments along the way
- Updated technology to keep in step with changing goals

The Road Ahead

Susan's Perspective: The American Red Cross

When it comes to mobile, what I get really get excited about is that moving forward, 5 to 10 percent of our catastrophic fund-raising dollars will come from mobile. But the application of this technology is not limited to receiving funds. We are also exploring ways to use mobile technology for the delivery of emergency services and other mission-related activities; that is what really excites me. I would like to see mobile used in ways that we have never seen before in preparation for future emergencies. I could see mobile used to provide people with information on how to evacuate, help them once they are in trouble, help them find their loved ones, and help notify blood donors of specific needs for their blood types.

I think there's so much more we can do with mobile. It is a platform for fundraising, but it is the whole ecosystem of mobile where I see great potential. We collect money that way, and we can also help people (even save lives) that way.

Wendy's Perspective: The American Red Cross

There is still much education to be done across emergency groups. Disaster management has been honed over the years, but the public hasn't been given a role. Social and mobile media allows everyone unprecedented opportunities to be valuable participants in disaster response, whether down the street, across the country, or around the world. Our job now is to figure out the processes that empower them. I think we are in the early stage of this, and I am seeing a shift. Citizens are aggregating information for us, and the public voice is being heard. Ideally, disaster response has to be a combination of both efforts. For example, people in Haiti who were trapped under the rubble used their cell phones to call or text relatives in the United States. Those calls were passed to the Red Cross via our Twitter and Facebook accounts. Though our core responsibility is to deliver aid services and not rescue, we want to facilitate that critical information correctly and quickly when it comes to us. Haitians also notified the Red Cross of 100 elderly people inland who needed water. It was good data to know and opened the doors for the public to provide situational awareness.

Organizations and citizens need to mix their efforts together. One place to look is the social Web, so if the information does come to you, how do you get it to the right party? This is the next area for us to grow.

Katie's Perspective: U.S. State Department

Sometimes things take a while to get approved because of all the different offices and agencies. But the foundation has already been laid, including relationships and responsibilities. We'll be able to do more programs like this in the future because everything is in place.

James's Perspective: Mobile Accord and Real-Time Social Change

Mobile strategy used to empower people to advance social change varies by where you are in the world, in the United States, Pakistan, or the Congo. We have a great mobile platform that allows us to do a ton of traffic, to be able to make an impact, and to do it in different places.

Our mobile banking system runs on the same platform as our donation platform. It drives social change to allow people to send money across the country or make billing transactions without having to be physically there. A person used to have to walk across the country to hand cash to a family member. Now they can just transfer from one cell phone to another whether they are in front of each other or 100 miles away.

The premise behind bringing mobile banking to developing nations is significant. Some countries have no banking structure at all. In the Congo, well under 1 percent of the people have bank accounts. Ten percent of the people have cell phones. In most developing nations, banking is 10 percent and mobile phone penetration is 40 or 60 or 80 percent. They deposit money in their cell phone accounts to make financial transactions. If they want to buy a Coke, money is transferred from the phone.

There are reasons why developing countries don't have a large bank population: First of all, they are poor communities; second, people don't trust banks; third, they don't have access to banks. Telcos are usually the most trustworthy companies or government agencies in developing nations. Citizens trust putting money into the account, and they know they can use it to purchase their calls.

The customer experience of being able to trust handing money over to someone else builds goodwill. It also starts business transactions which leads them down the path to be more efficient, which allows them to develop. For every 10 percent of mobile use you see, 1 percent of GDP increases in the country. As people start adopting cell phones more and more, their ability to grasp information is expanded, so their knowledge and education develop and their capacity to be more efficient and drive more economic value increases. It's a very empowering thing for developing countries that traditionally don't have developed infrastructure. You just put up one cell tower and now you can have education coming through it, real-time information, financial transactions. You can have connection points to the world. They drive accountability, economic development, health and human services. The mobile phone is the platform that folds it all together.

104

Assessment

The power of real-time layered onto the mobile platform and then propelled by traditional media has the force to create global awareness, reach, and results. When the three work in concert, they can deliver beyond expectations. In this situation, a virtual accelerated communication and donation cycle emerged and took on a life of its own. The Red Cross and the State Department posted tweets and Facebook updates, and they all lifted each other.

However, social platforms will take one only so far. In this extraordinary case, the personal relationships, whether old or new, formed the glue that pulled it all together incredibly quickly. Susan Murray of the American Red Cross had known David Diggs of CTIA for a number of years, whereas James Eberhard knew Kate Stanton at the State Department for only one week. Regardless of the length of time, relationships formed through traditional and real-time social platforms can coalesce to propel targeted campaigns for organizations and businesses.

Expand your social sphere, engage, and interact. Then nurture those relationships through social media that makes staying in touch and collaborating much easier. Professional and personal alliances that form over time could be the ones that sustain you through success or unexpected challenges.

USA Today: Publishing in Real-Time
Case Story: Transforming a traditional industry into enhanced journalism

COMPANY   *USA Today*

INDUSTRY   Media

OBJECTIVE   Move traditional journalist onto more cost-effective and reader-direct social media platforms

STRATEGY   Start by introducing one tool at a time, one department at a time

Acknowledgment

Special thanks to *USA Today* for recognizing how readers are changing the way they consume content and taking positive action to address it. Brian Dresher was hired by USATODAY.com as manager of social media and digital partnerships and has skillfully led the company's internal transformation. He has also formed strategic alliances with leading brands such as Yahoo! and *Forbes* and social media sites such as FARK.com. His participation as a speaker at several events across the country, including Gov2.5, SXSW, and 140conf, in USATODAY.com's social media efforts led our paths to cross and ultimately brought this valuable case story to our readers.

We appreciate *USA Today* and Brian for their willingness to share their journey of transformation one person at a time, one department at a time. You will see why *USA Today* chose this approach, how it managed it over time, and why it worked for the company. "Brian's perspective" offers insights along the way as well, of honest views of progress and resistance. (Note: Since this writing, Brian has transitioned to another company, continuing his role as change agent.)

Why This Is Important to You

Transformation begins with education and information. If your company has skilled professionals with years of hard-earned experience, it will be faced with the same challenge that the national newspaper *USA Today* faced and successfully addressed: educating and retraining the existing staff to achieve social media proficiency for the future viability of the company. Change is difficult, even if it is good

---

Courtesy of *USA Today.*

106

change, especially when it is combined with the task of getting seasoned journalists to adopt new skills. Reactions included, "Why should we be open?" "Why
should we learn these tools?" and, "Business as usual is just fine." The important
lesson from the *USA Today* case story is that the company's success with social
media introduction and adoption was contingent on respecting the employees'
values and tailoring the reeducation process specifically for the staff. Information
eventually led to empowerment.

USA Today had the courage and insight to buck the trend and become
teachable. Now it uses real-time social media in a variety of departments, including
editorial, corporate communications, customer service, marketing, ad sales,
and the college readership program, among others. By investing in its collective
knowledge base and taking a risk, it has become a role model in the "new" journalism without violating the traditional values of the profession.

There are lessons to be learned here by all companies, industries, and brands
that are considering real-time social media for their unique business purposes: Do
not skimp on your employees. Train and retrain the workforce to unlock the wisdom
and innovation that are waiting to be unleashed. Regardless of capitalization, businesses that are pondering these questions about how to introduce real-time tools
to a long-standing traditional staff would be wise to consider this case story as a
model strategy.

Background
USA Today was founded in 1982 with a mission to serve as a forum for better
understanding and unity to help make the United States truly one nation. Through
its flagship newspaper and popular Web site, *USA Today* engages the national con-
versation and connects readers online through social media applications. The *USA
Today* news and information brand also includes *USA Today* Education, *USA Today*
Mobile, and *USA Today* Sports Weekly. *USA Today* is owned by Gannett Co., Inc.
(NYSE: GCI).

Brian's Perspective
USA Today has a huge staff of really talented journalists who were used to doing
their jobs in a certain way. When the company saw that things needed to change,
we wanted to be sure this great staff knew they were valued. We knew that once
they became familiar with social media, it could help them do their jobs better and
in ways they never imagined.

The Challenge
Like many other organizations, *USA Today* has had to adapt to an environment with
limited resources, and so the challenge it faced was to get staff on board with the
value of social media and find a way to make time for it during hectic work hours.
For a news and information organization whose staff had formal training and years
of experience in journalism, the effort to introduce social media tools that might

contradict that training and experience added to the challenge of making social media a priority and a part of everyday workflow.

The Solution

USA Today recognized that to create internal buy-in, it needed to sell the staff virtually one at a time rather than attempt to institute an organizationwide mandate on the value of social media. At the same time that it wanted to ramp up its social media presence, particularly on Twitter, it had just launched a vacation "cruise community" that had many new features for the journalist Gene Sloan. It also provided the members of the reading audience an opportunity to interact with one another. Gene's acceptance and comfort with these on-site social networking features created an opening for the newspaper to work with him as an optimal internal test case to create an off-site social networking presence on Twitter (see Figure 5.1).

In a very short time, not only did the followers of Gene's Twitter feed grow, but he was recognized by the British newspaper the *Telegraph* as one of "the 50 great travel tweeters." Brian now had some tangible results to share with other staff members who might have been skeptical. He also had validation that with a little internal coaching *USA Today* could create meaningful relationships with its

5.1 Gene Sloan "The Cruise Log" represents the newspaper's first successful entry into social media

audience both on-site and off-site. Those early results would lead to an extensive yearlong internal education program to help the staff have a productive, effective, and enjoyable experience with Twitter.

One of the first areas of education involved the provision of biweekly hands-on Twitter training. It focused on the many ways the platform could bring the greatest benefits to the business, including the following:

1. Opportunities to build a personal brand while representing *USA Today*
2. What and when to tweet and not to tweet
3. Tools to manage and monitor Twitter activity
4. Impact of Twitter on traffic to USATODAY.com's Web site
5. Metrics interpretation

Despite the general ease with which one can create a Twitter feed and start tweeting, *USA Today* felt that this in-depth training was critical to override the widely assumed belief that Twitter was an irreverent, self-promotional tool instead of one that enabled true journalistic and business value.

The biweekly training sessions were the first hook used to educate and inform the staff members about Twitter's value to them. Equally important were ongoing efforts to share best practices, case studies, internal successes, competitive analyses, metrics, and new tools. Those posttraining updates—known internally as Twitter Tips—were distributed by e-mail once per week so that the staff members would feel empowered and encouraged to make Twitter part of their routine. Otherwise, they feared that Twitter itself or the training sessions would be treated as a one-off novelty without a need to stick with it and put it into practice.

Brian's Perspective

Staff was starting to catch on to Twitter, but there were still those who wanted proof that this really mattered to business. So we found ways to measure results that satisfied those concerns.

Measurement
Brian's Perspective

Implementation of the initial training and ongoing education were helpful to get staff up and running with Twitter, but we needed to quantitatively demonstrate an ROI—as measured by traffic to USATODAY.com—to warrant continued support of these efforts. First, they utilized an existing on-site analytics tool, Omniture, to measure the number of referrals from Twitter to USATODAY.com broken down by each section of our site. Over a several-month time frame, they observed notable increases in referrals to each section of their site. They also noticed a nearly perfect correlation with increases in their total number of Twitter followers to all of their Twitter feeds. Second, they turned to the off-site analytics tool Hitwise to compare the percent of traffic from Twitter to all of the news sites in their competitive set. Despite us having significantly fewer followers to our Twitter feeds

109

than the competitors, *USA Today* received nearly the same percent of traffic from Twitter. These two analytical measures informed them that Twitter generated a favorable ROI on traffic to the site and proper usage of Twitter allowed them to reap traffic benefits regardless of total follower count.

Lessons Learned

Although *USA Today* was fortunate to have many positive outcomes, there were a couple of steps in this process that it could have approached differently. First, the initial Twitter training sessions assumed that if a staff person opted to attend the training, that person had already bought into the benefits of using Twitter when, in fact, he or she just wanted to learn more before committing. Failing to recognize this resulted in some early lost opportunities to engage all the staff members at the outset. Tweaking the session by incorporating metrics into the beginning of the training session allowed the staff to realize quickly that there were tangible benefits.

Second, news organizations are very sensitive about the business side influencing the editorial side. *USA Today* speaks very candidly about the need to maintain separation of church and state. Having a marketing person train journalists on a platform for publishing content was at times met with resistance. Making it clear that this was the marketing department helping journalists learn a new tool to build their personal brands allowed greater comfort with adopting Twitter.

The successes in the training that were reinforced with their metrics in 2009 resulted in the creation of notable Twitter-related features in 2010. *USA Today* grew its number of journalists on Twitter to well over 100 and showcased them on its Twitter index page. Many journalists who have Twitter feeds incorporated their Twitter widgets onto their article pages or blogs. For the 2010 Vancouver Olympics, they created a Twitter hub that pulled in tweets from athletes, fans, journalists, and competitors. Plus, any journalist who attended the Olympics was required to carry a BlackBerry and tweet from the events he or she was covering.

Finally, some of the staff on the editorial side noted how the impact on the news-sharing process has evolved to a point where they may break news first on Twitter, flesh out additional details in a blog post, and then develop a thorough piece in an article for the next day's print edition or online.

This experience and experiment with the Twitter social media platform created a strong model. The paper has been able to point to this success as it continues to introduce other social media platforms to the staff members to distribute content, engage with the audience, grow its personal brands, and generate traffic to its content and USATODAY.com (see Figure 5.2). The successes of this Twitter model helped forge relationships and trust between marketing and editorial that no doubt have made other collaborations within social media much easier going forward.

5.2 USATODAY.com has extensive blog contributors interacting with readers

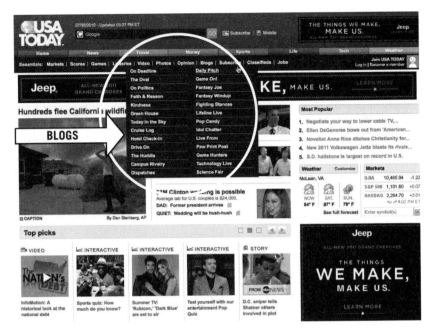

Assessment

Each enterprise is a unique culture unto itself, composed of the people and personalities that contribute to the whole. *USA Today* wisely and accurately assessed the personalities of its skilled and seasoned staff members to discover the best way to retrain them. This is an extremely difficult task for any business, but especially for traditional journalists who were probably resistant to using a computer instead of a typewriter not that long ago.

Brian served as the "mentoring up" guide, a sort of age and skill bridge. This is a huge issue that affects most businesses that are grappling with established long-term workers, many of whom like the status quo, as opposed to the young new hires who can serve as change agents. *USA Today* blended digital natives with seasoned professionals with the mutual and focused objective of growing its businesses. *USA Today* merits kudos for the following key points:

1. Acknowledged a change in consumer behavior in relationship to its industry
2. Created a new job category of manager of social media and digital partnerships and hired someone who could lead the transformation

3. Acknowledged the skills of current staff members and personalities
4. Committed to employee reeducation
5. Started small and then went big
6. Staff was committed to reeducation (most)
7. Continued educating staff on digital technologies as platforms evolved

It is evident that *USA Today* and its staff value the mandates of social media: openness, transparency, engagement, and giving something of value. It only makes sense that they would embrace real-time media technologies since they also value what a free press brings to society. The astounding finding here is that real-time social media can benefit even the most closed corporate cultures, as you will discover in the other case stories in this chapter.

EMC

Real-Time in the Enterprise

CASE STORY   The process of establishing and executing a strategy for social media proficiency at a Fortune 200 company

COMPANY   EMC Corporation

INDUSTRY   Data storage, technology services, and cloud computing for global clients

OBJECTIVE   Transform a wide range of business processes by leveraging the workforce's social media proficiency and "open" behavior models

STRATEGY   Engage internal knowledgeable employees for their expertise and perspective before going external

Acknowledgments

EMC's marketing CTO published the white paper *EMC/ONE—A Journey in Social Media* in December 2008. The author of the document kept a public blog of the experience at http://chucksblog.emc.com/a_journey_in_social_media. This document is still available to the public online and has become a popular best practice guide among those in the corporate social media space. The path EMC experienced is conveyed by Polly Pearson, former vice president employment brand and strategy engagement, who offers firsthand insights and commentary.

The foresight to document this process and make it available free to corporate peers and other interested parties highlights the shift in communications taking place in the corporate environment. It was not that long ago that corporations would not have even considered a transparent process like this regarding an internal business initiative. In fact, most still do not.

However, the tenets of social media—openness, authenticity, transparency, sharing, community, and more—would be betrayed by *not* making this material available. Inadvertently, or maybe not, EMC has created marketing goodwill in the friend economy that will have a lasting effect. Most corporations are just waking up to the fact that something big is going on here and will greatly appreciate the efforts of storage giant EMC's trailblazing efforts.

Why This Is Important to You

This case story describes how a very large global corporation successfully identified an emerging internal need, established a cohesive strategic approach, and saw substantial and compelling results throughout its business. In addition to the outward-facing corporate strategy of using social tools to interact with clients, partners, and other stakeholders, EMC's evolution in the social computing space has been unique and forward-leaning. The company realizes that operationalizing social technologies is the next step in the evolution of the workplace. It understands that the workforce of today and tomorrow is collaborative and social and that true innovation and high-performance execution will come from cross-functional interaction. The new workforce comes from the digital native demographic. Online, social, sharing, interactive, collaborative behaviors are the hallmark of what this workforce brings to the table. Understanding how to harness this inside a structured corporate environment is not easy. EMC shows step-by-step how its journey unfolds—internally and externally. EMC "gets it" and therefore exemplifies transformational leadership in this area. Competing on an international scale, harnessing global talent, understanding how to overcome barriers to adoption and prove the business value/ROI around social computing all epitomize transformational leadership. In addition, EMC has created a workforce that is proud of being part of a company that values training its employees and giving them a collaborative voice.

Every company, large or small, will benefit from the EMC experience. Its vision of introducing social media throughout the company instead of one division at a time was bold and risk-filled, but it navigated it brilliantly. You are encouraged to apply its best practices to your environment and enter the real-time zone with EMC.

Background

The DNA of EMC made it a fertile ground to adopt social media within the enterprise. It is an aggressive competitor in the information technology (IT) industry with 40,000-plus highly knowledgeable and technically proficient employees. In fact, some of the company's products (e.g., Documentum, RSA) support social media applications.

Corporate Challenges

EMC leaned to the conservative side when it came to adopting new productivity technologies. Its business protects and controls information for its clients, and many aspects of its traditional corporate culture were described as "command and control." In addition, certain audiences within EMC's management team were comfortable with controlling internal flows of information.

As the company grew and became more complex, communication, interaction, and collaboration across dozens of business units became increasingly difficult. As a result, most of the people in the organization did not know what the rest of the business was doing. A sense of isolation and frustration was growing quickly within the company.

Information became more difficult to find and share in a timely fashion. The one centralized intranet portal was not serving the company's needs. Meetings, conference calls, remote presentations, and extreme amounts of e-mail traffic were filling people's time and slowing business progress.

Employees who used outside social platforms were frustrated that EMC did not understand what those new tools could offer in a business setting.

Polly's Perspective

At the time I started working on the employment brand and connecting talent with EMC's strategy and potential, EMC was often seen as "old school" externally, and internally we had lost the purity of our identity in the years following the recession of 2001–2002. We had just entered many new markets, hired new leaders, acquired dozens of companies, and brought on thousands of new employees.

Though the company survived the recession and the dot-com bubble in 2001, the tone was described by one of my colleagues: "It doesn't feel hot in the halls." We brought 30 companies and over 17,000 people into EMC in just 18 months. They did not know each other or the company. With such a pace of growth and hiring, we needed to start branding the company as a great and "hot" place to work, but it became clear we had to connect with our own workforce first.

Responding to the Challenge

EMC senior management recognized that social media trends had to be better understood and addressed. The initial thinking was to categorize the problem to a single department (IT, marketing, human resources). It became clear that social media proficiency had unique aspects as a business challenge:

- It affected most aspects of EMC's business and was not isolated to a single division or department. Uses could be seen in marketing, customer service, engineering, HR, IT, sales, and more.
- It was apparent that social media could deliver positive results in key areas.
- Culturally, much of the company was uncomfortable with the idea of open and transparent information sharing and conversation, resulting in risk without careful governance.

These were all legitimate observations. Concerns stalled movement. As a result, an internal study was conducted to review the problem and propose a strategic approach.

Key Point *See social media as an overall business strategy, not the domain of a single department or function.*

Building the Initial Community

How does one go about building a social media strategy for a large company? Early on, EMC decided that its process of designing and implementing a social strategy should reflect the ethos of Web 2.0, which meant it had to be open, inclusive, and transparent.

The company engaged its own internal people who were interested in the topic, solicited their views, and enlisted their help.

To get the process started, the social media task force built a temporary and disposable free discussion forum site to engage other members of the domestic and global EMC community who were passionate and knowledgeable about these topics.

> **Key Point** *The use of social media techniques (e.g., the establishment of a community of passionate stakeholders) to address matters of policy and general strategy is a recurring theme. Simply put: Use social media techniques to solve social media problems whenever possible.*

Initially, the community discussion generated an extensive and undoable list of "must haves." However, out of the discussion came, "What should we do first?" That led to a clearer understanding of priorities and a logical order of execution along the lines of "if we want to do Y, then we have to get good at X first." A reasonably shorter set of concepts and ideas became the basis for an overall strategy that was manageable in size and scope, could be communicated in a few minutes, and formed the basis for an execution path.

> **Key Point** *As with any new topic, the natural tendency was to over-complicate key thoughts and activities. The team spent a great deal of time simplifying the expression and communication of ideas at every opportunity. Team members felt that it was better to communicate a few ideas effectively than fail at communicating several dozen.*

Key Principles

EMC came up with a handful of key guiding principles that it referred to throughout its social journey. As it encountered various problems and challenges, it returned to the core principles, which it still follows.

Rationale

The rationale for investing in social media proficiency was simplified to "exploiting the potential of transforming a wide range of business processes at EMC." The company saw social media as a business tool that it had to learn to get good at, just as it had to learn to get good at e-mail or navigating the Internet.

EMC saw how learning a new set of competencies could significantly reengineer many aspects of the way it would do business in the future. As a company, it could see great potential to do many things better, faster, and cheaper through what would be known as SMP (social media proficiency).

> **Key Point** Note the focus on proficiency versus tools or a platform. As with most productivity initiatives, the tools are of relatively low value unless people know how to apply them to the business.

The company spent a few weeks collecting dozens of potential examples from across EMC's business, spanning engineering, marketing, customer support, sales, HR, IT, and legal. Soon it was apparent that there was no shortage of substantial potential "big wins" if social media platforms were utilized strategically.

> **Key Point** EMC recognized that the only effective strategy would be a single platform for all internal aspects of the business—much like a single e-mail environment, a single corporate intranet, and so on. It was important to resist the natural tendency to build a platform along organizational lines.

Justification for Social Media Proficiency

Every company considering an investment in social media proficiency will at some point have to justify the investment to the business. This mandatory rite of passage was a key inflection point in EMC's thinking and is turning out to be important to other organizations making similar investments. This becomes a strategic topic for several reasons:

- Productivity investments are notoriously difficult to justify. Social productivity investments are perhaps even more difficult in this regard. This topic can bring out a natural skepticism in many individuals as well.
- There are few tools for measuring qualitative value: It is difficult to assess the value of a well-written document or a productive discussion with someone you didn't know existed or an open discussion that prevents an expensive mistake from being made.

Traditional measurement and justification frameworks were inadequate for measuring what members of the company all thought was ultimately important: improved interaction and conversation.

EMC decided to view its investment as analogous to productivity investments the company had already made: e-mail, file shares, conference calls, Webex, and conference rooms with multimedia support.

One of the most effective justification techniques tended to be slightly manipulative in light of the corporate culture. It frequently pointed out that because of the extremely competitive nature of EMC's business, it would not want to be in a situation in which competitors had a significant competitive advantage through social media proficiency that EMC did not. People tended to understand that concept in a visceral manner.

Using this approach, all EMC had to do was point out a few shortcomings with traditional collaboration tools to justify its goals.

Key Point *Many people are trained to produce the kinds of business case justifications that are found in traditional business school curricula. Those tools and thinking processes are difficult to apply to these types of projects.*

Key Point *As the required investments in this area appeared to be quite modest, EMC quickly realized that it could have ended up spending more time and effort justifying the initiative than it did by just moving forward.*

Key Point *When faced with a new proposition, many people respond by demanding to understand the "ROI." One should treat this as an understandable defensive reaction in response to a new situation rather than a de facto demand for a business case. On a more practical note, the actual investment was extremely moderate, greatly lessening the need for a traditional business case.*

Strategy Elements

EMC's overall strategy can be broken down to these key elements:

- *Focused on proficiency, skills, and behaviors* rather than tools, process, and measurement. Focused on the "social" in "social media."
- *Recruited and identified volunteers* who demonstrated proficiency throughout the organization and had them recruit and support others in turn.
- *Built proficiency from the inside out:* started inside the firewall, practiced a bit, and then ventured outside the firewall when internal proficiency was established.
- *Created separate non-IT functions* for both internal and external proficiency. Though EMC needed the help of IT at times, the overall endeavor was not solely an IT function.
- *Created a lightweight governance model* and used it sparingly. No governance would be dangerous in many regards; heavy governance would hamper progress and spontaneity.
- Resisted its natural corporate tendency to *organize, control, measure, and monitor* each and every aspect of the initiative.
- *Assumed that if people know how to behave in the real world,* they will figure out how to behave online as well. If not, HR or legal would be contacted.

- *Invested enough to learn* and use those experiences to guide future investments. EMC did not propose or ever consider a big-bang, end-to-end comprehensive road map. Instead, it positioned a series of incremental investment scenarios over time, based on what it learned as it went along.
- *Gave people enough time* to get comfortable with new ways of doing things. Patience is a hard thing to practice for many people. Attempting to push people too fast may result in an organizational backlash.
- *Resisted the temptation to overstructure, overorganize, overprocess, and overcategorize.* Many people associated with the effort had been taught to work in a linear, structured fashion. Although some of this is desirable, when taken to excess, it can lead to environments and efforts that are self-defeating, especially in a social media context. This turned out to be a very difficult mindset for some in the company.
- *Provided centralized funding for the required resources.* They persuaded the business to provide centralized funding by pointing to other shared resources that were not provided on a charge-back basis: e-mail, conference rooms, the corporate intranet portal, and related investments.
- *Made it fun* rather than making it look like work. People tend to give their best efforts when they are enjoying the experience.

Timing and Sense of Urgency

EMC felt a sense of urgency as it developed and studied these issues, resulting in a plan that was biased toward accelerating investments and results. Here were some of its concerns:

- It was evident that widespread social media proficiency could be worth potentially hundreds of millions of dollars to EMC's various businesses. It did not want to delay that benefit.
- Social media use was spreading across the company in a very viral and unorganized manner. The longer it waited to get started with an official and centralized capability, the harder it would be to align and coordinate existing efforts.
- Existing informal use of social media inside and outside the firewall was being done without governance and oversight, potentially exposing the company to unknown risks.
- It did not want to waste money on old ways of doing business when it was evident that social media tools and techniques would be more cost-effective.
- There were early signs of competitors showing an interest in these tools and techniques, and that raised additional concerns.

Execution of Internal Strategy

EMC had two goals: (1) to provide a platform for reengineering candidate internal processes and (2) to learn some of the core skills and behaviors required for eventual external proficiency.

An example of an internal business process might be launching a new product or collaborating on topics of mutual interest, such as the latest moves by competitors. Examples of core skills and behaviors included blogging internally and externally, contributing to a discussion or wiki, freely sharing knowledge and experience, disagreeing with people without being disagreeable, and starting a community.

What Kind of Collaboration?

EMC used many forms of collaboration in the workspace, including concalls (conference calls), e-mail, and document repositories, that are common to most large corporations. It needed an answer to the frequently asked question, "Why do we need yet another collaboration tool?"

Synchronous versus Asynchronous

Synchronous collaboration occurs only if everyone is doing something at approximately the same time. This includes meetings, concalls, videoconferencing, and instant messaging (IM)—anything they would have to be scheduled. Missing a meeting or a call put a person and a team at a disadvantage. It also reduced productivity.

Asynchronous collaboration models meant that people could freely join and participate when they had the time and the interest. There was no need to calendar or schedule defined interaction periods.

Text versus Rich Media

Many discussions in the social media world point to the effective use of video or audio formats for collaboration. Although those formats have their merits, EMC was primarily interested in text-based communication at that early stage. Text is easy to compose, read, share, and search. It also is amenable to use with international audiences among whom English may not be the native language.

Communities versus E-Mail

Although e-mail is a great tool for sending short messages and static information to known recipients, it does not easily support wide-ranging conversations, foster reusability of information, or prevent exposure of discussions and content to unintended recipients. For many people, it was hard to conceptualize the inherent limitations of e-mail in support of cross-functional collaboration. However, heavy e-mail users did see this proposed collaboration model as a way out of their "e-mail jails." More important information was finding its way to the corporate social media platform, reducing the need to save important e-mails.

Trust Boundaries

EMC came up with the notion of a "trust boundary": a predefined statement to all participants on the platform making it clear who was allowed to participate and who was not. The internal platform was restricted to "badged" EMC employees and selected badged contractors who had been vetted to access internal systems. People routinely would ask, "Who has access to this platform?" and would get a simple, logical answer.

Open versus Closed

This was an important and very controversial strategic issue. The natural tendency was for people to want their own private communities, specifically those in which the community owner could control who could view or participate. This innate need to control access, commentary, or participation was much more widespread and ingrained than the company expected.

There were two serious concerns with this approach. First, the administrative requirements associated with managing this sort of environment are not trivial. Maintaining detailed lists of who can see what and doing that with reasonable speed and efficiency represent a major investment of time and effort, besides being frequently ineffective.

Building tools for hiding information and discussion was not the core goal. On the contrary, EMC wanted to expose as many people as possible to multiple sources of information and discussion. It coined the term *the big conversation* to signify what it really wanted to do.

EMC already had a self-service document sharing capability in the form of its eRoom. It was met with great support from the company and moved the workforce toward the behavior of sharing files outside the e-mail tool. When it scaled out, however, it became a dumping ground for files bunched in organizationally aligned puddles. Despite the significant investment in eRoom infrastructure, the results were generally perceived as poor.

To avoid repeating the mistakes of the past, a "no private spaces" policy was implemented. This was very controversial at the time, but it ended up being a key decision and ultimately defined the essential nature of the internal collaboration efforts.

Initially, there was concern among members of the team that this policy would dissuade people from participating. They would tell people who felt the need to restrict access that they were free to use existing EMC platforms. In most cases, they thought about the pros and cons and ended up using the internal platforms.

Conversation-Centric versus Document-Centric

Many people tend to think of collaboration and information sharing in terms of documents and files. EMC recognized that there was a higher-order (and higher-value) collaboration model that focused on people's interests and dialogue. It ended up using the term *conversational collaboration* because it believed that documents supported conversation but were not the end goal.

The focus on conversational collaboration was perhaps the second most important decision EMC made regarding its internal social efforts. Here is an example: Imagine you went to a professional social gathering and all you did was push documents at other people and ask for comments. It would be very hard to start a discussion that way.

The company also came to believe that starting discussions would lead to the formation of communities of interest, which in turn would lead to very effective document collaboration if needed.

Keeping It Fun and Friendly

Since this undertaking was an effort toward social collaboration, the team felt it was important to make the user experience as enjoyable and friendly as possible. Users did not have to fill out any forms to use the platform or call the IT support desk if they had an issue.

Team members deemed it important that people use their real names in an informal and loose environment that was business-oriented but not stiff and inflexible. Members wanted to make sure that all users understood that those spearheading the effort were there to serve them and make their experience enjoyable, not to serve an abstract corporate mandate.

Impact and Measurements

The Importance of Establishing a Measurement Philosophy

Polly's Perspective

The original intent was to create a water cooler safe space where people could talk about work or anything else in an open atmosphere. However, we needed to come up with a measurement philosophy that would gauge "social productivity." We turned to our community to find out what they thought about the platform and what would represent success to them.

The entire topic of measuring business impact is very controversial in these types of projects. There is no consensus regarding generally accepted metrics for social media proficiency. Furthermore, this inherent lack of useful measurements and metrics can be used as an excuse not to undertake an investment in social media proficiency.

A key part of any initiative is establishing a general agreement regarding success factors. EMC developed a "measurement philosophy" rather than concrete measurements. It found this to be an important topic in considering an investment in social media for several reasons:

- Internal social media proficiency is largely about productivity, a notoriously difficult concept to quantify and measure, especially when the focus is on "social productivity."
- People may resist this sort of initiative and use lack of justification as a means of slowing or derailing an initiative.
- Typical and obvious metrics that might make sense in a traditional Web 1.0 world (e.g. page hits, unique visitors) fail to capture the unique value of expanded interaction and conversation.

Since EMC's goal was to make users of the social platform more productive in doing their jobs, who better to judge success or failure than the users? If you built a community to solve a business problem, how did it go? Or if you turned to the social platform to find answers, how did it help?

After three months of operation, EMC conducted an informal survey asking users to share how the platform had improved their productivity, brought value to their work, or created some other benefit. Dozens of anecdotes were submitted by the user community that turned out to have a far greater impact than any chart or formal analysis.

When people questioned the team about justification, they were sent a link to the discussion area where the responses were posted. This turned out to be an extremely effective technique, illustrating the broader principle of using social media to solve social media problems—in this case, providing justification. After six months, it was clear to any impartial observer that the platform had created substantial unique and differentiated value, and as a result, the demand for justification and measurement subsided.

> **Key Point** As with most investments in productivity, the value of social media proficiency becomes apparent once it's working. Although every corporate situation is different, the costs associated with an internal social platform may be viewed as an investment in an "experiment."

Examples of Specific Impacts
It is useful to share some examples of how the platform created value. Some were expected, and some were pleasant surprises.

Polly's Perspective
Our social journey was 95 percent behavior and 5 percent tools. Employees wanted to contribute. A few people started, evangelized it, and it soon grew virally into the thousands with participants from around the world. It increased a sense of community, shared mission, innovation, and connectedness. And in 2009, during one of the worst recessions ever, we believe it helped contribute to EMC's record levels

123

of customer satisfaction, and revenue. It made EMC a place where talent wants to work and to stay. Turnover is at a multiyear low.

The platform, along with the growing sense of trust and community among its users, shows value in the most unexpected ways. One of my favorite stories involves the founder of the company, an Artist Community within the EMC social network, and an individual contributor employee named Ian. Ian shared with me one day that he loved his job, and at the same time he wanted to do more. When asked what his true passion was, he said, "Painting oil portraits." I had recalled seeing photos of his oil portraits posted in the Artist Community and thinking they were wonderful. 'Ian," I said, "our founder recently passed away, and you know what? We don't have one portrait of him at the company." At that, Ian smiled. Three months later he presented his "volunteer act of passion"—an amazingly impressive portrait of our founder. Top executives soon knew Ian's name as they admired the painting and proudly showed it off to visitors. Today, that painting is hung in EMC's world headquarters lobby—a Fortune 200 company—with a plaque crediting Ian as the artist. When a member of the founder's family saw the painting, he said he was moved to tears.

The impacts arrived in distinct categories:

- Acceleration of time to value through better information dissemination and engagement: product launches, customer campaigns, and so on
- More efficient mechanisms for communication and certain forms of collaboration (replacement for concalls, e-mails, etc.)
- The ability to substantially reengineer certain business processes that required widespread engagement from multiple groups
- Establishment of a new and influential set of external "voices" through blogging
- The ability to tap an efficient corporate "social computer" to answer questions, find resources, and so on
- The ability to create and drive corporate initiatives more effectively with broader participation
- The ability to rapidly form "volunteer" efforts from motivated employees around topics of mutual interest
- Employees who were more educated, engaged, and satisfied with their work experience
- A profound change in the corporate culture

More Efficient Collaboration

As in most corporations, most information is shared via e-mail. However, e-mail had three problems in terms of collaboration (as opposed to communication):

1. E-mail is not discoverable by individuals who might have an interest in the topic but are not recipients.

2. It was very difficult to have a threaded discussion with many participants.
3. Searching and tagging capabilities tended to be limited in most e-mail environments.

Many people pointed out that it was easier to create a wiki (a Web page dynamically editable by anyone) and solicit improvements and comments or start a discussion on a message board than to blast everyone with an e-mail. The team was also told that when looking for information on a topic, it was far easier to scan the social platform for information and individuals who were relevant than to ask around.

Is EMC able to quantify this? Not scientifically, but enough people noted this effect and the significant level of improvement compared with alternatives. As an example of a "back of the napkin" calculation, imagine 1,000 knowledge workers who deem themselves 10 percent more efficient through the use of a social platform. At $100,000 per knowledge worker, that's $10 million.

Acceleration of Time to Value

EMC is making a significant investment in product development and enhancement, and the process of monetizing these investments requires a "launch" of the new capabilities to an extremely large and diverse audience. New product launches are conducted on the social platform. Marketing messages and positioning can be refined in real-time, questions can be posed and answered in minutes, and competitive responses can be tracked and responded to quickly as well. It has been an eye-opening experience for EMC to watch all the activity in a centralized location on "launch day."

The company believes that the business value of the social platform in this use can be best expressed as "shortening time to value." Being able to provide its sales and support organizations with real-time information as well as getting its questions answered in a swift and open fashion appears to have accelerated time to value considerably.

Getting quantitative proof can be difficult, but there was a consensus in the community that products were getting to market faster, sales and marketing organizations were becoming more proficient more quickly, and they could engage their partner communities more effectively than before.

Accelerating time to revenue of multiple $100 million business initiatives by even a few months or even weeks results in substantial sums.

Reengineering of Targeted Business Processes

Several high-value business processes became easy targets for reengineering by using the social platform. One early and high-profile adopter was EMC's competitive group. EMC does business in a highly competitive industry, and the gathering and sharing of competitive information is an important theme in its business. Real-time competitive information is now shared via discussion threads and wikis. Content

125

can be dynamically updated—sometimes several times a day—as new information becomes available. Participants can add their experiences and observations to the collective pool easily and efficiently. Finding an "expert" on a competitive topic takes only seconds, and getting a response does not require the use of a formal process.

The group manager of this function estimates that his group is now three to four times more efficient and impactful by simply using the social platform. In light of the fact that EMC has roughly 10 competitive analysts, this is a considerable improvement in labor efficiency, not to mention the quality of the competitive materials.

More recently, certain product groups moved to an "open" development process because all aspects of the product life cycle have been put online, including requirements definition, engineering progress, early customer feedback, bug lists, and pricing discussions—all in an open and transparent discussion. This "open product development" could translate into hundreds of millions of dollars in potential business value.

Other areas are councils and forums, face-to-face events that are expensive and time-consuming for EMC and participants, including customers, partners, analysts, and other important members of the ecosystem. They are going through a process of methodically complementing and/or substituting online community interaction for meetings in the physical world. These efforts result in cost savings (millions per year), better and more timely interactions, or both.

A Powerful New Set of External Voices

Most of EMC's business is predicated on finding new solutions to customers' problems. Therefore, it takes a serious interest in sharing and projecting its views on a variety of topics: technology, solutions, strategy, industry trends, and more.

Historically, the company has used traditional methods to get the word out: press releases, white papers, public speaking forums, and other traditional Web 1.0 mechanisms. Early on, EMC saw substantial value in the creation of an EMC blogging community whose members would share their views and engage external audiences on a wide variety of topics. EMC used its internal platform to help recruit new voices, let those people practice blogging in a safe environment, and then promoted them to represent the company outside the firewall.

EMC now has more than two dozen individuals blogging proficiently and bene- fiting the company outside the firewall, creating a substantial and formidable capa- bility in its market segment. These individuals can easily introduce new topics, refute competitor claims, and generally guide many aspects of the broader industry discussions. In EMC's first two years of building social proficiency in the workforce, it graduated new bloggers at a rate of roughly one per month.

The economic value of having a proficient blogging team in a highly competitive and fast-moving marketplace cannot be underestimated. EMC's blogging capability has become a key element of its overall marketing strategy and has transformed many aspects of how the company communicates with the outside world.

A reasonable estimate of the combined value of EMC's blogging capability (in terms of an alternative marketing investment) would approach $20 million to $50 million annually. Its current roster can be seen at http://www.emc.com/community/index.htm.

Asking Questions and Finding Experts

EMC's offerings span an impressively wide range of services and technologies. Even the simplest question can create difficulty if it is about something new to the person doing the asking. This process of asking and answering questions underpins core business processes at EMC: driving new engagements with customers, providing advanced customer support, and performing complex system integration.

Unlike e-mail, information shared on a social platform is available to all the participants at the same time, any time. Everything is searchable, tagged, and roughly organized by community of interest. Not only can questions be easily posed and answered, but experts are easily identified on certain topics or gaps are quickly found in the company's collective expertise.

An unexpected benefit in this regard has been the vetting of all answers. Since all information is shared in an open environment, incorrect or inaccurate information inevitably draws a heated response from "experts." In some cases, those experts have had to alter their official recommendations on the basis of input from field participants.

Putting a number on the business value of this open interrogation is difficult, but it probably runs into the tens of millions of dollars annually in light of EMC's large and diverse population of knowledge workers.

Driving Corporate Initiatives

EMC officially sponsors multiple initiatives that succeed or fail depending on the level of broader employee engagement. Its internal social platform has turned out to be a substantial magnifier in accelerating the progress of multiple corporate initiatives.

A clear example involved EMC's green and sustainability efforts. A limited grassroots attempt by a cross-functional volunteer community under the self-proclaimed name the Green Team garnered wide and passionate participation. As a result, an official corporate function was established to coordinate multiple sustainability initiatives across the company. One of the Green Team members, an engineer named Kathrin, was later anointed as the company's first chief sustainability officer. Kathrin got the job of her dreams, and given the deep and cross-functional nature of the work, the company's ranking on bellwether citizenship and sustainability charts soared.

Another example involved improving business efficiency in a tough economy. Corporate executives now routinely post official communications on the social platform and invite discussion in the community. Hundreds of suggestions for improving business efficiency at all levels have been submitted and evaluated, from the small and tactical to the large and strategic. One of the more lively discussion strings during the year was initiated by an individual contributor named Michelle and titled, "Do you have any constructive ways to save money?" She posted it on the "anything goes" area of the network called the Watercooler. This string has had more than 30,000 views and close to 400 ideas submitted. The CFO called attention (with a hyperlink) to this string in his memos to employees and reported back to the community with analysis and progress reports on their ideas. EMC exceeded its goals for cost reduction in 2009 by more than $150 million. Wall Street was pleased. The stock finished the year up over 60 percent.

A third example was enhancing EMC's formal innovation initiatives. The company's CTO office sponsors an annual competition across the company. It presented an interesting opportunity to watch how this happened twice: once without the platform and most recently using the social platform.

The first round of EMC's innovation conference had reasonable participation and engagement. By comparison, the second round increased to almost 1,000 proposals submitted, each of which was discussed, evaluated, and ranked using the social platform. The comparison was quite dramatic.

Collectively, EMC estimates the value of accelerating these corporate initiatives at tens of millions of dollars a year.

Grassroots Volunteerism

As with any large company, there are many initiatives that are important but cannot garner official corporate support and dedicated resources. EMC has seen that the corporate social platform makes it extremely easy to identify new initiatives and solicit participation with an absolute minimum investment.

These groups include hobby clubs (photography, cooking, etc.), affinity groups (employees who share cultural or other similarities), support for charities of all sorts, teams to look at cost-saving ideas, and teams to look at green initiatives, among many others.

Though it is hard to measure the business value of these hundreds of informal groups, EMC estimates the proceeds and benefits in the range of a few million dollars.

Employee Satisfaction

As noted by Polly Pearson, former vice president employment brand and strategy engagement, EMC takes the subject of employee motivation and satisfaction very seriously. It invests considerable effort in surveying employees on a variety of issues and using the results to drive change throughout the organization.

After a period of lower than normal employee engagement, initial observations have been extremely encouraging since the launch of the social platform. The company routinely receives unsolicited feedback from people who tell it that they have never felt more informed about EMC's overall strategy, that they now understand different parts of the organization much better than before, or that they feel they can openly discuss and engage in virtually any topic of interest. The company posted record employee engagement scores on its annual employee satisfaction and motivation survey, with over 90 percent saying they regard their coworkers and managers well and fully 95 percent reporting satisfaction on the job. The survey included 92 percent of the workforce, a population of over 30,000 people globally.[1]

Again, estimating the business value of tens of thousands of employees who are significantly and statistically more satisfied and engaged is a difficult task, but the number probably approaches tens of million dollars per year in terms of improved attraction and retention of talent, lower costs associated with turnover, and related aspects. Although EMC reports benefits in every area, it finds persistent, living evidence on a daily basis in the opinions, success stories, and acts of the employees as the true barometer of whether things have changed for the better within the company and for its success in the marketplace.

In the realm of metrics, there is another way to look at it. As Polly says, The biggest ROI in this new model is the "risk of ignoring" it.

Accelerating Corporate Culture Evolution
Everyone associated with EMC's initiative has observed that one of the undeniable effects of the social platform has been that it accelerated the evolution of certain aspects of EMC's corporate culture. Words like "open," "transparent," and "engaging" have been used to describe new aspects of how EMC is doing business both internally and externally.

Not every participant at EMC is entirely comfortable with these changes in the corporate culture. However, given the widespread popularity of the internal platform (and the social behaviors it encourages), EMC employees at all levels of management have little choice about accepting the new norm.

Cultural challenges for *employees* and *individual contributors* included the following:

- Becoming comfortable with the idea that spending time on a social platform would not be seen as "goofing off" by managers
- Learning to express personal opinions professionally and without fear of retaliation (other than occasionally a heated reply)
- Learning to communicate effectively on an open and public platform

Cultural challenges for *managers* and *executives* included the following:

- Being comfortable with the free flow of internal information and opinions independently of "official" channels
- Learning to be tolerant and resist the urge to control individuals expressing unique and/or unpopular opinions

- Listening and responding to feedback—some of it constructive, some of it less so

Within a year of general platform availability, the shift in the corporate culture and behavioral norms was profound and noticeable across most of the organization. It had accelerated its evolution into a more progressive and mature organization.

Common Attribute
Their team saw a broad range of impacts upon the business as well as patterns:

- It is far easier to find people to converse with on a broad range of topics.
- People are encouraged to reach out, engage, and discuss topics that interest them.
- The conversation is open and public and can be reviewed at any time by any interested participant.
- Brilliant perspectives and ideas emerged from voices that were never heard in the prior business model. Examples included the voices of introverted people who don't normally speak out in meetings and the voices of remote or globally distant employees who culturally are less apt to speak out in verbal forums or who were unknown to the wider company.
- Enlightened and insightful ideas often came from people whose job titles had little to no connection to the subject on which they were contributing. (Polly shared that some of the best employee engagement ideas originated from the engineering group.)

Many of the team members noticed that they had found a powerful mechanism to get "free" productivity from their workforce by simply enabling them to share and put to use their passions and ideas without the limitations found with strict command and control leadership. In reality, EMC has created a mechanism by which people do what they already want to do: meet new people, discuss topics of interest, and help one another. It is easy to do when everyone is co-located in a global "coffee room" to bridge inherent gaps in culture, time zones, and organizational focus.

The Road Ahead
EMC views investment in social media proficiency as a journey. Although the company has made significant progress, it realizes that it has much more to do in the future to fully exploit social media as a business tool.

Polly's Perspective
The way the world of business has been managing its workforce has remained relatively the same since the first sizable factories began to operate in the 1850s. In

today's knowledge economy, we have an opportunity—and a need—to leverage their minds as well as their hands. Today's norm of heavy-handed "employee policies" and "telling" employees what to do cuts off engagement. When employees are trusted, given business objectives and goals, and then allowed to participate in the problem-solving process, the business gets more . . . faster. The behavior models and tools found in socially networked organizations are the keys to that kingdom.

Following is a short list of proposed investments EMC plans to make in its social platform:

Internal Platform Enhancements
- More capacity, more performance
- A better experience for very remote users (e.g., Asia, India)
- Bidirectional e-mail bridging—e-mails can be sent to a predefined discussion area; all discussions and postings on a topic can be bridged to a predefined e-mail distribution list
- Better experience with newer smart phones that support a rich browser
- Done: more advanced social features: "following" people or topics of interest, expanded personal spaces
- Done: expanded customization of views, allowing users to create personal portals combining internal and external topics
- Done: photos
- Next: YouTube functions

Going External

As was mentioned earlier, EMC's overall strategy was to start with internal proficiency and leverage its experience as it moved outside the firewall. The team launched a highly successful external community known as the EMC Community Network (ECN) for partners, developers, and customers to engage with EMC engineers and one another. The ECN community can be reached from the landing page of EMC.com, has a consistent look and feel and a common mechanism for establishing identity, and makes it easy for users to browse other areas of interest across multiple communities. Membership is over 100,000 and on a growth pace of over 8,000 a month. Those numbers are an indicator that the company's customers were clearly ready for this new model.

Most important, EMC now has literally thousands of employees who are comfortable with social media skills, and as a result, the task of building effective external communities is more straightforward. An example of such an external community can be seen at https://community.emc.com/community/edn.

Enterprise Content Integration

Even though this particular initiative targeted social collaboration, document-oriented (or content) collaboration is still an important and relevant topic.

As EMC is an extensive user of Documentum products (EMC bought Documentum in 2003), most of its existing corporate content lives in repositories of one form or another. Over time, the company plans to expose more of its corporate content to the "social computer."

Industrial Strength Enterprise Wikis

If one considers the creation and maintenance of complex technical documents, it becomes obvious that an extended collaboration model would help greatly in having subject-matter experts provide source content as well as continually refine existing content. EMC, for example, creates many thousands of these complex technical documents as a key part of its business.

EMC has completed requirements analysis for this capability via a stand-alone wiki package for internal users.

Improved Analysis Tools

EMC had few tools to discover how people were using the platform effectively and realized it needed to provide better profiling tools to its community developers at both a content level and a user level.

Improved Knowledge Worker Client

As the platform became more successful, many employees became overwhelmed by the corporate feed. One of EMC's divisions, content management and archiving, targeted the need to manage literally millions of discussions (see http://www.emc.com/collateral/demos/microsites/software/centerstage/index.htm).

Assessment

The first wave of Internet technologies brought profound changes to the corporate world, and the second wave will do much the same thing. EMC believes it is a matter of strategic importance to invest early in understanding what these tools and skills can bring to the business world.

It believes that the very nature of work is changing to one in which the preponderance of value will be created by knowledge workers. Those workers will require different behaviors, tools, and platforms to be productive. In one sense, EMC viewed internal efforts as an investment in learning about this new world.

Understandably, there will be organizations that see little value in these sorts of capabilities or, unfortunately, see social media productivity as threatening to the business. Early on, though, EMC realized that people will use these technologies to communicate and share as part of a sponsored corporate initiative or not. Put differently, people are going to use this stuff whether you like it or not.

In the course of the EMC team journey, the company came across many organizations that were using social media tools and techniques to address one aspect or another of their business: marketing to customers, employee tackboards, and the like.

Although it applauds any investment in leveraging social media, a centralized and strategic approach across the entire business is a desirable state of affairs.

Finally, everyone associated with this initiative—whether on the central team, a prospective community builder, or any one of the many thousands of end users—recognized that working with social media environments is an entirely new way of working and can be fun as well.

Users reported back to the team that the social platform was intellectually stimulating, grew them personally and professionally, and can deliver impressive business value when used properly. And anything that's fun to do—*while making money for the company*—is destined for ultimate success.

Orange County Transportation Authority
Transforming Government

CASE STORY   Transforming government and transportation with social media; securing $212 million in stimulus funds while doing more with less

ORGANIZATION   Orange County Transportation Authority

INDUSTRY   Government agency

OBJECTIVE   Engage citizens to participate in transportation planning and use

STRATEGY   Develop a social media plan to reach citizens

Overview

The case story of the Orange County Transportation Authority (OCTA) is woven into the personal saga of Ted Nguyen, OTCA's public relations director. Orange County, California, is home to the largest Vietnamese population in the United States. Nguyen's father was a South Vietnamese military officer. During the fall of Saigon, on April 30, 1975, Ted, his father, and his family escaped certain death when they sought asylum in Orange County.

"I always knew that I wanted to give back to the country that embraced us," Ted shared. He worked for a public agency in which he became intrigued by the power of communication for both good and bad purposes. "I saw how propaganda was used in Vietnam," he recalled. "It created a distrust of government."

Ted went on to work for a U.S. congressman in Washington, D.C., and then in city government and public relations. An opportunity presented itself in which he would be able to fulfill his wish to give back: public relations director with the Orange County Transportation Authority.

Acknowledgment

The OCTA, Ted Nguyen, and his dynamic staff are to be thanked for their openness and willingness to share their story even as it continues to unfold. At this writing, the OCTA has received an award, to add to its many others, for outstanding social media implementation for public awareness and citizen engagement. OCTA, Ted, and his team are the new face of positive government in action. It is their experience and that of the citizens throughout the gold coast of Southern California that are the stars of this case story. We look forward to observing how the OCTA will embrace future real-time tools with the shared belief that it all starts with one person and that one person truly can make a difference.

Why This Is Important to You

Both commercial organizations and government organizations can benefit from the details of how OCTA decided to journey into social media.

Understanding one's target market and audience is a critical component of developing a strategy for social media outreach. OCTA has demonstrated a deep understanding of its market and embraced social media as a way to communicate directly to and with its customers: the transportation public. Citizen engagement is making a significant difference in the success of social media campaigns in the public service space. OCTA wisely used a pilot strategy to hone in on who its audience was and found a way to reach it.

The transformational leadership qualities exhibited by the department in terms of "just do it" are inspirational. Ted's personal journey and professional insights reveal an innate entrepreneurial spirit that is often antithetical to the practices of government agencies. Though it once was notoriously slow to act, OCTA has become a model for citizen empowerment, government action, and accountability.

Finally, for those who want to understand step-by-step what to do to implement a strategy, this is the case story for you. It also goes into great detail about the use of different platforms—creation of a YouTube channel and Twitter handles, how to organize a public live stream, and more. For behemoth organizations that are slow to change, the OCTA case story provides valuable lessons with tangible results.

Background

In 2007, the OCTA communications team utilized traditional tactics and tools for delivering information. The team communicated construction projects to stake-holders and the community through four-color printed brochures and flyers, direct mail pieces, and news releases. The area south of Los Angeles along the Pacific coast used to be a quiet suburb. It is now 3 million strong and provides more jobs than Los Angeles for residents all over Southern California. It is also the home to international technology businesses in addition to Disneyland in Anaheim.

In late 2008, the economic recession hit Orange County hard. Dramatic losses in funding from both federal and state sources left OCTA struggling to find ways to reduce costs while continuing to announce transportation projects. Because of the associated costs of traditional communications tactics, OCTA's team turned to cost-effective social media tools to achieve public involvement.

The department needed to do more with less while reaching out to a growing number of people who were engaged in political issues and talking to one another about matters that affected their lives. An additional goal was to engage those who were disinterested, disillusioned, or suspicious of government. Contrary to the popular "California girl" image of the blue-eyed blonde, Orange County has a minority-majority population composed of Hispanics and multiple Pacific Rim eth-nicities, predominantly Vietnamese and Chinese.

OCTA took social media for a test drive in a program to garner public support for Orange County to receive its fair share of federal stimulus funds from the American Recovery and Reinvestment Act. The campaign with on-the-street

YouTube videos, Facebook discussion boards, and a first of its kind interactive Web site helped OCTA secure $212 million in federal stimulus funds for transportation projects. It also became increasingly clear that the use of social media was an effective way to engage with the public. Using this successful experience as a springboard, the OCTA communications team developed a "Public e-volvement" program utilizing cost-effective high-tech tools to complement traditional methods and outreach tactics in an integrated communications approach. It is the birth, growth, and results of the Public e-volvement program that are chronicled in this case story about transforming government.

Ted's Perspective

In 2008, we embarked on a program to use social media to educate and inform citizens. We researched YouTube and found that enough people were aware of it at the time. Maybe it could work for us.

Research

The OCTA team researched social media by attending conferences, participating in Webinars, and reading blogs and articles written by some of the nation's leading social media experts. Learning the lingo of social media was one of the first challenges. Online conversations included "hashtags," "at mentions," and even "follow Fridays." OCTA dived head-first into social media by attending the first "tweet-up" with the Social Media Club of Orange County.

For practical hands-on research, a team of college interns created a Twitter account. Members began to learn the ropes of digital communications while others researched the latest online trends and still others investigated government organizations that used free social media. The research showed that it was not really about the individual tools. The common thread across all social media platforms was one-to-one human connections with the public. It was possible to cultivate and build fans one person at a time by breaking down the walls of bureaucratic communications and literally putting a face on the organization.

Ted's Perspective

So on my own time, I compiled a list of questions from citizens and taxpayers on transportation issues. It wasn't about pushing them. It was about hearing them tell us where we should go. We then created the Public e-volvement program." It was a way for OCTA to break out of the same old communications process of hosting special events in conventional ways. OTCA was the first in the nation to report on stimulus funding, GAO [General Accounting Office], making it relevant to people who pay taxes.

Challenges

Not everyone was onboard with social media. Executive management was hesitant to grant the public communications department access to Twitter, YouTube, and Facebook. Even members of the team resisted the shift to digital communications.

136

Planning

The OCTA public communications team developed the Public e-volvement program without the use of any consultant help. All materials and content were produced in-house. While laying the groundwork, a team of three full-time staff members and two interns devoted a couple of hours a day to outlining the Public e-volvement program. The plan included the following:

- Organize social media panel discussions and hands-on workshops for local government and nonprofit organizations.
- Position OCTA as a Gov 2.0 pioneer and a national model for government agencies using social media effectively to enhance transparency and accountability.
- Create an online tool kit to help other organizations start with social media.
- Develop a social media guide to help other government agencies get social media.
- Integrate social media into OCTA's public communications department's programs.
- Share with local universities and professional organizations during speaker presentations.

Ted's Perspective

We decided to hold a transit forum at Chapman University to ask the public, How do we deal with budget cuts? We e-mailed people to get sponsors. The event was streamed live so people could watch from home or at their office. Real-time questions were sent on TweetStream. Our meeting was the number one Trending Topic 11.6 minutes into the meeting! We had commentary and feedback from people watching from Russia, Western Europe, and Asia who have a stake or interest in transportation solutions.

The best hearts and minds of social media gathered in July 2009 at OCTA to discuss how to utilize social media to create transparency and accountability as well as bring a level of authenticity to the seemingly endless and faceless bureaucracy of government and public agencies. Billed as Gov 2.0, it hosted an over-capacity crowd of 75 Orange County professionals to exchange tips and share best practices for popular social media sites such as Twitter, Facebook, and YouTube. Hundreds of other people followed the event via live Twitter updates. It was the first event of its kind for government and public agencies in Orange County. Based on the overwhelming popularity of the first installment of Gov 2.0, the team invited local government agencies to attend hands-on workshops led by top experts on Twitter, YouTube, Facebook, and LinkedIn. A third Gov 2.0 panel discussion featured keynote speaker Dr. Mark Drapeau. The gathering was held in December for local governments, public agencies, and citizens with the goal of encouraging a more responsive and accountable government.

Ted's Perspective
The most important point from the meeting was that it revealed the global issues of being heard and connected in a shared experience.

Implementation

- Created a robust OCTA Twitter presence with a main account and several project-specific pages
- Developed a main OCTA Facebook page with subpages for major construction projects and transportation enhancement programs
- Created an OCTA YouTube channel and posted weekly two-minute videos highlighting current transportation projects and initiatives
- Communicated the importance of rail safety using social media sites
- Generated awareness of the stimulus-funded State Route 91 (SR-91) eastbound widening project by inviting Southern California social media practitioners to participate in a groundbreaking ceremony
- Created a personalized transportation blog that featured YouTube videos, audio interviews, and music slide shows
- Revitalized the CEO's weekly e-newsletter with an improved design and interactive social media tools

With the knowledge gained from social media research, team members were guided by a person from the California Association of Public Information Officials (CAPIO). Everyone worked together to set up accounts on Twitter, Facebook, and YouTube. To create awareness and visibility of OCTA's projects and services, the team established a main OCTA Facebook fan page to serve as the social media hub ("fans" became "likes" in spring 2010). Facebook would be the place to engage with the public by answering questions and sharing relevant and timely transportation information.

OCTA used Twitter as a communication tool for reputation/issues management, media relations, outreach for project studies, and construction communications. The primary goal was to enhance OCTA's reputation for being transparent. By monitoring conversations on Twitter, the communications team intercepted negative tweets and built lasting positive relationships with some of OCTA's critics. Just days before the groundbreaking, OCTA created a new Twitter account, @91fwy, to provide information about Orange County's largest stimulus project. The SR-91 groundbreaking event was OCTA's first attempt to utilize social media to share instant information via Twitter and Facebook. The @91fwy Twitter profile helped OCTA listen to the public and address questions and issues as they were posted in real-time.

Using an inexpensive Flip camera, the OCTA communications team shot and edited weekly YouTube segments called "Transportation in 2." Not only did those videos enhance the transportation agency's authenticity, but the team captured some major milestones on camera, including unveiling the Orange County Gateway sign, the high-speed rail press conference, and the SR-91 ground-breaking ceremony.

The following illustrations and elements convey the extensive planning, recruitment, awareness, influencer partnerships, and forethought involved in the use of social media by governments and nonprofits for building a social media base.

Digital Trends (Summary of Steve Rubel's White Paper)

Trend 1: Satisfaction Guaranteed
Customer and public relations are blending. Consumers use social media to demand service:

- Monitor Google: search OCTA, bus, rail, Orange County, West County Connectors, and so on.
- Find key blogs and communities: who's linking to our Web pages and sharing our stories.
- The new Web site model is "hub and spokes": a home-base Web site and lots of microsites and social media avenues branching off it.

Trend 2: Media Reforestation
The media is in a constant state of reinvention as part of the transition from paper to digital:

- Social and mainstream media are merging.
- Become a curator of one's own and related content in a niche to gain credibility and traffic.
- Most PR will soon be "direct to audience" rather than directed through the media.
- The average attention span of Web visitors is 20 seconds per page.

Trend 3: Less Is the New More
Media overload takes its toll. People don't visit that many sites to get information:

- The average person visits only 3.8 different Web sites per day, for a total of 115 Web visits per month.
- The prevailing theme is, "If the news is important, it will find me."
- Social media such as Google Gadgets will help you show up in searches.

Trend 4: Corporate All Stars
Workers flock to social media to build their personal brands, and employers use them as an effective and credible way to conduct community outreach:

139

- Corporate all-stars establish relationships online and serve as an early warning system for customer relations issues.
- Establish guidelines for ways to handle questions and comments.
- Give them independence but focus them. Give them the equipment and support to actively listen.
- Ford's Twitter (@ScottMonty) is managed by an employee posting under his own name and has a huge following. People find him a trustworthy spokesperson, whereas a post from "Ford" wouldn't be seen that way.

Trend 5: The Power of Pull

Where push once ruled, it's now equally important to create digital content that people discover through search (pull):

- People find information primarily through searches of social media sites and news aggregators such as Google News.
- Be discoverable. Having a bigger online footprint is the key.
- Write for searches, not just readers. People enter "headache," not "aspirin," so change your headlines and metatags so that Google can find you.
- Think relationships, not campaigns.
- Word of mouth 2.0: Friends and their shared experiences, rather than brand, will become the primary way we make decisions.
- Product utility is the key. Create resources that enhance the conversation. An example would be Walmart's blog written by employees.

Research Revealed

The team evaluated what worked and what did not and the latest trends via blogs, phone calls, and e-mails. Team members discovered that Californians are tech-savvy, with Orange County near the top of social media use. A search of periodicals indicated best practices of cost-saving social media tools and how OCTA could do more for less in the economic recession. Meetings with local early tech adapters helped OCTA establish close relationships that quickly gave it a leadership role in the Social Media Club of Orange County. Hands-on training from a social media pioneer in Orange County, Marisa O'Neil of O.C. Parks, cost only a half dozen Sprinkles cupcakes (see Figures 5.3 and 5.4).

OCTA conducted YouTube research to find meaningful statistics and discover how best to utilize the power of visual social media. The following points summarize YouTube statistics from 2008:

1. By 2010 Gen Y will outnumber baby boomers: 96 percent of them have joined a social network.
2. Social media has overtaken porn as the number one activity on the Web.

5.3 Marisa O'Neil: O.C. Parks cupcakes in exchange for social media training

5.4 Interns carefully dive into Twitter to take a test drive on social media

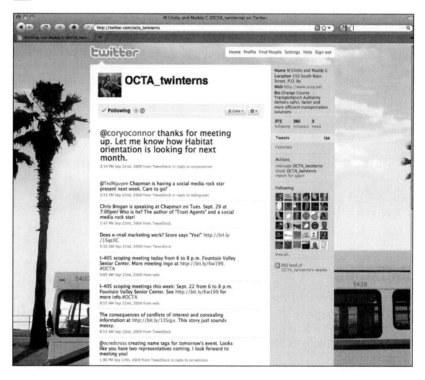

3. One of eight couples married in the United States last year met via social media.

4. Years to reach 50 million users: radio, 38 years; television, 13 years; Internet, 4 years; iPod, 3 years. Facebook added 100 million users in less than 9 months, and iPhone applications hit 1 billion in 9 months.

5. If Facebook were a country, it would be the world's third largest, between the United States and India.

6. Some sources say China's QZone is larger, with over 300 million people using its services (Facebook's ban in China plays into this, and stats are changing each month).

7. comScore indicates that Russia has the most engaged social media audience, with visitors spending 6.6 hours and viewing 1,307 pages per visitor per month. Vkontakte.ru is its number one social network.

8. A 2009 U.S. Department of Education study revealed that, on average, online students outperformed those receiving face-to-face instruction.

9. One in six higher education students are enrolled in online curricula.

10. Percentage of companies using LinkedIn as a primary tool to find employees: 80 percent.
11. The fastest growing segment on Facebook is females 55 to 65 years old.
12. Ashton Kutcher and Ellen DeGeneres have more Twitter followers than the entire populations of Ireland, Norway, and Panama.
13. Eighty percent of Twitter usage is on mobile devices. People update anywhere, anytime. Imagine what that means for bad customer experiences.
14. Generations Y and Z consider e-mail passé. In 2009 Boston College stopped distributing e-mail addresses to incoming freshmen.
15. What happens in Vegas stays on YouTube, Flickr, Twitter, and Facebook.
16. The second largest search engine in the world is YouTube.
17. Wikipedia has over 13 million articles. Some studies show that it's more accurate than the *Encyclopedia Britannica*. Some 78 percent of its articles are not in English.
18. There are over 200 million blogs.
19. Number of bloggers who post content or tweet daily: 54 percent.
20. Because of the speed with which social media enables communication, word of mouth has become world of mouth.
21. If you were paid a $1 every time an article was posted on Wikipedia, you would earn $156.23 per hour.
22. Facebook users translated the site from English to Spanish via a wiki in less than four weeks; that cost Facebook $0.
23. Twenty-five percent of search results for the world's 20 largest brands are links to user-generated content.
24. Thirty-four percent of bloggers post opinions about products and brands.
25. People care more about how their social graph ranks products and services than how Google ranks them.
26. Seventy-eight percent of consumers trust peer recommendations.
27 Only 14 percent trust advertisements.
28 Only 18 percent of traditional TV campaigns generate a positive ROI.
29. Ninety percent of people who can TiVo ads do.
30. Hulu grew from 63 million total streams in April 2008 to 373 million in April 2009.
31. Twenty-five percent of Americans said they watched a short video on their phones in the last month.
32. According to Jeff Bezos, 35 percent of book sales on Amazon are for the Kindle when available.
33. Twenty-four of the 25 largest newspapers are experiencing record declines in circulation because we no longer research for the news; the news finds us.
34. In the near future we will no longer search for products and services; they will find us via social media.

35. More than 1.5 million pieces of content (Web links, news stories, blog posts, notes, photos, etc.) are shared on Facebook daily.
36. Successful companies in social media act more like Dale Carnegie and less like David Ogilvy, listening first and selling second.
37. Successful companies in social media act more like party planners, aggregators, and content providers than traditional advertisers.

OCTA drafted this flyer to appeal to government workers' self interest, which included patriotism, public service, and participation (see Figure 5.5). They also sent online interactive flyers to save the date. They organized social media panel discussions and hands-on workshops for local government and nonprofit organizations (see Figure 5.6). The added benefit of planning the workshops was that it helped OCTA develop an extensive network of other agencies that were harnessing the power of social media.

In planning the tactics, this interactive e-form helped OCTA communicate ways to conduct an event faster, better, and cheaper.

To keep the conversations alive and stay top of mind, OCTA sent a follow-up e-mail with a helpful summary of the social media event to plant the seeds of online social engagement. It coordinated sponsored raffles, prizes, and additional news coverage through close relationships built through networking. With the help of the Social Media Club of Orange County's president, Morgan Brown, OCTA streamed live video for free (see Figure 5.7).

5.5 Social media public agency event e-mail tied in with online flyers

5.6 Interactive event e-vitation built awareness quickly for local government workshop at a minimal cost

5.7 Free live streaming video of OCTA Gov 2.0 meeting

OCTA drafted a Social Media Guide to share in the hope of receiving feedback from the local social media community and other potential users (Figure 5.8). The easy-to-understand overview literally illustrates step by step what OTCA did to become social media-savvy. The guide has information about Twitter for reputation management, media relations, bus schedules, transportation studies, and freeway construction. It shows how to link to Web sites and news clips. It also includes top-line tips for Facebook and YouTube plus a multitude of firsthand insights on doing more with less.

> We have created this information guide and online toolkit to share our thoughts and firsthand experiences using social media to strengthen public engagement, create greater transparency and enhance accountability at the Orange County Transportation Authority (OCTA). OCTA's social media program is integrated into our public outreach efforts.

*It does not replace—but rather enhances—our ongoing commu-
nications and outreach work. OCTA's Public e-volvement Program
optimizes community involvement and public participation utilizing
cost-effective social media tools to create opportunities for meaningful
public engagement. That means cultivating public participation with
two-way communications with community members, stakeholders and
other people.*

—OCTA Social Media Guide

Based on their research, team members created a professional Twitter
presence with a real human being who engaged with the public. One had the face
and voice of Ted Nguyen, the public relations officer (Figure 5.9), and another
profile was set up for OCTA news (Figure 5.10a). @OCTAYouth (Figure 5.10b) was
created to engage high school and university students and other young people to
share relevant information. Minority-majority Hispanic, Vietnamese, and Chinese
followers were targeted with relevant cultural news: "Lunar New Year Celebra-
tion, let OCTA do the driving for you." Other Twitter handles included @railsafesarah
and @91fwy, among the first highways in the nation to have a twitter profile.
@WCCProjectInfo tweeted construction projects in the West County for detours
and updates.

5.8 Social Media Guide cover

5.9 Twitter profile for Ted Nguyen, OCTA's public relations offer, gives a personal touch to messaging

Facebook served as the OCTA social media hub and the repository for updates, YouTube videos, links to project pages, audio, photos of construction milestones, slide shows with important rail safety information, and postings for events (see Figures 5.11a and b). Facebook offers the ability to reach people where they are every day and allows them to partake in conversations that are happening all over the site. Each day, Facebook has more than twice as many viewers as all the newspapers in the United States combined; only 13 percent of Americans still buy a daily newspaper. Additional Facebook profiles were made for services, such as OC Rail Safety. An ARTIC (Anaheim Regional Transportation Intermodal Center) profile was established that supports numerous transit services regarding the planned high-speed rail service. OCTA Social Media Guide Facebook factoid: "Not everyone will visit a company's web page every day, but 150 million people visit Facebook on a daily basis."

OCTA's chairman, Will Kempton, did not escape OCTA advances in social media. His blog underwent an extreme makeover with a new user-friendly format and saw a significant increase in engagement (see Figures 5.12 and 5.13).

148

5.10 Multiple Twitter handles such as @OCTANews (*a*) and @OCTAY Youth (*b*) provide important information to diverse followers

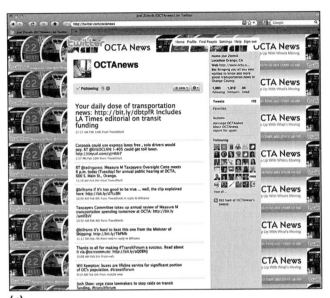

(*a*)

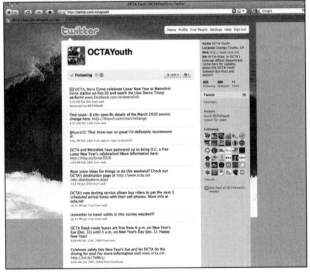

(*b*)

<u>5.11</u> One of multiple OCTA Facebook profiles that supported video (*a*) as well as the OCTA YouTube Channel (*b*). Video provided updates of the latest meetings and news for easy citizen access.

(*a*)

(*b*)

5.12 Audio podcast easily updatable and uploaded via iPhone app to audio Boo for even more real-time communication

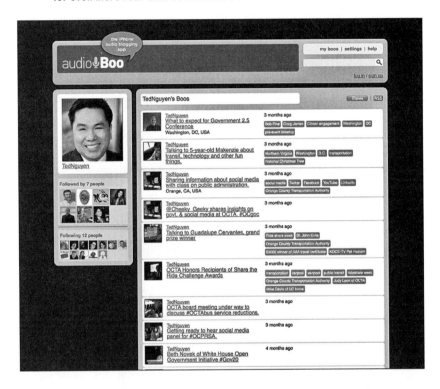

To show further commitment to its mission and share knowledge, the communication team presented OCTA's social media experience at the Cool Twitter Conference '09 to position Orange County as a social media leader. Team members also shared their story with Southern California public relations professionals [Public Relations Society of America (PRSA)] to demonstrate that a strategic approach and action can have tangible results. OCTA prepared a special handout for elected officials in Orange County to be part of a hands-on tutorial during an O.C. League of Cities meeting. With the goal of catapulting Orange County as a national example

5.13 Chairman improved blog format with easier navigation, thus increasing citizen interaction

of using social media to enhance transparency, OCTA carefully crafted the national keynote presentation at Gov 2.5 in Washington, D.C., on December 14–15, 2009, themed, "Using Social Media to Improve Government Services and Engage the Public." (See Figure 5.14.)

Evaluation

Social media humanized OCTA, making it an agency that was focused not only on improving roads, freeways, railways, and buses. It was also about communicating with the public and helping provide citizens with the information they need to make their lives better. In these times of greater public accountability and transparency, social media has provided impressive cost-effective results for OCTA. Social media,

<u>5.14</u> Gov 2.0 presentation leveraged OCTA as a national leader in social media for government

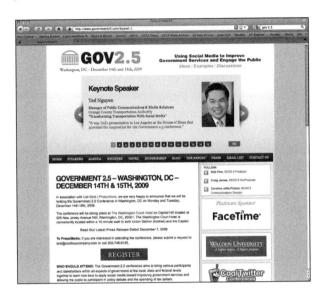

along with traditional outreach, have strengthened OCTA's ability to communicate with residents, businesses, the traveling public, and other stakeholders.

Because of OCTA's role as a steward of taxpayer dollars to deliver transportation solutions, public involvement drives its work. OCTA's efforts with social media should help advance the free flow of accurate and truthful information by serving the public interest and contributing to informed decision making. It has built a credible reputation, demonstrated expertise, shared information, helped people, and, most important, listened before talking. Conversations about OCTA transportation issues in Orange County and traffic on the I-5 are already happening online, and if team members are not there to engage, the public will lose out:

- An overwhelming number of participants agreed that the Gov 2.0 events were relevant, engaging, and well organized.
- @TedNguyen reached 59,874 people with 94,035 impressions during the first Gov 2.0 panel discussion.
- Tweets containing the hashtag #ocgov reached 43,166 people with 260,845 impressions during the third installment of Gov 2.0.
- As a result of highly successful Gov 2.0 sessions, local government agencies and nonprofits, including the City of Anaheim, the Orange County League of Cities, and the Orange County Sanitation District, have joined social media networks.
- OCTA shared its social media guide and Public e-volvement tool kit with 500 people with highly positive feedback.
- The OCTA team led the way with 21,296 Twitter followers, the most for any transportation or public agency, and was listed among influential people by Twitter applications.
- OCTA utilized social media tools for construction groundbreaking of the SR-91 freeway by maximizing news and social media coverage; 295 clicks to videos uploaded by social media practitioners and tweets during the press conference reached 20,738 people with 228,480 impressions.
- After a positive relationship was built through social media with former critic and "trans-enemy" Steven Chan of the Transit Advocates of Orange County, he now frequently posts OCTA project information to his blog with kudos to the OCTA communications team.
- News stories generated by local, state, and national publications provided media credibility for the program.
- CEO's e-newsletter tripled readership to 4,000 people, with 90 percent saying that it provides timely information.
- Comments and responses from presentations exceeded the goal of demonstrating OCTA as a leader by sharing social media.
- The *Orange County Register* regularly features OCTA as a social media leader with a news value of approximately $112,000.

Future Planning

Now that the framework has been created, social media is being integrated seamlessly into all OCTA projects and programs on a daily basisas with any other outreach tactic. At OCTA, the communications team members are not the experts on social media; however, the team has picked up some nuggets of knowledge and garnered success along the way. As a public agency serving Orange County's taxpayers, it is compelled to share its successes and challenges with other government offices and agencies because OCTA cares about enhancing the community. According to OCTA, that's the point of it all: to help each other "get" social media and share their experiences.

Ted's Perspective:

The individual can impact change on a local level. We wanted to build relationships of trust one person at a time. Leadership involves mobilizing people. Finding out what are their aspirations and getting citizens involved. Then you reach a groundswell or tipping point. One person can make a difference.

Here is the way to set up a social media program:

1. Research the issues and opportunities
2. Plan
3. Implement
4. Analyze

Assessment

There are a number of striking elements that contributed to OCTA's success in its social media journey. The first was having an advocate and visionary in the public information officer, Ted Nguyen. His wartime and firsthand experience of how propaganda controls communication and stifles conversation and human progress is freed and unleashed in social media for the greater good. Orange County is fortunate to have him as a citizen.

The second success element is commitment. You will recall that some coworkers resisted moving in this direction. This is a very common reaction in companies that are faced with change. Enough of Ted's supervisors and staff made a full commitment to learn and master as many social platforms as possible to improve communication to their stakeholders. It is evident that they took their responsibility to keep Orange County moving very seriously. It may be surprising to find so many people interested in transportation issues when most of California is notorious for having insufficient mass transit. However, that is precisely why citizens appreciate having a voice and embraced OCTA social media efforts. In addition, the communication team did not abandon traditional media. They were aware of different levels of social proficiency and blended the two tactics.

155

5.15 What does Gov 2.0 look like?

As a public agency, OCTA tracked expenditures for every item in its social media launch, honoring accountability and transparency. It also demonstrated the cost-effectiveness of free digital platforms with the exception of labor time and sweat equity. In social media, conversations are real-time currency. OCTA benefited from relationship building that translated into free streaming video of one of its meetings. The *Orange County Register* wrote about OCTA, giving it $112,000 of free ink. Add that to the value of Internet presence, blogs, tweets, YouTube, Facebook engagements, podcasts, and photos that are all shared in the digital ether as far away as Russia. What was an attempt to serve citizens in Orange County, California, has had a real-time impact on citizens around the world.

One of our favorite articles from the OCTA social media journey is a *Register* blog by Jonathan Lasner and Jeff Collins called, "Can Twitter Shake Up City Hall?" with a Ted Nguyen interview. The article poses the questions, "What does Gov 2.0 look like?" (see Figure 5.15) and, "What will Citizen 2.0 look like?" The answers are unknown, but one thing history tells us is that when citizens are given a voice, change happens.

Costs
- Various office supplies: $5–$50
- Podium sign: $5
- Evaluation materials: $5
- Donated flowers and raffle tickets: $150
- PRSA presentation and meeting: $140 waived for presenter and staff

Wahoo's Fish Tacos: Community Building through Extreme Sports

CASE STORY Evolving a thriving business in a competitive industry by discovering customer trends and securing key partnerships
INDUSTRY Restaurant, franchise, fast food
OBJECTIVE To make a living while being able to go surfing
STRATEGY Align with famous extreme sports athletes

Acknowledgment

He has been described as "the coolest CEO in America." Immediately upon meeting Wing Lam, CEO and cofounder of Wahoo's Fish Tacos, one can see that this is absolutely true. Usually in flip-flops and surfer shorts with long hair flowing down to the middle of his back, Wing is the epitome of the Wall Street meets extreme chef surfer lifestyle (see Figure 5.16). Though he looks like a surfer fresh from the waves, Wing calls himself a bean counter because of his undergraduate degrees in finance and Spanish at San Diego State University. Wing has also taught at Pepperdine's MBA program. Before college, he attended high school in Orange County, California. Always aware of the ROI of PR, he calculates in his head where he wants to expand his business and how.

Wing is an authentic humanitarian and savvy businessperson who keeps a sharp eye on trends; that is evidenced by his phenomenal track record. He was the first to spot today's world-famous extreme sports stars and Olympic champions when they were kids in his restaurant or at events Wahoo's sponsored. As his business continues to expand, Wing is evolving into a philanthropist who gives back to his community and numerous charities. As he says, "Not bad for a little Chinese kid from Brazil who didn't speak a lick of English." We thank Wing for letting us share his classic family success story and transition into social media in his own untraditional style.

Why This Is Important to You

Go with what you know with a passion. Add free real-time social media to interact with customers in the lifestyles they love. Toss in celebrity endorsements. Align yourself with key partners. This is a mix destined for success. As odd as it sounds, the Lam brothers' objective was "to make a living while being able to go surfing." This was the overriding passion that drove everything that followed. Much has been written and said about passion. When this intangible is supported by a sound

5.16 Wing Lam, "the coolest CEO in America," in front of Wahoo's Fish Taco Restaurant serving up a surfer lifestyle

business foundation, patience, and a unique offering to customers, passion can become profitable, especially when it is connected to an aspirational lifestyle. Some people aspire to be identified with luxury autos. For other people, it is buying a certain brand of wine. For yet others, it is the Southern California surf scene and having a backstage pass to a concert.

Real-time social media heightens access to aspirational lifestyles by supporting the communities where they thrive regardless of the degree to which a person actually participates in the lifestyle. Whether a wannabe or fully engaged, anyone can take part in the conversation if he or she has a true interest. Wing has much to share about how he has been able to create fervent generational customers in the surfer lifestyle space by listening to them. His commitment to paying close attention to their interests led to discovering extreme sports in its genesis before anyone else. Then, as Wing continued to observe and hear how customers were communicating with one another on emerging digital platforms, he and his team stepped into social media to interact with them too. This active participation built tremendous conversation volume and activity that lifted the local Wahoo's Fish Taco brand to global awareness.

Background
Wing Lam literally grew up over a restaurant. Home was on the floor above his parents' Chinese restaurant in São Paolo, Brazil. He and his two brothers, Ed

and Mingo, stood on crates peeling shrimp. In 1975, the family immigrated to the United States and moved to Southern California, where they opened one of the first Chinese restaurants on quaint Balboa Island. Movie star John Wayne lived in neighboring Newport Beach and walked into their Shanghai Pine Garden Chinese restaurant. That unexpected celebrity connection changed his parents' business forever and placed the restaurant on the map. A photo of his dad with John Wayne would hang proudly in the restaurant for years.

The brothers' life was split between the restaurant and the beach. Addicted to surfing, they would travel south to Mexico to surf and there were introduced to the fish taco. Years of surfing trips to Mexico created a craving for the specialty of char-broiled fish, salsa, and tortillas.

Since being in the restaurant business was natural for them, the three brothers opened their first Wahoo's Fish Tacos restaurant in Costa Mesa, Orange County, California, in 1988. Their menu was finalized the night before to reflect the flavors of their beloved fish tacos along with their Brazilian favorites and Asian-inspired items. No formalized focus groups or sampling was involved. They chose to trust their own taste buds plus those of family members and friends. It proved to be a winning combination. In 1994, Wahoo's started franchising, and it currently has 1,500 employees in 50 restaurants in California, Colorado, Texas, and Hawaii, with plans for additional locations.

Having witnessed the power of celebrity endorsement for his parents' restaurant, Wing thought that someday he would like to have just one John Wayne. Now he has hundreds of athletes, rock bands, and celebrities who are fans of Wahoo's Fish Tacos, including

- Shaun White: gold medalist snowboarder
- Tony Hawk: world-famous skateboarder
- Rob Dyrdek: professional skateboarder
- Patrick Dempsey: TV and film actor
- Green Day
- Offspring
- Blink 182
- Jack Johnson: world-famous surfer/musician
- Kelly Slater: nine-time world surfing champion
- Jeremy McGrath: six-time world Super Cross champion
- Robby Gordon: world-famous NASCAR driver and off-road driver
- Carson Palmer: former Heisman Trophy winner and starting quarterback for the Cincinnati Bengals
- Jordan Palmer: backup quarterback to brother Carson Palmer
- Matt Leinart: quarterback for the Arizona Cardinals
- Mark Sanchez: quarterback for the New York Jets and former USC football star

Wing has been on the *Ellen DeGeneres Show* and has been featured on the Food Network shows *Food Unwrapped* and *Beach Eats* and in local magazines, the *Wall Street Journal*, *BusinessWeek*, and *USA Today*. He has appeared online and offline touting company leadership that has pushed his ROI per square foot off the charts.

The Challenge
There was no place for surfers to eat like the places they loved in Baja California. Surfing takes a lot out of a person and can build a ferocious appetite. Surprisingly, cities along the coast did not have a fast-food restaurant that served healthy food. The brothers knew they loved surfing more than anything else and that eating was not far behind. The question they posed to one another was how could they surf, eat, and make a living and let friends know about it.

The Strategy
Open a restaurant that serves healthy fast food that a person can eat right after surfing. That meant serving the fish taco, the surfer's hamburger. This would be a differentiator and a challenge for three young men in a sea of hamburger outlets. Though popular in Baja, Mexico, the fish taco was exclusive to surf aficionados or tourists who traveled south of the border.

They would target 18- to 24-year-old males since they are the biggest consumers of fast food, eating out approximately five times per week. The brothers decorated the restaurant with surf paraphernalia and equipment given to them by nearby surf companies. To sell fish tacos, they would present food as part of a lifestyle and look for events to participate in and build awareness of their restaurants. The arrangements had to be free (or affordable) and be authentic to their passion for the surfer lifestyle. To achieve this, they would (1) follow trends and (2) develop partnerships.

Wing, Ed, and Mingo started with surfers, skateboarders, and snowboarders and expanded to other extreme sports. Customers and friends were starting to talk about the new sports they were trying out and finding very exciting. Couple that with surf culture and fish tacos from Mexico; they would keep things very clear and simple.

Wing's Perspective
We treat young, undiscovered talent like professional athletes. That means a lot to them, and they remember us. We end up creating pop culture for kids.

Strategy Execution
Approximately 99 percent of their event partners wanted Wahoo's Fish Tacos, and so before the X Games became popular, Wing volunteered at an event when

Shaun White was a little kid. He gave Shaun his first free skateboard. Kelly Slater, world surf champion, was another early customer Wing supported. Wing made a personal and strategic decision to support anything with kids and protecting the environment. This would serve him well.

Wing's Perspective

I grew tired of telling people about events. There had to be a better way to share the news about what we were doing.

The Internet was in its very early stages and was used primarily for company information. At the time, Wing found word of mouth to be the best way to advertise to his target customers. For example, when Monster energy drink was a start-up, it wanted to sponsor an event, and Wahoo's tagged along by providing food. In turn it gave other people, fans, and customers a chance to tag along with Wahoo's and share the event experience. Everyone would have a great time, and the participants would talk about it in their own language to their friends.

Soon social media started taking shape with MySpace. Now Wahoo's could interact directly with fans and view information about what they liked or where they lived. This helped geotarget promotional giveaways that included backstage passes for concert tours across the country and around the globe. The restaurant would give people the opportunity to have a great experience and share it with friends in their social networks. Then Wahoo's would be mentioned in the conversation for making it all possible.

It found another fun way to reach people. One day, Wing and his crew suggested posting pictures of themselves as kids on MySpace. People especially liked the photo of Eddie Santos, Wahoo's art director and Internet media guru, sporting a mullet. The photo got passed around and talked about and evolved into RockdaMullet ultimately becoming the number two persona on MySpace with over 110,000,000 clicks from around the world (Figure 5.17).

RockdaMullet engaged with fans in conversations about rock tours, concerts, parties, events, and everything else that Wahoo's lifestyle embraces. To engage fans even further, Wahoo's jumped onboard new social media platforms along with fans. Wahoo's is on Twitter at @Wahoos and on Facebook.com/Wahoo's. It became very active in new media postings, status updates, blogs, video, and photos. Wahoo's team members created a steady flow of content that was interesting to kids, teens, and young adults. Their fans collaborated and provided user-generated content filled with backstage concert experiences, compliments of Wahoo's, for bands, including Blink 182 and Green Day. A wide variety of events, music, action sports, charities, and celebrities provided plenty to talk about in the Wahoo's community.

Wing's Perspective

Early in social media, people would try to sell me a $5,000 ad that would only go to a few people. I told them, "Why should I do that when I can send out one

5.17 Eddie Santos, aka RockdaMullet; Wahoo's popular persona created a way to talk to fans and customers on MySpace

message and reach 5 million?" When they heard that, they wanted to be part of what I was doing.

Wahoo's Now

MySpace, Facebook, and Twitter ended Wing's search for a better way to get the word out for events quickly and at no cost. Wing has never paid for traditional advertising. He does some trading and co-oping. He describes the old way of advertising an event: "I did Project Playhouse for charity at Fashion Island in Newport Beach. It won awards, got some press, and raised $37,000 for Tony Hawk's charity. Now that we have evolved to the Internet and real-time social media, Eddie put us on MySpace, Facebook, and Twitter, and millions of people hear about it. We'll be able to raise more for charities."

Wahoo's brick and mortar restaurants average $3,500 per store sales per day. Wing and his brothers are prominently featured in a multitude of interviews on a variety of YouTube channels extolling their success story. Though a recognized, skilled businessman, Wing prefers to describe himself as "a tribesman, not a leader." The brother trio stays focused on packaging an experience. As Wing describes it, "Wahoo's is like a getaway to our favorite places in Baja California. Our friends give us their boards (surf, ski, skate) that we put throughout the restaurant. It's a great hangout as a surf environment, and our customers enjoy healthy good food." Wing and Eddie also use their ocean of fans in restaurants and the social space to crowdsource ideas and the next trends.

Internal Observations

When asked how Wahoo's stays relevant, Wing replied, "When we see new athletes or sports trending up, our interest in them is genuine. They know this and actually seek us, rather than us seeking them. These new athletes know we will support their events, and the partnerships grow from there."

His advice to businesspeople and marketers about real-time is authentic and transparent: "Always stay ahead of the curve. Align with certain brands. I learn from my customers. My early customers have kids of their own who are into new things, like comic books. We have a partnership with TopCow, a leading comic book publisher, and do events around Comic-Con San Diego, the largest international comic/animation/scifi show. So we can spot the next trends. It's a give-and-take relationship. Most important, it's about making their overall experience better."

He also sees a huge opportunity for the next generation to figure out how to monetize the real-time platforms that are his primary source of interacting with his customers in the digital space. Wing will have the opportunity to share his entrepreneurial approach when he evolves into academia. He will teach marketing in the MBA Program at Concordia University, Irvine. No doubt, wherever the surfing CEO travels, Wing will be true to his comment: "It doesn't matter where you are around the world; you need to support the community and the community will support you."

Assessment

"Find a need and fill it" has been sage business advice for decades and certainly applies here. The Wahoo's story is a classic study in building an online and offline community of fans, brand advocates, and influencers by knowing what they want and then providing it by appealing to both their basic needs and their aspirations.

It is also significant that the need for basic communication and the rise of social media were embraced by an already successful company as a way to stay relevant and increase the fan base. Many companies looking at social media may be thinking that things are just fine the way they are, so why change? The Wahoo's story shows that a good company can get better by using the new communications tools that social media brings to the table. Go where the customers are both online and offline is the new mantra.

Among the many best practices from Wing Lam and Wahoo's, four are quite prominent:

1. Follow your passion.
2. Be a trend spotter.
3. Build a community where your company and brand can add value to "hang out with the cool guys."
4. Use social media for social good. Wing Lam is in the enviable position of providing support to causes that matter to him because he has built

a business foundation around giving to the community. His philanthropy is renowned—from children's issues, to fighting diabetes, to feeding the needy in the community. He is the first to admit that it brings him personal satisfaction to do good. He is also now fulfilling another passion by becoming an educator at Concordia University.

By operating in real-time and being a part of the community, both online and offline, Wahoo's knows its customers like nobody else and passionately provides relevant products and services to them that ensure continued success.

Mazda North American Operations:
Social Media Restart

CASE STORY   Building a community around a challenger brand's loyal enthusiasts (moving from a challenger brand to an enthusiast brand through virtual and real community building).

COMPANY   Mazda North American Operations

INDUSTRY   Automotive

OBJECTIVE   Have a social media presence that fulfills Mazda dealers' request for leadership, guidance, and presence

STRATEGY   Let the brand support the passion expressed by brand enthusiasts

CONTRIBUTORS   David Harris, group manager of digital and alternative media, Mazda North American Operations; Josh Levine, CEO, Rebel Industries

Acknowledgments

The connective tissue that happens in social media is one of the elements that continues to fascinate. It is due to Josh Levine, CEO of Los Angeles–based Rebel Industries, that the connection to Mazda North American Operations materialized and to David Harris, group manager of digital media, Mazda North American Operations. Both contributed to the insights shared in this case story. David and Josh live social media, which means they are open and transparent in all their business undertakings. This is an extremely significant move in the highly competitive global automotive industry in its current unstable condition. Their accessibility and willingness to share insights most likely are due to the fact that Mazda, Josh, and David had been involved in real-time social media in its early stages and before all their paths converged.

Why This Is Important to You

Join us as we step into Mazda North American Operations in phase 2 of its social media voyage. There are a number of significant reasons why this case story is filled with lessons for global and local businesses across every industry. Two noteworthy points are mentioned here, though it behooves the reader to benefit from other insights by examining this chronicle thoroughly. First of all, the Mazda experience is particularly important for companies that took a bold step into social media and set up profiles but are disappointed that those platforms are not delivering on objectives or living up to expectations. For Mazda, that meant researching and reassessing interaction with all stakeholders (auto dealers, customers, business partners). The call to evolve social media bubbled up from the dealers at the grassroots level as well as flowed down from top corporate offices.

Second, there are lessons in how Mazda wisely recognized snags in competitive social media outreach and integrated those lessons into its efforts. Mazda placed the focus on supporting brand enthusiasts who celebrated Mazda rather than pushing the brand itself. Counterintuitive thinking has led to tremendous traction on its sites.

Mazda's case story is unique in relation to the others in this chapter because it is the only business that already had social media in place. All the other case stories are about taking the daunting first steps to introduce real-time social media in the enterprise or organization. Mazda's journey provides valuable messages on the need to stay committed and make adjustments to a real-time social media marketing strategy. Its wise action also illustrates how a company can recuperate from social media malaise and become a viable supporter of a passionate enthusiast community.

Background

Mazda's parent company, Toyo Cork Kogyo Co., Ltd., was founded in Hiroshima, Japan, in 1920 as a machine tool manufacturer. It evolved into producing trucks and then consumer autos when the first Mazda vehicles began arriving in the United States in 1970. The auto company has maintained a reputation for uncompromising quality and outstanding value. Mazda is ranked in the top 20 global auto manufacturers based on sales. Though the United States and Canada are separate regions, they are combined under the Mazda North American Operations umbrella. Media agencies considered Mazda a "challenger brand," though "enthusiast brand" is more appropriate because of the passion its customers have for it; this is attributed partially to the auto's presence in grassroots and professional auto racing with MAZDASpeed. The company continues to evolve styling and technology with sporty and subcompact models, lower emissions, and hydrogen fuel innovations.

The Challenges

Before David Harris arrived at Mazda, the automaker had created profiles on the main social platforms in 2007 on Facebook, YouTube, and Flickr, adding Twitter in 2008. Some campaigns had been executed at the time, but the brand's presence had not been maintained. It was about name acquisition, not about conversation. Nothing was happening on the sites. Unfortunately, the profiles were stagnant. Also, local Mazda dealers were asking the brand for guidance, leadership, and a social media plan.

167

Mazda in the United States and Canada is part of Mazda North American Operations. Canada had blazed the trail in social media before its U.S. counterpart and actually had someone dedicated to social media before David's arrival. The United States had some catching up to do across the board. They discovered that there was no consistent social media presence before December 2009. There were individual campaigns such as the Mazda Design Challenge in 2007, but they were treated as one-offs. Some of the initiatives were deemed successful on the basis of impression counts and consumer sign-ups but did not create a lasting conversation.

David's Perspective
Someone called me a "spoon." I'm the spoon that stirs the pot. I do think differently, from an interactive viewpoint.

Responding to the Challenge

Restart Strategy
David entered Mazda in its interactive group after working as a senior advertising manager at a competitor. He hit the ground running with the support of Mazda senior executives who were aware that the dealers were anxiously looking to them for guidance and a social media plan. Corporate embraced real-time platforms and wanted to move forward aggressively. It was also evident that a more effective adoption of social media within the enterprise was necessary.

David and his team started reworking their social strategy from the inside out. They put together a quick social media plan and established the corporate policy governing platform use. They outlined a liberating policy that set boundaries yet encouraged employees to go out into the social space and utilize the tools. They also formulated a task force to usher in a cultural change within the company and did not let themselves be limited by departmental boundaries.

During David's first week at Mazda, he attended an owner appreciation event called Summer Stock. The entire parking lot and spillover areas were filled with motoring enthusiasts. The scene was filled with Miatas, RX-2's, and three generations of RX-7's and RX-8's. David saw firsthand how the brand had been democratized by so many people over multiple generations. David and his team would tap into this passion when building Mazda's social communities. Next, they refreshed their Facebook, YouTube, Flickr, and Twitter accounts. Though there are hundreds of communities and video-sharing sites on the Internet, they focused on these primary ones to keep things simple and maximize their effort. They recognized that Facebook was a hub because of its size and dominance. Since social media is all about interests, if a Mazda enthusiast has an interest in photography, it makes sense for the brand to have a presence to support that customer. Therefore, the team narrowed down photo-sharing sites to Flickr instead of trying to be all things to all people and ending up scattering time and resources.

Forrester had researched and reported on auto brand presence in the social space. The reports revealed that Mazda already had tremendous traction. Though it did not have a lot of volume, it had excellent activity, which was ascribed to owners expressing pride in their vehicles in the same way that Mazda's engineers expressed their pride about the vehicles they built. Also, over 75 percent of car buyers research Mazda on the Internet before making a car purchase. Generally, people look for information and validation on their potential purchases, in this case a car. Validation comes in the form of both professional and consumer reviews of the product.

The most credible, authentic, and influencing element occurs when a Friend or family member owns the product and gives his or her opinion (note the capital F in Friend). The second most influential group consists of friends who fall within one's social space (note the lowercase f here). As more people confirm a choice, confidence is built. Based on the Forrester reports revealing excellent positive traction, social platforms could be very potent for building pride, community, and purchase confidence when combined with family/friend recommendations.

Josh's Perspective
Mazda really is a brand that is owned by the community. That makes it the perfect brand for social media.

Before David arrived, Josh Levine of Rebel Industries had worked with Mazda on a 2007 Facebook program called the Mazda Design Challenge. Soon after David joined the company, he pulled Josh into the social media fray. Dealers already had a very dynamic presence in their own cities and towns. Moving them over to social media would add another connection to their communities and further that involvement. David and Josh found remarkably high levels of engagement between the brand and local dealers and owners. This amounted to a very high sense of ownership for the brand outside the company. Rebel's job became one of facilitating that engagement by nurturing it on a daily basis.

Restart: The Brand Voice
David did not want one specific person to be the Mazda brand voice on social media. It was not about placing one executive or personality front and center, as some auto companies do. He insisted that Mazda speak to the voice of the "community," that is, the multiple voices of the company: business partners, dealers, and especially owners. His intention was to create an authentic Mazda voice to support the community. He held fast to the belief that the brand is not owned by any one person and that it is instead truly a social brand. His purpose then became to support community passion rather than be a heavy-handed dominant voice for the brand itself.

169

Building Community: The Dealers

David's Perspective

Our dealers are integral to us. We have many dealer advisory councils or groups where the dealers participate to help guide the business. Their success is our success.

David looked to Mazda dealers and associations as great information resources for the rebranding efforts. They were taken into partnership, and their voices were heard. His team wrote a handbook describing the social media vision that was distributed to the dealers when David met with them in the field. His group designed an education plan to give dealers a better understanding of the platforms and explain how they could start participating along with Mazda corporate.

David and his team also advised dealers that if they participated in the social space, the focus needed to be about their brand. Mazda and the local dealers would be linked. They could share content, but authentically; the social space represented an opportunity for them to voice everything that they do within a community that is good. They were counseled that their businesses would not be criticized or treated negatively. When they sell a car, they should be mindful that taxes go back into the community in addition to the taxes paid by their employees. With a true community grassroots perspective, they sponsor little league teams, Rotary Clubs, and a multitude of civic activities. Placing the Mazda brand within the social media community where tangible involvement and interaction could grow would benefit everyone.

Building Community: Customers

When monitoring platforms for conversations about the brand, they decided to go beyond influencers and look for those who were celebrating the brand. Mazda's strategy was not to find one keystone person. Rather, it was to find the person who celebrated the brand with enthusiasm. Mazda, in turn, would celebrate the customer. The authentic and honest engagement with brand enthusiasts would be an essential component of the community restart.

Restart: Execution

After all the main platforms had been rebranded, a launch date was slated for December 2009. They had zero followers or fans. Within six months of the launch, Mazda had 70,000 fans on Facebook. David was quick to point out, "It's not about the number. It's about the fact that these fans are engaged, and the volume of conversations that were happening was primarily among themselves. It's heartwarming."

Postlaunch

Monitoring

Rebel Industries continues to work very closely with Mazda's marketing department. They have a team that constantly moderates conversation and makes sure questions are answered in a timely manner. If people have concerns that the community cannot solve on its own, Rebel delegates them and makes sure those in the community get an answer from the brand. When that occurs, Mazda forwards the problems to its customer assistance team, which is headed by the manager, Tom Hannah. His team engages those customers directly to help them resolve their complaints. Its goal is to satisfy the customer.

Josh's Perspective

A unique element about the Rebel-Mazda relationship is that Mazda has given us an enormous amount of access into its social profiles but is also very hands-on, posting content and communicating with consumers directly.

Content

Rebel also posts content for the brand on a regular basis. It may be in the form of retweets or responses or original content to fuel the conversation. There are a number of people within Mazda who also contribute content. Jim Jordan, the alternative marketing manager, is known to go out to a race and post photos live from the event to the social channels for the brand. Mazda's public relations team will post a news announcement directly into the social channels.

The company supports a very fluid environment where there are about half a dozen people both internally and externally who have access to the profiles and can add content whenever it is appropriate. They all adhere to the same social media policy, which gives them both guidelines and flexibility.

Conversation Starter: Celebrate the Customer

Mazda started an owners group on Flickr specifically for sharing photos of cars, which is standard for an auto manufacturer. The twist was to create a space specifically for owners that recognizes and celebrates them. This requires that the company regularly comb through photo submissions to find great pictures of Mazdas, get permission from the submitters/owners, then share those photos on Facebook and acknowledge the owners. It moved photos from a small owners group into a much bigger audience. Once there, people talk about the cars, mostly giving one another compliments. They also trade notes and share conversations about the photos. "These are real people, real car owners," Josh Levine comments. "It is much more about them and celebrating the fans than it is about just pumping out marketing messages. It is very different from uploading images that are owned and approved by the brand."

Outreach: Blog

In addition to updating status and content on the social profiles, Mazda and Rebel do substantial hands-on communication with bloggers, forum moderators, and dealers. There is an extraordinary amount of conversation on the forums about Mazda, partly because it is an enthusiast brand and a strong racing brand. Rebel and Mazda directly contact forum moderators, usually by e-mail. They respond, and a relationship is nurtured. As Josh describes it, "These are guys who started Mazda blogs on their own. They're doing it for the love. Mazda feeds them content, and bloggers receive content from the brand. They give us feedback. We bounce ideas off of them." These influencers have turned into a vital part of the Mazda community and are essential to the brand's long-term engagement goals.

New ROI: Return on Involvement

David's Perspective

The ROI is not about selling the car today. It truly is about building the brand in a very collaborative manner with all partners involved: owners, dealers, business partners, and more.

What makes Mazda unique is the relationship it has with its dealers. Many auto manufacturers are either afraid of their dealers or have contentious, resentful exchanges. Mazda embraces its dealers to achieve a full understanding of their priorities and creates an environment where all the participants realize that they need to work together. Social media will only enhance this. Mazda continues communicating the roles each party has to play and respecting those lines of responsibility. The dealers have a role that is important yet different from the role of the brand. In addition, a customer's connection to a local dealership is different from his or her relationship with a brand that is more or less faceless. Mazda's ongoing presence on real-time social media platforms supports and encourages involvement, interaction, and conversation across all lines among all parties.

When asked about the ROI of Mazda's social media efforts, David responded, "At the end of the day, if communications are done with credibility and authenticity, it lifts the brand in the mind of the consumers who see them. Will it [social media] sell cars today? There are two ways to look at that: First, go into the Mazda Facebook forums. People are asking, 'What do you guys think of Mazda 3?' The forums become discussion points for the product and the brand. Second, this is generating a volume of organic content that is not looked upon with the suspicion of traditional advertising and is helping to build our share of voice in the Web sphere. That is true ROI."

David recounted an actual car sale that came from someone at GOSO22 who is a consultant to dealers. The message read: "Will someone please sell me a car?" Mazda picked up the message on its social listening tool, responded immediately, and sold that person a car. He predicts that the real ROI will come in one or two years as the brand continues to build and people see a constant positive message that will give them the confidence to buy. Mazda wants customers to feel proud to have a Mazda and not think of it as a discounted vehicle.

Internal Summary

Both David and Josh agree their social media efforts constitute a work in progress. As Josh describes it, "There are things you have to figure out on a daily basis. You've got to go out there, see the results, and come back. Between my team and David's team, we're constantly in a state of optimization." They regularly look at the weekly and monthly data. The data is reviewed to determine what worked, what is going to continue to work, what will improve, what did they learn, and how will this apply going forward. Josh observes, "It's not a situation where the client says go out and sell me some cars and don't come back until you do. I know for a fact that a lot of client situations are like that. This is very much a partnership where we are all working for a common goal; we all have different pieces we need to deliver in order to ultimately make the brand successful."

The Future

David's Perspective

There has been a lot of education happening on a global basis. I am very collaborative with some of our European counterparts.

Mazda is a global brand that is working collectively to share knowledge about the impact of social media because it is a worldwide phenomenon. The European Union is investigating these platforms and trying to wrap its arms around opportunities on that continent. Japan is also asking about social media, looking to Canada and then the United States as pioneers in the space.

Dealers are members of their local communities, and so geolocation will be extremely important to them going forward and at some point will be essential. Mazda has been doing mobile marketing for five years and is currently reevaluating those opportunities since mobile has changed dramatically with the popularity of e-readers, tablets, and notebooks that go beyond the iPhone and Android. Car clubs and the culture of the car have been around for as long as the car itself. Enthusiasts will continue to talk about Mazda, and the brand intends to be there when that occurs.

As more dealers adopt social media, the company will try to encourage them to find their dealerships' voice and authentically utilize it. Mazda is looking at how it can support dealers in those local brand-building efforts. "This recipe is not complete," David observes. "We're still figuring out how to make it better. We are trying to work together with our dealers to help them celebrate our brand and their brand."

Assessment

As the social channel matures in terms of execution of a brand management plan, many companies are finding themselves in a similar position as Mazda North American Operations in terms of recalibration of the brand's message and engagement on the social channel. Companies are realizing that social media is not a fad and that serious strategic and tactical planning is critical for success.

Mazda had a team with the foresight to make course corrections in real-time, building on the strengths of customer enthusiasm. This story also highlights the fact that consumers are talking among themselves about your brand whether your company is in the conversation or not. Mazda clearly understands that and has positioned itself as a "credible convener" in the conversation. Other companies should take note.

Finally, working with an agency that understands social media and your business is key. The agency landscape is furiously trying to keep up with the changes brought about by the social channel, sometimes to good effect but often not. Because David already understood the social channel, he was able to spot the intrinsic credibility Rebel Industries brought to the table. Couple that with the willingness of a large multinational corporation to sign off on social media plus real-time efforts, and it's a winning story!

THE ROXY THEATRE

Entertainment and Business Revitalization through Customer Sharing and Social Media, or How Social Media Saved the Sunset Strip

CASE STORY   How a small business revived its brand and energized businesses in the whole community by using social media platforms for real-time customer relationship management and awareness building, resulting in co-opetition rather than competition.

COMPANY   The Roxy Theatre

INDUSTRY   Live music entertainment

OBJECTIVE   Revive a brand that once commanded great respect and save a local business from extinction

STRATEGY   Embrace new social media tools to listen to and retain customers plus build awareness

Acknowledgment

Nic Adler, owner of The Roxy Theatre in Los Angeles, California, is a businessman for his time and generation. Nic is reinventing his club, his street, and eventually his city by using the fundamental concepts of community building inherent in social media.

He made a giant leap of faith when he shifted his thought process from, "We know best on our own," to, "How can we improve together?" Nic's journey is not finished. He is now working with his local municipality, West Hollywood, to share his knowledge and help other struggling businesses improve the overall economic climate in their community.

Nic first presented his amazing business revitalization story in coauthor Beverly Macy's UCLA extension social media marketing class and subsequently presented it at the Gravity Summit in 2010. He is now a sought-after speaker for both the entertainment and tech industries, where he conveyed his rebuilding through co-opetition at SXSW 2010, in Austin, Texas, as well as in municipal government circles at Government 2.0 in Washington, D.C., in 2009. He has been featured in the *New York Times*, Mashable, the *Los Angeles Times*, and NPR Radio and in cover stories in *Venues Today* and *Nightclub and Bar*. Both Nic and his story are inspiring for their energy, determination, and hope.

Why This Is Important to You

Government and business leaders agree that small business is the engine of economic growth. However, small businesses in general are taking a beating in the current global downturn. Finding, attracting, and retaining retail customers are especially hard. In this case, one must combine those with an established older brand that was set in its ways in terms of marketing and customer service. It fell into the trap of always expecting business to stay robust by operating with the competitive habits of the past. It was a formula for a slow demise.

It takes vision and leadership to try something different. This story details how the owner of the famous Roxy Theatre on Sunset woke up to the harsh reality that his family's business could fold and took immediate steps to chart a different path. It started with opening a platform to listen to customers, face the fears, and take constructive action. These are things that resonate with business owners everywhere regardless of company size. For small business owners, however, the risks of making mistakes feel greater because there usually is not an enormous amount of financial resources to fall back on if strategies fail. Errors hurt small businesses, but nothing motivates like fear.

What began as a way to just stay alive has blossomed into more business for everyone. It is hard to believe that there had never been a Sunset Strip Music Festival until 2008, but that is a fact, and it came about through the "Social Strip" community built by Nic and fellow business owners. The festival attracted over 10,000 music fans, boosted retail sales, and renewed awareness for the entire music scene in Southern California. As Nic says, "Initially I thought the goal was online advertising, which turned into a conversation, which has changed people's perceptions."

Small businesses that may be hesitating to invest time and energy in social media will be especially intrigued by this story. The entire business climate in the community was lifted by the Roxy's leadership. Not only did the Roxy rebuild, but other local businesses joined in the social media journey and helped support one another. This signifies the power of one person saying yes to cooperation and change and the subsequent positive spillover effect that can generate.

Here you will find out how increased ROI and financial stability came from an open attitude to education, strategy, and the use of social media. All this melded into a cohesive brand identity, an information hub for the LA music scene, and a new way to communicate with existing fans and bands directly, attract and retain new customers, and save money by reallocating traditional media dollars for free platforms that target customers to draw standing-room-only audiences. You may not be in the music industry with famous people lining up outside your door, but there is a great deal to learn about real-time cooperation and customer sharing that completely flips the traditional closed, competitive model.

Background

The world-famous Roxy Theatre (known as The Roxy) on the Sunset Strip in Los Angeles was opened in September 1973 by music producer Lou Adler the year his eldest son, Nic, was born. Hundreds of famous acts such as the Doors, Rolling Stones, Bob Marley, Bruce Springsteen, Nirvana, X, David Bowie, Tin Machine, Warren Zevon, My Chemical Romance, Chickenfoot, Korn, 30 Seconds to Mars, Brian Wilson, Tori Amos, Elisa, Foo Fighters, Meat Loaf, Motley Crue, Guns N' Roses, Al Stewart, Van Morrison, Avril Lavigne, Papa Roach, Linkin Park, Jane's Addiction, Jay-Z, Bad Religion, NOFX, Steve Aoki, Jonas Brothers, the Pussycat Dolls, and Them Crooked Vultures have played this highly prestigious venue.

The Roxy is one of the most legendary and influential music venues in America and around the world. From the 1973 opener featuring Neil Young to Bruce Springsteen's classic 1975 performances, the history of The Roxy Theatre is paved with icons: the Guns N' Roses prestardom shows, Miles Davis, Jane's Addiction, and Pearl Jam, among many others. Over the course of time, the club has also been a popular performance mecca for other entertainment, including stage productions, comedy shows, and performance art. Lou Adler was responsible for bringing the stage play *The Rocky Horror Show* to the United States. It opened its first American run at The Roxy Theatre in 1974 before it was made into the movie The Rocky Horror Picture Show the next year.[3] Back then, the club was so successful that it had very little competition to worry about. Even John Lennon was a regular. The company had a long run.

Nic Adler took the helm at The Roxy in 1998 and has remodeled its interior to encourage conversation. Among the club's unique features are comfortable booth seating, a full-service and draft bar, and a menu that features a modest array of dishes to keep appetites satisfied. The Roxy's open dance floor and superb sound facilities offer fans one of the most intimate entertainment experiences around.

There is also "On the Rox," an on-site after-hours facility that has been the setting for some of Hollywood's hottest parties. Located above The Roxy and overlooking Sunset Boulevard, On the Rox features its own full-service bar and DJ booth with a proprietary sound system. Always in touch with its past, The Roxy lets fans glimpse its legacy when they enter the club thanks to an extensive collection of performance photos that adorn the walls.

The Challenge

In 2007, Nic started to realize that he was faced with reviving an iconic 35-year-old brand. It needed an injection of new life in an event-driven entertainment town. At the time, The Roxy relied on traditional public relations for relevance and placed an expensive print ad in the *LA Weekly*. Though The Roxy was a staple venue for mainstream music executives, its target audience was composed of digital natives who consumed their information online. Nic and his team had made few changes in their media habits for over a decade with minimal outreach to audiences or bands. The Web site was static and had no ability to receive feedback.

The club was losing market share to venues in the Silverlake area in East Los Angeles. Trending bands perceived the venue as unhip. Ticket sales were down, and ROI was dwindling. Clubs like The Roxy suddenly fell out of style. The neighborhood's music and comedy venues, hotels, and restaurants rarely spoke to one

177

another and regarded each other as competition, not as a community. Police were cracking down on auto cruising along the Strip, and that was pushing customers out of the area. The turning point came when Tower Records on the Sunset Strip closed after 36 years in business. Tower had been the epicenter of Los Angeles music discovery and distribution, ergo the world, with albums and CDs by multitudes of great performers. Nic knew that The Roxy could be next if something drastic was not done immediately. The Roxy was in "stasis," as in the science fiction definition of the term meaning "hypersleep."

Nic's Perspective

I want The Roxy to be around for another 30 years. I've been handed a legend along with a legacy to fulfill.

The Solution Evolution

Charged with reviving this storied venue that had made music and Hollywood history (Jack Nicholson is Nic Adler's godfather), Nic decided to take charge and lead both The Roxy and the Sunset Strip into the digital age. Because the times and music scene had changed, Nic realized that The Roxy needed to change its outdated policies and embrace the future. Who else was going to do it?

Nic could see that the hill to climb was steep. The problem was finding a way to revive a brand, make it current, and reenergize the customer base to generate revenue. The Roxy brand was remembered fondly by some and dismissed as passé by others. Just setting up a Twitter account would not do the trick.

Nic's Perspective

If The Roxy were a person, what would it be like? How would it act? We used these answers to create a "social personality."

Nic and his team began to change The Roxy's image radically from the inside out. They launched a blog as their main Web site: theroxyonsunset.com. At that time, they had only a calendar-style Web site that consisted of one page and had not been updated in two years. Blogging was a huge step, and it taught them about content development and distribution. It also helped the company acclimate to the two-way conversation that comments on a blog will bring. Initially, the feedback was less than favorable. Nic recalls, "I wanted to stop! I didn't want to hear the negative comments. But I was told to keep calm, hold tight. Now I want to know if a customer complains because that means I can do things better."

Part of rebranding The Roxy with real-time social media required discovering and adopting a social personality based on community building. This meant being true to the following social media values and behaviors:

1. Transparency
2. Authenticity
3. Openness

4. Community-centric mindset
5. Recognizing and engaging others to create two-way communication
6. Participating in conversations that create community
7. Collaborating altruistically

The product mix needed to change as well. Since indie bands had migrated to hipper parts of Los Angeles, Nic began booking acts that appealed to a new audience. Shows started selling out after being announced on Twitter. The "velvet rope" attitude disappeared, and Nic started allowing fans to take photographs to share in real-time, as opposed to his father, who had barred public cameras from the exclusive haven. Overall, Nic replaced the former closed, mysterious celebrity-centric Roxy behavior (cult of personality) with open, authentic community behavior (cult of conversation). As was mentioned in Chapter 4, while monitoring tweets about and within his club, Nic read a customer complaint about a weak drink. He looked at the person's profile picture, found her in the club, and delivered a new, stronger drink. A tweet immediately followed: "The Roxy is great! The owner just brought me a new drink!" As of this writing, The Roxy is the most popular club on Twitter, with over 32,000 followers.

Direct competitors in West Hollywood decided to engage in social media, particularly the Viper Room (@theviperroom) and the Comedy Store (@thecomedystore).

Nic's Perspective
The tipping point came when the Viper Room tweeted a message that I could have ignored. I thought for a second, "Should I answer them and help a competitor?"

To answer would be absolutely counterintuitive. Nic could have operated as in the past: every company for itself. But ultimately, The Roxy decided to openly welcome the Viper Room into the social space.

This was truly a turning point for both Nic and the local businesses on the Sunset Strip, because the open strategy worked. Nic launched the term co-opetition to describe the cooperative competition evolving in their midst. Taking the co-opetition route ignited collaboration online that spilled over into the offline world. The right people were brought together at the right place at the right time. The Roxy, the Viper Room, and the Comedy Store all possessed a social personality. The trio made the same philosophical shift and dedicated their business mindsets to social media. They shared a special geography, saw the benefit of banding together, and connected their networks.

The "Tweet Crawl" came about through this new mode of doing business. It started in July 2009 when several local businesses collaborated to invite the Twitter community for an all-night event on Sunset Boulevard with free access to the clubs, specials on drinks and food, and hidden prizes with clues on Twitter. A number of participating clubs and businesses had started their own social media efforts by then and participated in building awareness. The co-opetition efforts helped make the Tweet Crawl a success at that time and up to the present.

Another outgrowth of co-opetition put The Roxy in a position to collaborate with the Sunset Strip Business Association on the 2009 Sunset Strip Music Festival. In its second year, the Social Strip created history when it was able to shut down the Sunset Strip from Doheny to San Vicente. This had never been done for a music event and was possible only because former competitors came together as a team. It resulted in approximately 10,000 people spiking sales for local businesses and partying in the streets, enjoying an unforgettable show by Ozzy Osbourne.

The Sunset Strip VIP Pass program is another example of co-opetition working for the business community. To encourage tourists to stay in the area, customers who book accommodations at participating hotels on the Strip get free front-of-the-line access at participating clubs.

Analysis: Current Social Media Execution

Today, The Roxy is a shining example of a company transformed by the use of social media. From customer service, to who should be the next band at The Roxy, to initiatives for fans, to content for daily blogs, Nic has learned what works for his audiences. Based on fan tweets, Facebook comments, photos, and videos, his team crowdsources and uses customer material to update The Roxy blog.

Nic also uses social media in the everyday operation of the club. He takes the feedback received through social media seriously and shares it with his staff. Bouncers, cocktail waitresses, and back office staff all have a deeper appreciation and understanding of how the work they do during their shift may reflect on the club in public forums. This internal engagement has changed their attitudes and behaviors.

The club has free Wifi that Nic uses to distribute live streaming shows. The Roxy developed a VIP program via social media and an "all you can eat" pass for Club Rox. The passes were advertised only on Twitter and sold out in three days. The club also uses the Twitter hashtag #ontherox so that fans can talk about the shows. Twitter provides snapshots of behind-the-scenes activities and access to staff. It is a powerful tool to reach large groups of qualified followers and provide them with immediate information. Twitter is also a handy way to respond quickly to requests, complaints, and comments. The Roxy Facebook page is where more in-depth conversations take place among friends that cannot be facilitated on Twitter in 140 characters. Nic and his crew also use Facebook for market research and customer service. Their blog roxyonsunset.com operates as a Web site with show announcements, music samples, videos, photos of bands, and any long-form news or information their customers might want. Links to former competitors (the Viper Room) are also on their blog. TheRoxyChannel on YouTube also is home to videos from the venue. They are dabbling in Foursquare and other geolocation opportunities.

The Roxy still has a publicist and a street team, but social media is a no-brainer, according to Nic. He embraces the conversational aspect of social media and encourages other small businesses to find what works for them. Overall, for businesses just getting started with social media, the key point is to start slowly:

"Starting small was key for us," he says. Nic also believes that defining your business's personality is essential to developing an online voice. As he did at The Roxy, Nic suggests thinking of your business as a person. How would it act and interact with people?

Though they may be steeped in social media, there are still businesses in his radius that do not understand the tools. Being ahead of the curve can be isolating while waiting for everyone else to catch on. With effective use of social media, however, The Roxy found itself teaching others, which will further increase consumer loyalty and clout.

Impact on the Bottom Line: Driving Business

Nic's Perspective

If it were up to me, I wouldn't spend any money on traditional advertising or a dollar on print. But we have agents in New York and LA who want to see a print ad with a photo of their artist. They don't realize I've sent their artist's links to 5 million people in the last three weeks.

Nic loves the paid ad platform on Facebook and has the ability to finely target a desired audience. He says he can laser down to 1,500 people who will like an artist and sell out his shows because "getting very specific works." He described a recent sold-out concert promoted with social media: "I had a band that was friends with Paris and Lindsey. They got them to tweet the show. There was no talk of the show on Thursday or Friday. Between noon and show time on Saturday, we hit 4.5 million followers for free. No show is totally gone while the doors are open. There's always a chance to get action." Nic went on to say, "What's great about social media is you don't have to worry if someone is going to stop and read a print ad. They are talking back to me about it, so you know if they read it. The shift has happened already."

He commented, "At first, I thought it [social media] was advertising, that doing the blog was an advertising tool. It turned out not to be that. It turned out to be more of a road map of what we should be doing and who we are." Reflecting on the whirlwind nature of his journey, Nic admitted he needed social media education in the beginning: "I would come home every night at one in the morning from The Roxy and stay up three hours for an entire year until I understood how to speak the language, retweet, know every network, do Facebook. I already understood marketing. I've been marketing shows all my life. But I needed to know how to use these new tools. The feedback was amazing. That's really what has changed what we do."

Civic Evolution

Nic's real-time social media leadership has led to greater municipal involvement for him as well. He is currently serving as vice president of the Sunset Strip Business

Association. It is a private, nonprofit corporation run by Sunset Strip business owners in West Hollywood with approximately 200 members consisting mainly of businesses in the hotel, restaurant, retail, valet/parking, and nightclub areas and the associated tourism industry.

He is being tapped to share his insights, business experience, and social media expertise to guide, empower, and evolve companies into real-time commerce. All this from deciding to respond to a Viper Room tweet.

Assessment

If Nic Adler continues to be open to the changing needs of his audiences and the tools they use to communicate and consume music and media, The Roxy Theatre will be around for another 30-plus years. His team has made the correct moves over time to systematically stretch beyond traditional business systems and communication habits. Being tasked with saving a family business from closing its doors, making a difference in the customer experience one person at a time, shifting brand perceptions, and adjusting product offerings in a recording industry that has vaporized would cause anyone to run away to the nearest deserted island.

But there was a legacy at stake: family history as well as music history and global relationships. Though daunting, the solution was as simple as talking to and, more important, listening to customers. This is a lesson for every small business even if your customers are not Ozzy Osbourne. When the commitment was made to implement real-time social media as platforms for building community, the drop turned into a cascade. Instead of failing together, they averted the fate of Tower Records by reinventing individual businesses and rising as the Social Strip. Competitors offered one another a digital olive branch. Education, starting slowly, and cooperative competition are the main features of this case story. Real-time social media marketing was and continues to be the instrument of remarkable change.

DIRECTV.
SATELLITE TELEVISION

DIRECTV
Customer Interaction Transforms Business

CASE STORY   How listening to customers can have far-reaching positive effects, from building prepress buzz that amplifies results to refining current business practices drawn from crowdsourced knowledge to directly affect the bottom line.

Note: Multiple case stories will be conveyed for DIRECTV:

1. Launch of the DIRECTV DVR Scheduler for the iPhone: informs customers first to generate follow-on press interest
2. Broadcast service delivery and recovery
3. Cocreation in-product feature testing and deployment

COMPANY   DIRECTV, Inc.

INDUSTRY   Entertainment: multichannel video programming distribution

OBJECTIVE   Build a knowledge bridge between the DIRECTV customer service organization and customer-run communities online

STRATEGY   Listen to customers for information and feedback and to inform influencers

Acknowledgment
Credit goes to DIRECTV and its customer care team who are truly committed to stellar customer service. DIRECTV first showed up on our radar when Charles E. Miller, director of digital care at DIRECTV, presented at the Gravity Summit at Stanford University in May 2009. His compelling understanding of social media and groundbreaking integration of these platforms into customer service have put DIRECTV on our list of best practitioners in the social media channel.

Why This Is Important to You
Regardless of how one defines customers (B2B or B2C), using social media to follow, like, join, listen, and respond to customers in real-time can and will affect

consumer brand confidence and ultimately brand loyalty. In addition, the power to discover influencers and develop them into brand advocates will change the way companies think of and execute word-of-mouth marketing, service, press, and publicity. If you are considering stepping into social media for customer service, the path that DIRECTV carved out will be most pertinent. If you are actively using social media for customer service, you will discover lessons for refining current practices.

What started as a way to enhance customer service led to the implementation of social media for service monitoring, delivery, and recovery as well as creating opportunities to inform product development and delivery life cycles. When encouraged and supported by the highest executive levels and executed correctly, customer service through social media can be an important touch point with consumers and clients, providing a wellspring of ideas for the overall business. This has been the case for DIRECTV. Its vision of putting the customer experience first continues to reap rewards beyond expectations. For the tenth year in a row, DIRECTV scored higher in customer satisfaction than cable companies measured in the American Customer Satisfaction Index.[4]

Background
Launched in 1994 and headquartered in El Segundo, California, DIRECTV is the world's most popular video service delivering state-of-the-art technology, unmatched programming, the most comprehensive sports packages available and industry leading customer service to its more than 26.3 million customers in the United States and Latin America.

Early in the social media phenomenon, DIRECTV found its customers talking about the brand on these new, emerging social platforms. In 2005, DIRECTV launched its social media efforts in customer service by establishing a branded peer-to-peer forum. The objective was to build a knowledge bridge between the company's technical support organization and DIRECTV customer-run technical communities online. The forum linked subject-matter experts within DIRECTV's technical support organization with highly knowledgeable existing customers, new customers who were just getting started, and longtime customers who wanted to enhance their setups. It also helped build relationships by enabling DIRECTV to provide accurate information and clarify new initiatives. Trust was built and relationships deepened.

Those community contacts linked DIRECTV with other leading influencers and brand advocates who enthusiastically tested early product releases. Because advocates were included early, those customers had a vested interest in spreading the word when a product was launched to the general public. Currently, DIRECTV employs social media platforms to listen to customers as they comment on core and innovative features of the satellite service. The strategy of listening, acting on issues, and then sharing what is learned throughout the organization enables DIRECTV to transform its business to be in sync with its customers' ideal view of a video service.

Charles's Perspective

Socially connected customers have access to more information on the details and nuances of businesses than ever before, and as a result can collectively assemble and interpret communications and rumors to inform their buying decisions. DIRECTV recognizes this and continually adapts to engage customers in ways that clarify communication and build long-lasting relationships.

CASE STORY 1: PRODUCT LAUNCH

Launch of the DIRECTV DVR Scheduler for the iPhone: inform customers first to generate press interest to amplify reach and outcome

DIRECTV's Perspective

DIRECTV has been active on Twitter since 2008, helping customers and listening to find out which product features resonated most with them. As the launch of the DIRECTV DVR Scheduler for the iPhone approached, we sought out customers who were also iPhone enthusiasts.

Responding to the Challenge

DIRECTV's digital care team monitored Twitter, blogs, and various social media, taking special note of DIRECTV customers who were passionate about using their iPhones but were unaware that the DIRECTV DVR Scheduler for the iPhone was due to launch. It did the following:

1. Sought out and engaged customers with whom It had interacted previously, who updated from their iPhones or listed an iPhone in their profiles
2. Identified and engaged those who mentioned using the iPhone in their public conversations or profiles
3. Identified and engaged iPhone "power users," defined as those who lived and breathed the iPhone

It was deemed that these customers would be the most excited about getting the early word out about new iPhone app functionality from DIRECTV. One customer who stood out was Jessica Gottlieb. She is a top mommy blogger who has been recognized as the person responsible for coining the Twitter hash tag #motrinmoms in her tweets and has been noted in a well-known case study criticizing Motrin's campaign suggesting that mothers who choose to carry their babies in slings can have back pain, which resulted in a controversial public relations situation for Motrin.

Months before the iPhone app launch, DIRECTV, via Twitter, helped Jessica resolve an issue regarding a sports subscription that she wanted handled before the season started. The DIRECTV digital care team managed it quickly and made a lasting impression on Jessica, who continues to advocate her loyalty to the

185

service in the social media space. The DIRECTV team periodically listened to her in the social channel to discover what kinds of topics were important to her. Team members noticed that Jessica was regularly using her iPhone to post blog entries about her "everyday mom" experiences. She was then selected to be one of the prime blog influencers for the product launch because of her connections as well as the fact that she was very active with the iPhone.

When the time approached to launch the DVR Scheduler for the iPhone, DIRECTV's public relations department started to build a plan to get the word out on the new service. It put together a short list of reporters with whom it had existing relationships and who might pick up the story, but it also wondered if there were other ways to break through the clutter of the thousands of other branded iPhone apps making their way into the iTunes app store. That is when the public relations department approached Charles, who had coordinated with them on issues emerging online, and asked whether he could assist with getting the word out regarding the DVR Scheduler for the iPhone, given Charles's previous use of Twitter and other social media channels on behalf of DIRECTV. "We know you've put the word out there on Twitter and other sites in the past. What do you think you might be able to do with this?"

DIRECTV's digital care team assisted the public relations department to develop a plan that would distribute information through various social media contacts and other blogs within hours of the app launching on iTunes. At the time, of course, it was considered highly unorthodox for a Fortune 500 brand to reach out to influential bloggers and Twitter users profiled as avid iPhone users to announce the pending iTunes app before doing a formal corporate press release. Charles's team moved into action. Part of the work involved finding previous DIRECTV topics that had prompted discussion in the social space and observing how long it took those topics to reach widespread exposure. It could take as little as a few minutes to as long as a couple of days for a brand topic to reach its social media peak. Based on those prior experiences, his team estimated that this campaign would require about 10 hours to achieve peak distribution. His team strategized as follows:

1. Determine the date the app would be available in the iTunes store
2. Coordinate efforts around the time the iTunes store typically uploaded new apps
3. Back up the launch from that point by 10 to 12 hours

It was ten o'clock on a Sunday morning in Los Angeles when the team started ramping up its efforts. Preparations had started days earlier when DIRECTV reached out to customer-run community sites where influencers gather who actively try out new company products and services as part of a customer-run beta program. Those highly engaged customers were looking forward to receiving early word about the DVR Scheduler launch and already had created screen shots from the beta test program. At DIRECTV's request, they agreed to hold the information regarding the launch until DIRECTV gave them the green light to post the news.

Charles sent word to these long-term advocates that they were "good to go" and, within minutes, screen shots and an announcement were posted prominently on their home pages. Charles knew these sites were often where lead bloggers looked for breaking news about DIRECTV.

Simultaneously, Charles reached out to Jessica Gottlieb, whom DIRECTV had already identified as an important brand advocate. Charles sent her the following direct message on Twitter: "Hey there Jessica! Not sure if we got this to you yet. [A demo of] DIRECTV's DVR Scheduler App for the iPhone video is online to check out. I just put it on YouTube, which walks you through it. Want to be the first to tweet it? DIRECTV's DVR Scheduler App for the iPhone will be on the Apple App Store just after midnight tonight." Jessica responded, excited but also time-constrained, "I am at a car lot right now, can it wait?" she answered. "How much time do I have?" Charles had prepped her days before, alerting her that something iPhone-related was brewing. He said, "She knew to look for a message from me about something coming up, so when I gave her the specifics, she said, 'Okay, I'll do it.'" She then posted it on her blog: http://www.jessicagottlieb.com/2009/03/DIRECTV-releases-their-iphone-app/.

DIRECTV's Perspective

DIRECTV's product lead for the iPhone app created a YouTube video on how to navigate the DVR Scheduler app. Charles and his digital care team stressed that this video should be a straightforward "how to" video zeroing in on the features customers would find most useful. By tightly focusing on his hands, using app functionality with a voice-over that guided the user through all of the features, the video was knowledge-rich rather than promotionally rich.

Just days before, Charles had alerted Jessica that something iPhone-related was brewing. Shortly after receiving the message with the details of the iPhone app, Jessica "liked" the YouTube video, wrote a short blog statement, and tweeted about the video and the new app. Those mentions helped get the ball rolling. Just 45 minutes into the launch plan, DIRECTV saw multiple customer tweets being posted about the iPhone app. DIRECTV then reached out to four key iPhone app review sites. Those sites had also been prepped three or four days ahead of time, so they were aware of the upcoming launch. Since they were primed and ready for the app introduction, each site knew it had a limited window of opportunity to spread the word and make the most of it. Charles conveyed a sense of urgency in his messages since he knew momentum was building quickly. He reserved an hour for the review sites to make as much noise as they wished about the product. After that, DIRECTV confirmed the news from its official Twitter presence.

Charles's Perspective

Creating exclusivity was very important. This approach recognizes the value we place in our trusted influencers. The buzz they generated gained such significant reach prior to launch that some customers refreshed the iTunes store multiple times just to be among the first to confirm and download the app.

The app was greatly anticipated and well received when it did launch. A formal press release was issued four days after the launch, when the first 100,000 downloads were achieved. The goodwill of influencers and press pickups led to nearly 500,000 downloads by the end of the month. Within weeks, the DIRECTV DVR Scheduler for the iPhone would be named a Forbes Top 10 app for 2009.[5]

What might have been just another iPhone app announcement for traditional media was instead a roar of digital excitement led by customers and enthusiasts, eventually achieving DIRECTV's objective of amplifying and subsequently defining the traditional press pitch.

CASE STORY 2: BROADCAST SERVICE DELIVERY AND RECOVERY

It was opening night of the 2009 college football season. Fans across the country were seated in front of their televisions, ready to enjoy the opening game, when DIRECTV lost the signal to a popular high-definition (HD) sports channel.

Charles's Perspective

Twitter is the live breaking news feed for many brands. Nowhere is capturing customer trends in real-time more important than for high-volume marquee events broadcast on DIRECTV. Reliability is an important aspect for any company, and at DIRECTV, broadcast monitoring is core to delivering quality service. Monitoring online mentions of our broadcasts is now another touch point to identify and define issues quickly, respond faster, and engage customers on alternatives, if necessary.

Rising to the Challenge

DIRECTV has long observed public mentions of its brand on Twitter and keeps a close lookout for mentions of broadcast service quality. The company has a dedicated team that monitors signal delivery through various means: directly watching channels, keeping up with escalations from call center agents, and now using Twitter. Using Twitter to monitor broadcasts not only creates a wider lens to monitor hundreds of channels simultaneously, but it also adds a new verification point to traditional broadcast monitoring efforts and a method to reach out directly to affected customers.

That became crystal clear during the first college football game of the 2009 season. In the opening minutes of the game, the HD version of the broadcast was completely lost and went to a blank gray screen. DIRECTV's digital care team saw immediate chatter about the channel outage in the online social space. Team members coordinated with customer care's command center and DIRECTV's broadcast operations team to confirm and scale the issue before moving into channel-recovery mode.

While the broadcast team worked to resolve the root issue, DIRECTV's customer care organization responded to customers on Twitter, directing them to the standard-definition (SD) feed of the game and immediately notified agents about the issue. This situation provided a great opportunity for the company to reach out to customers. Using social media, DIRECTV advised customers, "The SD version of the game is available on the following channel. When HD returns, we'll let everybody know here online." That message was tweeted and retweeted. One customer reported, "Thanks so much for letting me know! My father was getting ready to throw a chair through the TV, and you just stopped him from doing that!" Another customer responded, "Okay, we appreciate it, let us know when the HD is back."

The digital care team also updated top forum moderators along the way, leveraging their online presence and influence. Accurately informing customers online provided an opportunity to avert calls, reduce wait times, and prepare customer care representatives to handle questions about the issue. Being out in the real-time social space and actively letting frustrated customers know where they could go to temporarily alleviate the problem helped DIRECTV mitigate the overall customer service issue.

DIRECTV's Perspective

DIRECTV's national command center team are the real social media stars. While the digital care team can talk to a number of customers in plain view of others as we assist people online, the broadcast stream has the ability to affect a much wider audience whether they are online or not. In recognition of this scalability we have changed our established business practices for monitoring broadcasts to include looking at issues escalating on Twitter.

CASE STORY 3: COCREATION IN PRODUCT FEATURE TESTING AND DEPLOYMENT

The ability to quality-control new products and features before launch to the general public is often a private and controlled process. How did the social channel help DIRECTV improve in this area?

Rising to the Challenge

Externally, DIRECTV has collaborated with an online customer-run community to refine early versions of its receiver software for many years. The company then turns to its peer-to-peer customer community to offer early support and gather feedback. After rollout, customers share tips and experiences about using new advanced features while DIRECTV works behind the scenes to inform top contributors on updates and refinements.

DIRECTV also seeks the opinions of its most avid, technically savvy followers. For example, it was discovered that one customer is a remote control aficionado who owns over 200 remote devices. He is now part of the DIRECTV influencer

189

community and is asked to test and write about new DIRECTV remote devices in the company's peer-to-peer forum. These interactions with the customer-run community and techie influencers continually give DIRECTV an opportunity to listen, learn, and improve the products and services it launches.

Customer Service Halo Effect

Though they are not case stories, the following two descriptions merit recognition as outgrowths of initial real-time social media use in customer service.

Internal Service Support

DIRECTV uses social media tools within its call centers to facilitate communications within and between teams. The company has the ability to scale and scope the feedback it receives during these interactions. The result has been improvements in employee training and communication.

Service Monitoring

Twitter and Facebook are common platforms for entertainment brands and sites where customers are actively sharing. DIRECTV customers engage with one another via @DIRECTV on Twitter, and Facebook "Like" interactions continue to grow. Posts, reads, author engagement, subject proliferation, and sentiment are all important to understanding where DIRECTV is making a difference and where to improve service and communications.

Social Media Analysis

Here is a comparison of the before and the after. The before is that when DIRECTV used to monitor service incidents, it often relied on a customer service organization to surface glitches that were happening and being called in on the floor. This process usually took time to identify and size up an issue, resulting in instances in which an issue would occur and be solved by the time it was adequately identified and communicated to the customer service agents and affected customers. In this scenario, the customer experience could be terrible, with customers calling regarding an issue about which an agent may not even know. Customers would quip, "What do you mean you need to make a report? It's right here in front of me!"

Through the use of social media platforms, DIRECTV is able to detect service disruptions within minutes or sooner. With this near real-time information, DIRECTV is able to address service anomalies immediately using social media as an early warning system that complements the established monitoring process.

The broadcast team is able to craft messages for wider-impact incidents that go to all customer service representatives faster so that they are more aware of what is happening. DIRECTV's agents are empowered to respond, "Yes, I just received an alert about that," or, "Our broadcasting team knows about it. They are working on it, and I'm sure they will resolve the issue soon." Real-time information improves the experience for both the customer and the agent.

Assessment

Customer service was a logical first step for DIRECTV to test real-time social media. The company is well positioned to continue embracing existing platforms and develop innovative approaches. Its latest products include portable and mobile devices that provide a platform to socially empower customers, such as the DIRECTV DVR Scheduler, iPhone apps, and NFL SUNDAY TICKET™ game streaming. DIRECTV's early efforts have created a strong foundation to meet the call of mobile social customers who prefer to support themselves when possible and, when they cannot, interact with companies on social platforms.

Gathering feedback is more valuable than ever to ensure that products are ready to launch and that support services are in place and tested. DIRECTV makes certain that all services are executed well across the board, not just online. Embracing their customers' ideal view for the best video experience and trending how those expectations change over time allow DIRECTV to adapt and retain its status as the leading innovative video service brand in the industry.

Using social media to follow, like, join, listen, and respond to customers in real-time has worked well for DIRECTV and promises to continue to do so in the future.

CHAPTER 6

Analytics and Measurement

n July 2010, Isaiah Mustafa, the "Old Spice Guy," appeared in a series of commercials on YouTube, breaking all the rules about how agencies and brands could talk directly to influencers through social channels. The campaign became famous overnight and went global with millions of views, comments, tweets, and likes. This was groundbreaking for the advertising world because it merged social media, creative teams, and a brand in real-time. After the commercials were uploaded on YouTube, the creative team from the campaign's agency, Weiden+Kennedy, shot over eighty 30-second messages featuring the actor Isaiah Mustafa responding to specific Twitter posts and comments. It then used social media to communicate and deliver those personalized messages to specific celebrity influencers and members of the general public.

Peering through the Now Lens at the ocean of conversation and engagement data can provide a valuable frame of reference for current and future trends and outcomes. Reporting and tracking these outcomes in real-time can lead to extremely powerful results and is increasingly possible, as the Old Spice Guy commercials are proving. This has given birth to an entirely new social media measurement layer that calculates sentiment, volume, activity, velocity, and influencer dynamics.

These new services are aimed at helping businesses make sense of the data rush that many executives in the C-Suite feel has blindsided them. Analytics and measurement tools provide familiar data for those in media, sales, finance, and other practices who need to justify dollars, time, or both when allocating budgets. One can almost hear a global sigh of relief when decision makers are reassured that conversations can be measured. After digesting this chapter, readers will have a better understanding of the why, when, and how of social media measurement.

Savvy marketers want to know what is happening both now and next, plus have the ability to adjust accordingly, in real-time, based on metrics that matter to them. As a reminder, real-time social media can seem counterintuitive; this means that traditional hard-number measurement often will be elusive in quantifying a proven, highly successful campaign. In real-time social media campaigns, "success" is measured by how one delivers on the stated objective. Since companies increase revenue from two sources—increased sales and reduced costs—social technologies are poised to gain traction in the enterprise as they execute in terms of both contributing to added revenue and/or reducing costs.

Before a discussion or understanding about social media analytics and measurements even begins, one must ask: What will success look like for my company, brand, or organization? Will the results be quantitative, qualitative, or a blend of both?

Advertisers and marketers have long searched for proof that their campaigns are effective. After all, accurate reporting is critical in segmenting markets and optimizing media buying. However, the methodologies with which most media are measured today are decades old. Some new tools have been implemented because of DVR use as in play+1 or +2 to measure audiences that time-shift viewing. For example, total viewers for a particular show are being calculated from the night the original airing takes place plus one or two days later to account for playback and viewing from a DVR. Even with adjustments such as this, unbelievably, not much has changed in the world of basic media measurement.

In the real-time competitive atmosphere in which targeting very specific markets is increasingly important, these out-of-date methodologies are rapidly becoming less relevant, primarily because they are too slow. From social media to streaming video, the Internet and mobile phones have changed the way users consume, produce, and share content. Standard metrics such as clicks and page views are giving way to the demand for engagement, sentiment, and interaction analytics in real-time.

Jodee Rich, founder of PeopleBrowsr, a social media analytics company based in San Francisco, states, "Social media is creating a global collective consciousness consisting of social media data, real-time search data, and public online conversations that are ripe for advanced analytics." Converting that data into actionable intelligence is the challenge. Therefore, the success objective will determine which tools to use, whether existing free platform analytics are sufficient, and whether third-party research insights will be needed.

Right now the market is grappling with a patchwork of free tools and multiple paid services. Since real-time platforms are relatively new and free, analytic tools offer only limited to moderate amounts of information. That is why third-party companies are surfacing to fill in the gaps. For example, to gain the full view and impact of a Twitter campaign, one would need a sentiment and volume service (based on sampling), a hashtag-tracking service, and a total activity service to measure all the tweets. Some companies are merging tracking systems but are campaign-specific. This is changing as social media grows and companies are starting to combine services—to everyone's relief. Wisely taking time to choose research tools and companies that deliver analytics will help the budget by minimizing redundancy or avoiding premium charges caused by an unforeseen emergency.

The emerging consideration inside large organizations is determining the best way to create a social layer in the enterprise architecture that lifts all internal priorities. Traditional CRM is data-centric and grew out of the need to track and report on critical information about customers. Social CRM is conversation-centric, creating the need for a brand-new metric. Tracking and reporting relevant conversations, sentiment, velocity, influencers, and so on are proving disruptive in most companies. That is because conversations cross traditional internal corporate divisions and boundaries. Deciding who "owns" or cares about a conversation, as well as who will be in charge of measuring and distributing the data, is a complete process change. For instance, a conversation on Twitter may be a customer service "complaint," but is being tracked by marketing. This, in turn, requires building an internal escalation procedure for real-time spikes.

Organizations are also realizing that they need to learn how social media conversations convert to site traffic, downloads, sales, and other desired outcomes. Social CRM results will be calculated from Web, e-mail, mobile, search, and video metrics combined with conversation analytics to help marketing, customer service, and sales teams post positive business results (see Figure 6.1).

The next factor is to determine just what areas of the enterprise could be affected by the social channel. This is a very broad overview that helps the company begin to think through measureable data and business results:

6.1 **Questions to ask before social media implementation to determine if measurement is required**

> **Measurement Evaluation Questions**
> 1. What is the objective?
> 2. What constitutes success?
> 3. How do we measure it?
> 4. Do we have tools required or do we need a third party?

1. **Customer service**
   a. Increased retention, loyalty
   b. Intervention in customer issues to deflect service calls
   c. Customer satisfaction improvements

2. **Sales**
    a. Lead generation
    b. Referrals
    c. Engagement of influencers
    d. Incremental purchasing from social channels
    e. Measurable lift from coupon/promotional offers
3. **Product development**
    a. Idea generation via crowdsourcing and contests
    b. Product defects awareness
    c. Product research—focus groups
4. **Marketing**
    a. Product information
    b. Brand messaging and positioning
    c. Sharing of comments and reviews
    d. Linkage of sharing and traffic generation

Measuring Influencer Dynamics

In July 2010 the online and offline magazine *Fast Company* launched the Influence Project to find that year's Most Influential Person Online. Although the project received mixed reviews, it did bring to the foreground the question, "What is influence, and how should we measure it?"

Indeed, one of the most intriguing new developments in real-time social media measurement is that of the Influencer. Influencers might be key writers, bloggers, podcasters, Facebook users, Twitter users, LinkedIn groups, viral videographers, or others who could have a major impact on a brand or product launch, as recounted in the DIRECTV case story in Chapter 5. Understanding exactly who is spreading the word about a brand in the digital universe is now possible and should be part of every analytics program. Finding and measuring those Influencers is becoming vitally important because of the rising "just like us" review-based marketing and buying dynamic. Brands need to reach out to the Influencers as well as consumers. The same holds true in a business-to-business (B2B) environment. In that case, Influencers could be industry and stock analysts, research firms, trade associations, or clients. Since we have established that customers today trust one another more than they trust the brand and listen carefully to Influencers, we are indeed witnessing a new value chain that requires listening to the customer in all his or her permutations.

Monitoring influence is starting to figure more prominently in social brand management. Companies that already are tracking influence can now incentivize and optimize advocates and brand ambassadors in real-time. Thus, we are seeing companies such as Starbucks and Virgin America partner with start-ups like Klout, a company that measures influence on Twitter, to identify influential social media users. Klout's Web site explains, "The size of the [influencer's] sphere is calculated by measuring True Reach [engaged followers and friends versus spam bots, dead accounts, etc.]. Amplification Probability is the likelihood that messages will generate retweets or spark a conversation. If the user's engaged followers are highly influential, they'll have a high Network Score."

David Harris, group manager of digital media and alternative media for Mazda North America Operations, offers his take on Influencers: "At Mazda, we go more direct than influencers. We are looking for those who are celebrating the brand. It's not about finding that keystone person. It's all about here's another person who is celebrating our brand with enthusiasm. Then we want to celebrate them." Harris and his team have had great success turning Mazda from a challenger brand to an enthusiast brand. His journey is featured in Chapter 5.

We will see more Influencer/brand enthusiast intelligence put to use. Smart companies are already monitoring social platforms to segment and target their influencers and learn how to support them. Mommy bloggers are high on the list, but it doesn't stop there. No matter how broad or narrow your target market is, influencers abound if you know how to search for them. If "reviews are the new advertising" and "influence marketing" is taking center stage, then the sentiment in those reviews and among those Influencers should be included in the overall picture as well. Some, such as Stephen Kruger, CEO of Interactive Buzz, call it "return on influence" as opposed to "return on investment." Kruger says his company spends time educating clients on the fact that a social media campaign is not a binary process. Social media lives beyond the campaign, and the influence should continue. It is important to take measurements after the campaign stops because the campaign elements continue to be searchable and actionable. The influence, good or bad, lives on and needs to be monitored and managed.

Measuring Data Insights: Scale, Scope, and Sentiment

Companies, their advertising agencies, and marketers realize that social media also has the ability to provide deep insights rather than simply tallying how many consumers, friends, or followers have been acquired. Marketers need to leverage the vast amounts of behavioral data contained in the social streams for more accurate audience targeting and measurement. There are real-time platforms like Social Mention that provide these insights for free. If your customers are fantasy sports fans, meet them on their turf while activity is taking place. If they are parents, find them at events and in discussions that matter to them. This is smart marketing regardless of traditional or emerging media. The Now Lens allows a company to appraise behaviors, objectives, measurements, and results ahead of the competition.

As was mentioned before, social and real-time marketing allows access to a vast network of pervasive, collective intelligence 24/7, with billions of contributors coming online every second. This collective metadata cloud (the flock of birds) is ebbing and flowing with global data from blogs, tweets, reviews, opinions, likes, Web sites, check-ins, and games. It is rich with real-time statistics and real-people sentiment about every topic under the sun in every language in the world. It includes raw insights that are fascinating, robust, and filled with promise. It is also clogged with random, frivolous, superfluous noise. Separating the two and then mining the intelligence that matters most to your organization are what analytics and research companies are tasked with doing.

Blake Cahill, formerly with Visible Technologies, a social media research company based in Seattle, Washington, wrote in May 2010, "Social media has exploded in recent years and brands are realizing that this is critical for many parts of their organization. While taking the initial 'plunge' into social media is not difficult, enterprise adoption, success and ROI calculation can only be achieved with proper planning, deployment, and careful measurement." Visible Technologies heard the cry for tangible measurement tools and devised a social media calculator to determine whether a company could realize financial benefits by using them. Other measurement platforms are helping clients leverage social channels and positively shift brand perception, increase sales, and strengthen customer relationships.

"Before having monitoring software in place we couldn't talk about the scale and scope of issues as they emerged online," recounted Charles Miller, director of digital care/social media strategy for DIRECTV in El Segundo, California. His company is responsible for satellite distribution of program content around the world, charged with "delivering the best TV experience" for its customers. When glitches happen, his company hears about it. "Having measurement tools that allow us to deliver feedback to management in real-time is very helpful when we've had both negative and positive feedback," Miller explained. DIRECTV has seen positive sentiment on social platforms for 3-D. They are also able to watch the effects of disruptions as they happen and see how much negative impact an event has on the brand by monitoring trending over time. A major success factor in DIRECTV's use of measurement is a commitment to monitor on a steady, consistent basis: "Scale, scope, and sentiment really matter to our management."

Commitment to measurement is an investment in long-term brand success based on true customer satisfaction. If a company experiences a glitch that adversely affects customer satisfaction, a quick response via real-time social media handled in an honest way can not only mitigate the problem, but also create brand goodwill. Sentiment and volume measurement tools will reveal whether the problem has truly abated or is steaming and ready to explode.

As noted earlier, brands have recovered in a few days or a week. In other cases, regaining customer confidence can take months or years or never happen. That is why, at a minimum, social media sentiment, volume, and trending need to be added to every brand analysis mix delivered weekly or monthly. When a company is in reputation management mode, taking an hourly or daily pulse reading may be required.

Developing Standards

Measuring success varies with the objective for each business and is now further complicated by the fact that social media analytics and measurement mean so many different things to different people. Unlike traditional marketing programs such as TV advertising, direct mail, and other one-direction media, measuring social media and real-time trends can be complex and less than straightforward. Networks spread from person to person and community to community. There is an element of geometric dimension in how these seemingly random bits of information coalesce and flow, then separate, then cascade. Businesses that have made a commitment to social platforms are hungry for standards that will assess campaigns effectively and help inform future strategies and tactics. At this stage, social media and real-time marketing lack across-the-board standardized metrics that have served as a primary advantage for online advertising.

Some familiar Internet measurements apply: unique visitors, reach, frequency, site "stickiness," click-through, sales conversions, impressions, engagements, time spent on site. Some of this data is available in Google Analytics or Facebook Insights, but these metrics may not capture the subtle information available on real-time platforms: nature of the likes, followers, comments, tone, frequency, velocity, personal interests, brand love, or distaste. That is where personal assessment comes in, with a researcher making a judgment call on whether a comment is positive, negative, neutral, or mixed. A number is assigned to each judgment, and then those numbers are calculated to determine overall sentiment.

Establishing a format for making that call is critical. Deciding if a sarcastic comment is mixed, negative, or positive is a challenge and depends completely on the assessor's point of view. It is important to know who is doing the measuring and the criteria for decision making. Some measurement companies are automating sentiment evaluation by analyzing five to ten words prior to the main search term.

What to measure will vary depending on campaign objectives. Some categories are listed below. When applied to multiple real-time platforms, one can begin to see how time-intensive tracking can be:

- Demographics, technographics
- Geography of participating consumers
- Sentiment, passion
- Shift in sentiment at the beginning, middle, end, and beyond of a campaign
- Media mentions
- Influencer reach
- Growth rate of fans, followers, friends, and likes
- Virality and "share-ability"
- Number of embeds
- Number of downloads
- Number of unique authors
- Hashtags
- Top users
- Engagements (which can be uploads, comments, passalongs)
- Comments
- Ratings

- Blog posts and links
- Photo, video sharing
- Digital buzz

How to measure is being addressed as well. One example is the Social Advertising Best Practices and Social Media Ad Metrics established in May 2009 by the Interactive Advertising Bureau (IAB) (http://www.iab.net/iab_products_and_industry_services/508676/801817). The IAB's definition of a social ad is "an online ad that incorporates user interactions that the consumer has agreed to display and be shared. The resulting ad displays these interactions along with the user's persona (picture and/or name) within the ad content."

Its guidelines go on to describe five key factors:

1. Data used for social ads
2. Ingredients of a social ad
3. Context for delivering a social ad
4. Consumer control
5. Privacy guidelines

For metrics, the IAB breaks the social media space into three sectors:

1. *Social media.* These sites are "characterized by the inherent functionality that facilitates the sharing of information between users within a defined network."
2. *Blog.* This "is a type of Web site used by individuals, groups or business entities to publish opinions and commentary on various topics."
3. *Widgets.* These are "applications that can function on any site that accepts external content, including social networks, blog platforms, start pages [e.g., My Yahoo], desktop platforms, or personal Web pages," whereas social media applications "are software programs designed to work on one or more platforms"

but that "work only on the platform for which they are designed."

By using these three categories, the IAB further breaks down measurement criteria. Some interesting newcomers to the world of online media measurement include the following:

- Games played
- Uploads (e.g., images, videos)
- Poll votes
- Invites sent
- News feed items posted
- Comments posted
- Friends reached
- Topics/forums created
- Number of group members or fans
- Earliest post date for conversation-relevant posts
- Latest post date for conversation-relevant posts
- Meantime between posts
- Growth
- Influence

The Social Media Advertising Consortium (SMAC) grew out of needs identified by those in the social media advertising industry: providers, publishers, and agencies. They came together and created a governing body to help bring clarity to their industry. SMAC's focus is on three primary areas, which sound similar to the IAB's:

- Terminology
- Buying units
- Measurement metrics

SMAC hopes that the resulting standards will allow the social media industry to scale, innovate, and evolve responsibly and effectively.

Text and Data Mining

Another intriguing source for measurement is traditionally known as text and data mining: the extraction of often unseen information residing in large databases for the purposes of predicting behavior. Data mining tools are powerful and have been around for quite a while. This process allows businesses to make informed, data-driven decisions and possibly predict future customer behavior. Now the metadata that underlies Twitter, Facebook, and other social technology platforms offers huge potential for business production, sales forecasts, and political strategies. Social media data is being extended beyond its original applications into a tool for predicting the future.

We have ascertained that the exponential growth in social media has helped create a large body of content that reflects the trends, experiences, evaluations, and sentiment of the marketplace. In March 2010, HP Labs published a paper (http://www.hpl.hp.com/research/scl/papers/socialmedia/socialmedia.pdf) describing how it used data captured from Twitter posts to predict box-office revenue at the movies. Using this data as a predictive model, the team was able to demonstrate that it could forecast opening weekend box-office revenue with 97.3 percent accuracy. This compared favorably with a well-known prediction tool for movies, the Hollywood Stock Exchange (HSX), which had 96.5 percent accuracy.

The exciting aspect of this study is not that this particular application used social media to predict box-office revenue but that a model has been developed to use social media to predict a wide variety of outcomes.

An initial analysis of the tweets revealed the following:

- The tweets built up in volume the week before the movie release, peaked at the time of the release, and fell during the two weeks after the release.
- The average number of tweets made by individuals about a particular movie was 1 to 1.5.

- The distribution of tweets by individuals showed that a handful of individuals made many tweets; the distribution followed the "long tail" power distribution that frequently occurs on the Web.

The team then proceeded to analyze the data for predictive power. Here's what didn't prove to be very good predictors of box-office success:

- Before the release of a movie, studios promote the film heavily via TV, print, news releases, interviews with the stars, and trailer videos. The research classified tweets according to whether they contained URLs, indicating that they could reference trailers, movie reviews, or other PR about the movie. It turned out that although 22 to 40 percent of the tweets contained URLs, those tweets were only mildly predictive of box-office success.
- The percentage of retweets was in the range of 11 to 12 percent and was even less predictive of box-office success. This is surprising in light of the fact that retweets are indicative of word of mouth.

There were three factors that proved to be powerful predictors of box-office revenue:

1. *The tweet rate or the number of tweets about a given movie per hour.* This is indicative of the overall attention and interest the movie is generating. This factor is particularly important in predicting the box-office revenue for the opening weekend.
2. *Positive sentiment about the movie.* The researchers created a customized method for analyzing positive and negative sentiment about movies for the purposes of this study. Sentiment

proved to be an important factor in predicting box-office revenue in the weeks after the opening.

3. *Distribution, or the number of theaters in which the film screened.* The wider the distribution, the more opportunities for revenue generation.

The researchers concluded: "While in this study we focused on the problem of predicting box office revenues of movies for the sake of having a clear metric of comparison with other methods, this method can be extended to large panoply of topics, ranging from the future rating of products to agenda setting and election outcomes."

These findings can be confirmed by the direct experience of one of the authors during a Super Bowl campaign for a global auto manufacturer. Twitter buzz and retweet frequency, volume, and reach increased the week before the TV commercial aired during the game. Twitter activity was responsible for over 50 percent of digital buzz for the automaker, which surpassed that of all other car makers over the Super Bowl weekend and the following week. Awareness building increased Web traffic and foot traffic to the showrooms. Just tracking Twitter requires the following measurement for a comprehensive view:

- Embed links in tweets to Facebook, favorable commercial blogs, articles
- Track hashtag strategy with key words
- Tweets per hour
- Brand tweets
- Celebrity tweets
- Followers
- Retweets
- @mentions
- FB shares
- Listed

- ○ Overall tweet reach
- ○ Overall tweets
- ○ Twitter syndication organic and paid, if applicable

In addition to tracking and measuring tweets for the information listed above, PeopleBrowsr will be creating a tool that will search a person's tweet in real-time while it is being written. Jodee Rich describes this new service for consumers as a way to mitigate the 60 to 70 percent Twitter drop-off rate: "We think consumer analytics are evolving around giving consumers tools they need to make them more interesting in their public posts and more connected to the interest groups they are thinking about today. This will now be possible. When a person enters a tweet or post on Facebook, our 'T2D2' feature will look at all their relationships and connections based on the words within the message. It will take all the key words out of that post and it will look up what their friends are saying about those topics, then present a PeopleBrowsr data stream. Before sending the post, the user can review if there is any related information from the people in their social sphere they may add to make the tweet more interesting." This amounts to an analytic tool that combines real-time search with sophisticated crowdsourcing.

Organizational Alignment

An emerging issue that companies are faced with is to determine where measurement and analytics fit within the organization. Since social media campaigns and metrics are developing and being implemented primarily in marketing or customer service, they appear to fit there more naturally. However, most IT departments normally own data mining and analysis, especially in large corporations. As Enterprise 2.0 puts more emphasis on cloud computing and supporting mobile deployments, social analytics could shift to IT.

In June 2010, Forrester Research released findings on social media users that "IT staff increase productivity by adapting Social Computing to their role." Forrester acknowledged that CIOs should enthusiastically embrace social media as a means for boosting IT productivity while also giving IT staff the experience needed to support Social Computing initiatives across the enterprise."[1]

Clearly, organizational alignment is proving to be a critical consideration among corporate communications, marketing, customer service, IT, eCommerce, and so on. Internal escalation procedures that fully integrate real-time communication need to be in place. Finally, organizations must have senior leadership support for social media interactions. Even something as seemingly basic and simple as whether or not to respond to negative comments needs to be thought out well in advance. In September 2010, AT&T in the United States sent 10 million e-mails announcing upgrades and inviting customers to post comments on their Facebook Wall. Hundreds of comments came pouring in, and most were negative. AT&T"'s policy, apparently, by looking at the Facebook page, was to respond to each one. Why is this significant? It shows a strategy. Other brands moderate comments, and some do not allow negative comments at all. It is obvious that AT&T leadership, cross-functional teams, and other internal groups were prepared for the outcome.

Tracking and the Physics of Velocity

Think of the rich rewards for brand managers, advertising agencies, C-level executives, and other stakeholders who can harness the text and data mining, analytics, and measurement required to produce intelligence from all this information. Piercing the cloud of global consumer velocity, sentiment, and connections, combined with what is trending at any given moment in any part of the world, will ultimately enable companies to develop strategies that engage more meaningfully with communities—both customer-facing and those within the enterprise.

Whereas most measurement is targeting sentiment and volume, Culture Jam has tapped into the significance of velocity and geolocation for its clients. Currently, CEO Matt MacNaughton focuses his efforts on Twitter. His company tracks and measures a number of activities on Culture Jam's proprietary "tweet for a reward" platform, particularly "velocity." As MacNaughton explained, "If you think about it in the physics mind set, our whole tracking suite adds up to a velocity of sorts. The velocity of a social campaign has to do with speed and mass. How quickly messages are syndicated is powered by a mass of participants that continues to grow impressions. The more people participate, the faster it rolls along, so we are looking at mass and energy. We calculate all the elements we track to gauge velocity and how it impacts the success of the quality, reach, and success of the promotion for our clients" (see Figure 6.2).

The success of this very young company speaks to the power of piercing the global cloud of consumer sentiment. It specializes in building applications that allow social media marketers to create an exchange between a brand and users. It is a classic barter relationship adapted to social platforms; however, this barter deal is designed to go viral. Consumers, or users, become "syndicators" when they spread the special offer and message to their friends and followers. The result is that brands increase followers to create further conversation and marketing opportunities. Users (syndicators) receive something of value for free—music, video, a coupon, or an experience, whatever the item of "value" is perceived to be.

In mid-2009, MacNaughton's company launched the first ever "tweet for a download" application, featuring a free mix tape by Travis Barker of the rock group Blink-182 and DJ AM. After only one year, Matt's company now handles promotions for studios, clothes companies, sports franchises, and others who use its extensive tracking system to discover previously unknown markets, adjust concert tour

6.2 Tracking systems aggregate into "velocity" as measured by Culture Jam

Real-Time Tracking and Velocity Chart

velocity = change in displacement(speed)/time

1. How many people hit the special offer page
2. How many tweets are going out to gauge the syndication activity level of the promotion across twitter
3. The exact follow count of each person that tweets at the exact time and aggregates that for the exact potential tweet reach and eyeballs
4. Sponsor follower growth
5. Geolocation to determine number and volume of users and what cities, towns they are coming from

marketing, and find hot and cold consumer groupings on a global level. For example, Culture Jam crafted a promotion for the NHL champion Pittsburgh Penguins. If users chose to tweet, they could view never-before-seen photos from the seventh game of the Stanley Cup series the Penguins won in 2009. Though the campaign was centered in Pittsburgh and the U.S. northeastern corridor, the data they tracked showed other markets where it was reaching, spreading, and grouping. They saw heavy activity in Canada. But since they were tracking international traffic as well, they also saw activity in Russia and Eastern bloc countries where the strongholds of the hockey fans live; these are potential untapped markets.

We know that on-the-job learning and education are of primary importance for employees and stakeholders in organizations. Imagine the opportunities for continuous improvement that would surface as a result of tapping into one's consumers' collective knowledge. Crowd-sourcing and collaboration would identify new market needs and service opportunities and benefit from community feedback. Technologies exist to facilitate data collection in diverse social media, but there are no silver bullets. Extracting market intelligence from real-time ideas and community feedback as a means to drive products and services requires receptive product managers.

Some might comment that all this sentiment analysis and influencer hunting is merely an outgrowth of the old customer evaluation forms, and it is. For the last 20 years, customers have been bombarded with evaluation forms and surveys for purchased items or services.

Most companies still use a customer evaluation form but have learned to "game the system." Performance is tied to customer satisfaction. Recently, an associate relayed that she bought a luxury car on the East Coast and was told by the salesperson, "Nothing but a 5 will do. If you give me anything else, it's like I've failed." The buyer felt pressured to give a 5, but she said that the customer service was substandard. In fact, the salesperson did not fix a minor problem, and her overall experience did not merit a 5. Rather than fix internal problems, this dealership was bullying customers into giving false ratings. Its sales bonuses are tied to customer satisfaction ratings. The strategy appears to be to pressure the customer and not fix the problems. Today, she and legions of others with similar experiences can and will go online to name the dealership and the salesperson and to warn others.

Consumers have become weary of evaluation forms that do not seem to help improve their service but are used instead to collect data, sell their names to other mailing lists, or justify employee incentives. In the 1990s companies began to improve customer relationship management by making it more of a two-way street. Instead of simply gathering data for their own use, they started giving back to their customers not only by attempting to provide improved customer service but also in the form of incentives, gifts, and other perks for customer loyalty.

To be sure, consumers have also figured out how to game the system and in many cases have become overly demanding and quick to threaten a lawsuit because their hamburger was not cooked the way they wanted it. It seems like both sides of the pendulum are out of whack. Perhaps social platforms and real-time measurement will help regain the balance with its rules that require authenticity and transparency.

In the early days of social media (way back in 2007), a common question was, "Is social media worth the time and effort?" As someone wisely put it, "Would the CFO get as excited about social media as a CMO would?" Unfortunately, some companies are still making casual forays into social and real-time marketing. They run it separately from their broader strategy, which is a mistake, and largely without a measurement strategy in place, which is another error. When asked to quantify the value of the time and effort, they cannot. Until recently, real-time metrics seemed to offer random bits of information rather than actionable business intelligence that mapped back to business goals.

Luckily, this field is evolving rapidly. It is imperative that companies become focused on how they are marketing to both consumers and other businesses via social channels as well as how consumers discuss brands among themselves. This will allow marketers to make informed decisions about their social marketing initiatives through the Now Lens of smart measurement. At the very least, displaying customer sentiment will let companies know where they stand.

CHAPTER 7

Viewing the Future of Real-Time Social Media: The Next Lens

N ow that we have studied how the complex trends at the intersection of social technologies, global connectivity, and innovation are shaping the present, we come not to the end of our journey but to another beginning. The migrations and formations of our flock of birds continue to grow and amaze us as we watch the dynamic data collect and disperse around us throughout the world. It is evident that real-time social media marketers will need to be "future warriors" by being nimble and embracing ongoing change because none of this is going to stop. Social platforms will evolve, people will continue connecting, and language will change. We are already seeing the beginnings of the new marketing language touched on throughout this book:

Former	New
Return on investment	Return on interaction, return on influence
Share of voice (a media buy)	Share of conversations on social platforms

Microblogging   Tweet
Advertising   Consumer reviews
Customer relationship management   Consumer real-time muscle

The Next Lens provides a view of what the outcomes of this living, breathing collective consciousness—this global brain—could look like and where it might take us. Right now, a handful of businesses have appointed conversation officers, directors, and managers. The digital habits of Millennials and digital natives are informing new thinking in how education, knowledge distribution, and organizations should be reconfigured. Your mobile device is already communicating with your calendar, and apps are tracking your health and the health of your family. Geolocation is serving up products and services in your own personal hemisphere that matter to you in real-time. Today's knowledge workforce—lawyers, doctors, accountants, marketers, researchers, and executives—is expected to be solution-based and fully connected. Indeed, society in general will be fully connected, and the silos between platforms will begin to dissolve.

Very soon, all of us will be receiving customized information from the global brain:

1. *Industry:* medicine, education, financial services, etc.
2. *Topic:* entertainment, travel, food, information, etc.
3. *Person:* thought leaders, celebrities, designated authorities within social circle, new connections

Right now, new businesses are emerging around content aggregation and curation. These innovative companies will provide an ever-increasing service to those looking for a personalized qualified selection of the best and most relevant content or resources on a very specific topic.

We will see conversations and engagements grow in social functionality within companies, organizations, and learning establishments. Businesses will continue to boost their market position by expanding their footprint in real-time social media. After years of getting axed, vital employee training will be brought back to corporations as a way to remain solvent, competitive, and gain market leadership. Immediate opportunities for businesses, brands, and marketers will include the following:

○ Content development, production, and syndication for mobile devices as they become the "anywhere" hub of choice
○ Back-end financial management of mobile transactions as global consumers move into the era of the digital wallet
○ Ratings and review monitoring as the new advertising
○ Managing and designing globally and socially connected collaborative workplaces, education learning environments, and systems
○ Designing, implementing, and programming socially enabled media everywhere and thus transforming traditional media: outdoor, print, e-mail, TV, radio, OOH, online, and digital
○ Programming social gaming and virtual currency to fully integrate advertising and brand experiences
○ Programming 3-D and alternative reality technology for business and consumer use
○ The growing global brain metadata will spur big business in content aggregation and curation
○ Customer relationship management will evolve to customer experience management
○ Measure and deliver customized dashboards: followers, mentions, retweets, mutuals, trends, sentiment, velocity, likes, links, time of engagement
○ Privacy and security policy guidance and implementation
○ Storage development, archiving, and smart retrieval for mounds of real-time global search data
○ Americans and other westerners will seek the new lands of opportunity, specifically China, India, South America, and Australia

Social Media Dream Life

Let us strain our eyes to catch a glimpse of what waits for businesses, governments, societies, cultures, and individuals down the road. Jodee Rich, CEO of PeopleBrowsr in San Francisco, California, spent time in the 1980s with the Extropians,[1] a group of people who have assumed that advanced biotechnology will give us extended life and whose purpose is to envision how human behavior will evolve: people experiencing longer lives that translate into multiple careers and relationships. They postulate that we will become less concerned about midlife crises because extended life will supply us with more years to follow our dreams and get it right. The perception of more time will enhance the appreciation of real-time.

A recent think tank at Tim O'Reilly's Foo Camp used the Extropian construct as a model from which Rich and a small group of digital anthropologists established the "Sotropians." The theme was "How would social media affect life in 2040 after 30 years of real-time development and adoption?" The group speculated that

o   Our greater connectedness will lead individuals to become less judgmental.
o   The availability of public profiles and data will accelerate relationship building.
o   Geographic boundaries will become transparent, and virtual villages will rapidly evolve and decline around issues.
o   We can all tap into the collective stream of consciousness to enhance how we learn, shop, make decisions, and even select airline seats based on those around you.

Rich shared more findings discussed within the group: "We know now that global conversations are evolving into a 'collective consciousness.' The earlier thought that people are separated by approximately 6 degrees of separation has been narrowed down to 2 degrees.

218

As an example, real-time social media will give a person the ability to look around a room rapidly and see the relationships, connections, and backgrounds of all present. A person will then receive instant information and make those 2-degree connections that are most valuable at that time. As a result of being better informed and connected, friendship groups will both quickly form and break down because people can move on to other groups more easily. Understanding each person based on their social profiles, both positive and negative, could reduce judgment and prejudice. Open and more complete public knowledge will help us realize that all of us have 'skeletons.' If people became less judgmental, that would be an extraordinary thing for human beings.

"Another outcome of social-media-infused technology will be the ability to walk into a room of 200 people and activate software that will do face recognition, look up all the data on everyone so you will be able to connect with the people you specifically need. This will let a person instantaneously find people you have met before, who share mutual friends, or similar interests. Real-time friendships will 'power up' around whatever is occupying our focus today."

Rich further explained the Sotropian view: "For instance, in an advanced civilization there will be very little difference between *privacy* and *publicness*. The universe is open. So it really becomes a difference between being *public* and broadcasting your *publicness*.

"Currently, PeopleBrowsr receives every tweet, blog post, every Myspace and most of Facebook's public stream, all at the rate of more than 10,000 posts per second. Every post is scanned and a metadata cloud created around links, retweets, hashtags, and other keyword markers. The metadata will provide the opportunity to see the world through the eyes of another human or the connectedness of two humans. Rather than a bleak Orwellian future, ubiquitous social metadata will realize deeper human interaction."

The Sotropians anticipate a world full of people hyperlinks. "In the past," Rich explains, "digital storage space was not available to support this torrential data. However, current multi-terabyte servers are receiving over half a terabyte of data per day. In the future, they will store every bit of metadata locally about your friends, friends of friends, and friends of friends of friends. Analytics will become more about studying relationship and connection data between different types of consumers or companies. The business applications for real-time social media marketers and businesses are unfathomable."

Rich concludes, "Insects achieve a higher collective intelligence by prioritizing group interaction. Language brought humans out of the jungle and, until recently, we have been restricted by slow verbal communications. Optic fiber between computers has dramatically increased the collective power of computer networks. Any technology that increases the band rate of human exchange will move our collective consciousness to the next level. We are moving from word-of-mouth speed to faster social network speed. I think it is imperative that we use this collective consciousness or we will not survive as human beings."

The next evolution in measuring underlying conversation metadata will be the ability to measure truth. The Los Angeles–based social media producer and content strategist Rome Viharo predicts a time when we will "measure the potential truth value of a phrase, statement, or idea based on discussion patterns and behavior that happen around it. This, of course, brings up the questions, what is truth? How and who defines it? What is true to one person is not necessarily true to someone else. First, it is important to distinguish truth as the most honest and rational idea, as distinguished from an opinion. Then, what is rational must include honesty and some form of a win-win scenario. Social media is perfect for this. Social media is about being open, authentic, and adding value. It is the ability to discuss in your own self-interest as well as that of someone else. If a company is only marketing in a way to extract as much money as possible from the consumer, this will be measured as win-lose. If someone is unable to argue in their own self-interest, this will be analyzed. Literally, we will be able to determine if a person does not 'measure up' as being truthful."

Viharo goes on to foretell accurate lead generation: "Lead generation will be tracked by gauging behavior of metadata. In social media, people are so focused on what people are saying. A more notable metric is their actions related to a brand. If you want to know what people are really up to, pay less attention to what they say and more to what they do. I look at the flow of people's behavior on social media."

Rodney Rumford, cofounder of the highly popular real-time photo-sharing site Plixi (formerly TweetPhoto) contributes these thoughts: "As I look forward, I see opportunities for brands in real-time search and location-based marketing. It was only a few years ago that I used to say 'Google is so yesterday.' Well, that is no longer true. Google is surfacing this data in a matter of seconds. Real-time services will make the data hit users when and where they want it. Search is becoming less important and the data that matters to me will find me. Based upon a variety of things such as location, user demographics, social graph intelligence, and preferences that have been learned by a variety of services through my participation now will be able to serve me data that matters most."

At the moment, the market is very focused on the now of real-time in social media. Consumer feedback and conversations on social technology platforms are exciting and new. Marketers are now or soon will be evaluating the power of social media tools as a continuous part of the integrated marketing mix. Creative marketers and technologists will continue searching for new and compelling experiences for consumers. With storage capacity expanding from terabytes to petabytes, imaginations supported by collaboration will be empowered in ways we have not yet seen. Let's look at immediate next categories, such as social gaming and virtual currency, social mobile, and social location.

Social Gaming and Virtual Currency

Contrary to popular thought, the majority of people who play video games are women age 18 to 43 and stay-at-home moms. Facebook is the most popular destination for online games. A *social* game is a structured activity with contextual rules through which users can engage one another. Games such as FarmVille, Bejewled, Texas Hold'em poker, and Mafia Wars have proved that social gaming is a fast-growing and quickly maturing pastime for an ever increasing number of people.

Recently, the casual game maker PopCap Games commissioned the Information Services Group (ISP) to survey exactly who plays social games online. It confirmed that the average social gamer is a 43-year-old woman. (This is not to be confused with the young male gamers who dominate the Xbox action game field.) The ISG survey found that 55 percent of social gamers are female and 45 percent are male. Females are more avid gamers, too, with 38 percent of females saying they play multiple times a day, compared with just 29 percent of males.

Advertisers and major brands are taking notice and starting to steer budgets toward social games as a way to interact and engage with these customers. Brands offer virtual goods currency to the game players if they become friends of their pages. Gamers are also being rewarded with free virtual goods currency for watching video advertising within games.

Along the lines of trading goods or points for items is the experiment done by a major U.S. auto manufacturer. It tested converting leads to sales by creating auto gaming online. As an in-market (potential customer) goes to the manufacturer's Web site, that person is engaged to play a competitive game that requires him or her to answer questions about the model in which he or she is interested. The players get ranked as an expert or a novice on a leader board as they answer more questions. Points are converted to discounts on car features when a player decides to purchase the car.

This gaming and virtual currency market is expected to become a multi-billion-dollar business and is already exploding seemingly overnight, driven mostly by social gaming. Virtual currency is also the newest revenue stream in the monetization of online social sites. Most games were based on a monthly subscription until virtual currency and virtual goods came along. Major game makers and studios such as Warner Bros. are opting to release new online games by using the free-to-pay model instead of the subscription model. Right now, the companies Zynga (FarmVille, FrontierVille, Texas Hold'em) and PlaySpan are dominating the game development and virtual goods/currency space. Playspan's Ultimate Game Card is a popular multigame prepaid card used to facilitate the purchase of virtual goods in social games.

According to the ISG survey mentioned earlier, 28 percent of social gamers have purchased in-game currency with real-world money. Players pay real-world cash for virtual (fake) currency to purchase virtual nonexistent gifts, items, and goods. To restate, people are paying real money for things that do not exist. Social gaming is indeed serious business.

In fact, virtual currency is such a market disrupter that the South Korean supreme court has ruled that the fictional "cybermoney" used in online games can legally be exchanged for actual cash in the real world. The ruling stipulates that players of online games can sell their in-game currency to other players for real-world money. According to an article in the *Korea Times* on January 1, 2010, it also means that the South Korean government is going to tax the proceeds of those sales.

The Korea Game Development & Promotion Institute says that more than 830 billion South Korean won ($732 million) worth of cybermoney was exchanged online in South Korea in 2006 and that amount might have exceeded 1 trillion won ($882 million) in 2008.

In China, the supervision of virtual currencies has been under regulation since 2006 as well. The official Xinhua News Agency reported in November 2006 that the Chinese central bank would begin to supervise virtual currencies as they could affect the value of the yuan. Virtual currency could be used only to buy online game items, according to the Ministry of Culture. It is disconcerting to know that the currency value of one of the strongest economic forces in the world could be affected by social gaming. This fact alone speaks to the power of social platforms.

Another example of how big this new market might become is that of social network Hi5, which announced in July 2010 that it had raised $14 million in a second round of funding as it shifts into social games and virtual goods. The company is making free-to-play games that users start playing for free, but they pay real money for virtual goods such as decorations. This network does not have much of a chance to unseat Facebook in social games, but it might have a good chance to set itself up as a diversification opportunity for social game developers that do not want to be entirely dependent on Facebook.

Brands, advertisers, and marketers have zeroed in on this emerging opportunity to reach new audiences. *Sports Illustrated, Family Feud,* ESPN, and Discovery Channel all have plans for social games. In July 2010, MTV bought a social gaming company and Disney agreed to acquire Playdom Inc., one of the largest makers of social games.[2]

Businesses will look to real-time marketers for guidance and development ideas because some form of social gaming will be built into most content. It encourages engagement, increases conversion from leads to sales, and is proving to be a reliable revenue path for social media and real-time companies.

Social Mobile/Social Tablet

Mobile has taken on a broader meaning. Cell phones are center stage at the moment. However. the iPad, the new PlayBook, the Amazon Kindle, and other portable e-reader devices have expanded the reach, capability, and interactive experiences of mobile. According to Reuters, Apple sold approximately 3.3 million iPads in the second quarter of 2010.[3] Amazon claims to have sold more e-books for its Kindle device than hardback books as of June 2010, as reported to ZDNet.[4] According to ABI Research, in July 2010 there were over 4.8 billion mobile subscribers worldwide, and with continued advances in devices, services, and billing models, the mobile Web is inspiring a new age of anytime, anywhere information access.

Consider this: The U.S. Census Bureau U.S. & World Population Clocks as of October 3, 2010, counted 6,872,647,238 people on the planet. The ABI Research just mentioned goes on to predict that by the end of 2010, mobile subscriptions will reach 5 billion, mostly coming from developing markets in Africa and the Asian-Pacific region. That translates into approximately 72.75 percent of the world's population with mobile devices in their hands. If you are an app developer, think about creating a couple for Asian and African markets.

The world is also witnessing an explosion in real-time social media services as users are seeking novel ways of interacting with their friends and families around the globe. Easy-to-use interfaces, visual elements, dynamic and current information in real-time geolocation, coupled with delivering the right interactive data are setting the bar for the consumer and business experience.

As Rodney Rumford says, "My cell phone knows where I am and what I like as well as what my friends like. This represents an opportunity to provide value to mobile users in real-time. My keys, my wallet, my cell phone will soon all be the same device."

With mobile penetration already reaching 100 percent in many developed markets, the mobile phone will soon be in virtually everyone's pocket. And emerging markets are undergoing the leapfrog effect. They are leapfrogging over the troubles of inadequate infrastructure directly into 4G Wifi. They will not be relegated to the traditional economic evolution of subsistence → agrarian → industrial → service → technology path. As noted by James Eberhard, CEO of Mobile Accord in the American Red Cross Haitian relief case story in Chapter 5, mobile is delivering information, education, and economic growth in developing countries and will continue to do so. The rise of mobile social networks presents the full integrated experience anywhere, anytime.

The number of users on these services is growing fast. In fact, a new study by InStat is predicting that by 2012 there will be nearly 30 million Millennials in the United States using a mobile social network of some sort, and a *Computerworld* report confirms that worldwide, the number will soar to 975 million. Though mobile social networking is still commonly thought of as something for the youth market, 35- to 54-year-olds are the most active demographic on mobile social networks.

Prognosticators have been trying to determine when mobile for business and associated advertising will hit a critical mass. It is actually happening now, though at different adoption levels around the world. As use grows, technology will change simultaneously. We foresee the development of 3-D holographic technology embedded in mobile devices. When a person is called on a phone or on an e-reader, a 3-D holographic image will stand on the phone surface and interact with the caller. The same engagement technology will be used for products, brands, political candidates, and medical services. Imagine contracting an ailment while on vacation and calling your doctor, who can diagnose the problem and recommend treatment in real-time. Long-distance diagnosis is already taking place with the use of Skype-type Internet video services.

Holographic technology already has been developed by Jason Opat at Integrated Media Group in Wichita, Kansas. A former special effects expert who worked on 3-D and interactive computer screens for Hollywood films, including *Transformers* and *Ironman,* Jason and his team have developed holographic avatars, or a virtual concierge, who can answer questions in real-time. Though the device is restricted to a kiosk, a Wichita hospital is testing the virtual receptionist to direct visitors throughout the facility.

Holographic technology will also affect home entertainment and the in-theater experience. Instead of current theater stadium seating with the stage at one end and seats rising to the back, the stage will be in the center with seats surrounding it. The holographic movie image (no longer film) will come alive at center stage. Before the movie even reaches this shared experience point, fans and consumers will have had the opportunity to interact with actors, producers, musicians, and stakeholders through social sites and mobile apps.

In virtual reality worlds, 3-D technology really shines. In 2008, Carl's Jr. fast-food restaurants experimented with virtual reality by creating a shopping and home environment. Fans could create their own avatars, enter the virtual world, and interact with one another. It was a limited campaign, but the parent company, CKE Restaurants, is consistently on the cutting edge of virtual worlds and gaming to engage its young male target demographic. Expect to see more virtual world ideation and implimentation across all industries.

Animation is also being used to convey concepts in the financial world. Designer and flash animator Rob Feldman of EarWorm Media created a persona for a client in asset liability management. The persona is a hero called ALM Man who takes special care of his clients, guarding them and their assets. In a social media integrated world, anticipate traditional business and real-time marketers seeking the benefits of animation, 3-D, and holographic technology to enhance brand engagement and trust.

We are already seeing industry segments as early adopters, specifically in health care. In July 2010, Manhattan Research released this regarding its "Physicians in 2012" report:

Physician adoption of digital media shows little signs of slowing in 2012—quite the contrary. While the last few years have seen a rapid uptake in Internet-related media and devices, the next few will see the emergence of a maturing physician audience, one that is more proficient and has more extensive experience with online professional products and services.

Growth in newer media adoption has been particularly remarkable in the last two years, and is in many cases limited only by the availability of professional content in these formats. Participation in social networks that are dedicated to physicians has almost doubled from 2008 to 2009. Mobile trends are equally impressive, with smartphone/PDA ownership growing significantly between 2008 and 2009.

Even more change lies ahead. In 2012, physicians will be more immersed in online media in several respects. Physicians will use online resources more frequently and will reduce or eliminate their use of offline sources as the Internet becomes a primary rather than complementary resource. A higher number of physicians will perform a broader and more complex range of functions online, including on mobile devices. User-generated content will become a mainstream source of information and influence, and professional social networks may well start to evolve into hubs of content, service, and connection. All of this at a time when manufacturers are aggressively seeking a new sales and marketing model, and the overall product and payer landscape is shifting.

There's an App for That

It was estimated in May 2010 that the market for mobile device software programs should rocket to $17.5 billion within three years. Downloads of mobile applications to handsets will leap from slightly more than 7 billion in 2009 to nearly 50 billion in 2012, according to an independent study commissioned by GetJar, the world's second largest app store.

Mike Zeinfeld is the founder and CEO of Complemedia, a company that has been developing iPhone apps for brands since the beginning. Recently, Complemedia was invited to Apple headquarters in Cupertino, California, to discuss the current impact of apps. Zeinfeld made these observations:

When the iPhone was introduced, it presented a marriage between an innovative mobile touch screen interface and small computer programs designed specifically to run on this interface, called "apps." This combination solved the problem of accessing information on the go in a manner that rivaled the non-digital counterparts.

Just as the iPhone (and, later, others like the Palm Pre and Android powered devices) solved the problem of accessing information from anywhere, "apps" evolved to a greater purpose. From calculating tips at a restaurant to magically finding out what song is playing on a radio, mobile apps now seemed to be solving ubiquitous problems.

Whether that task is "catching up on the latest news," "seeing what our friends are doing," "shopping for a new car," or even "reading an MRI," we can achieve these tasks anywhere, anytime, in an extremely convenient format.

The power to solve life's "big" problems in such a compact and mobile solution has changed the landscape of many industries. Many processes, features, and activities which were once challenging when you needed help at a critical point now seem simple.

To name a few industries which dynamics have changed because of mobile information consumption:

Healthcare: This class of users is quintessentially "on the go" and "information hungry." Now, healthcare professionals can access patient information, prescribe medication, learn about new therapies all in the place that they need it most: point of care. Apps have been extremely effective in reaching physicians. Complemedia's own apps have over 100,000 downloads primarily by medical professionals and see utilization rates much higher than their online counterparts.

In a digital holographic world, expect patients to be able to scan their own injuries and feed information to emergency evaluation centers or physician groups to determine on-the spot care and treatment.

Auto: The traditional cat and mouse game of dealer vs. auto-buyer changes significantly when you factor in an all-knowing mobile consumer device. Try this experiment: go into a dealership and ask what inventory they have available for a new car you are planning to buy. Then, watch the salesperson as they walk into the showroom office and access the computer to pull the latest inventory list. While you are waiting, pull out the Cars.com iPhone app and you will have the answer before they do. Not only do you have easier access to their data, but you also have access to third-party data which will give you a leg up in negotiation.

News: Mobile applications may be a potential new revenue source for newspapers and magazines. Apps effectively "package" up a news or magazine property into something with a higher value than simply reading on a computer screen. The convenience of an app gives publishers another way to monetize their content. Time will tell if the revenue source from mobile apps will be significant for publishers.

People want to know "what's going on," especially in breaking news situations. News organizations need to create and sell real-time rate increases when escalation on their sites or apps occur.

Retail: Shoppers are now armed with real information to make purchase decisions. At point of purchase, shoppers can pull up as much information as they need to make a buying decision, from warranty information, editorial reviews, user reviews, and pricing. For example, shoppers can utilize a phone's camera to scan a bar code and retrieve all of the relevant information without even typing a keystroke.

The version of the retail app mentioned above is being used by restaurants in San Francisco. They place a QR Code on a menu posted in the window. Tourists scan the QR Code with a phone to get food reviews from prior diners. In the future world, the QR Code will call up a 3-D chef to tell you about the day's special. Real-time social media marketers will be called upon to align advertisers with the appropriate app that will add value to their target consumers.

When Kia Motors America launched its edgy Soul model, the Korean auto manufacturer was the first to advertise on the imeem mobile music app for the Android phone. For social media, it will continue to be about mining pertinent lifestyle opportunities.

In April 2010, Pampers announced it was launching the iPad application "Hello Baby," which lets parents track the growth of a child and was Pampers' first mobile device application. The move reflects parent company Procter & Gamble's push to position its brands at the forefront of new and emerging technologies. The packaged-goods company sees this as smart business and is allocating more marketing dollars for digital, mobile, and social media. P&G is the parent company of Old Spice and gave the green light for the hugely successful YouTube/Twitter Old Spice Guy campaign described earlier in this book.

For consumers, the iPad/PlayBook concept is that of leaning back versus leaning forward. Leaning forward is what users do when reading or watching their computers and mobile devices. Leaning back is what they do with the iPad-type devices. Why hunch over a mobile device to see a YouTube video when you can lean back in a chair and watch it on the iPad? In fact, photo, video, and user-generated content are actually the new e-ink. For years, media agencies have been trying to find a way to make paper come alive. Short battery life, inability to update, and expense have hampered efforts. The iPad is the new e-ink. Links, video playback, audio, full color, and just-around-the-corner 3-D functionality make the iPad and future devices the replacement for luminous ink.

Be on the watch for how iPad/PlayBook apps will plug into business processes. The devices are more affordable than standard laptop computers. That is the key. E-readers with Wifi capabilities will change the way companies, government offices, and education institutions function and manage services internally and externally.

Location Awareness Platforms

Geo-Loco (geographic location awareness) is already here, and its use is starting to spread. Foursquare and Gowalla are the big brands right now, but many others will emerge. Most utilize the mobile "check-in" system and reward users for registering an arrival at a store, restaurant, or event. Brands and advertisers are learning how to offer sponsors a chance to get customers to the door with easy directions and mapping. Subscribers have the ability to arrive in an unknown town or city and be able to look up where their favorite, trusted brand of coffee shop, restaurant, gas station, movie theater, retailer, or bank is located in direct relation to where they are at the time.

The ability to target consumers on the basis of their locale is in the very early stages and will continue to have a significant effect on the way companies advertise, and not just in the mobile medium; it will also shift their entire advertising strategies, channels, and budgets. As Rodney Rumford said, "While 'checking-in' real-time to locations is quickly gaining traction as a normalized behavior, the next step is auto tracking of where you are and signaling back to services that will provide relevant value based on what you are actually doing at that time in the real world. It will move from where you are to what you need."

Few brands seem as dedicated to testing location-based services as Starbucks, which has used Foursquare, Loopt, and Brightkite. The company runs promotions where users compete for a Frappuccino badge by tallying the most check-ins. Starbucks has been pushing its VIA packaged coffee whenever Brightkite's users check in at supermarkets. In Safeway, Walmart, Target—anywhere you find groceries— you can now buy VIA. Programs like these are an efficient way to tie social media to the bottom line. The data can be collected, analyzed, and applied to finding the best way to allocate budgets to social media efforts.

Entertainment companies such as the *Today Show*, Travel Channel, Bravo, and the History Channel are engaging users with location-based services. As part of their e-government solutions, the city of Torino, Italy, has created a welcome application for visitors as they arrive at the international Sandro Pertini airport. The welcome application offers the following: Welcome, Tourist Information, What's Going on in Torino, and Emergency Phone Numbers.

The Next Lens

The chaos theory and the butterfly effect have no ending but instead reconfigure and transform in an endless flow. We have learned that companies cannot stay mired in a comfort zone for the future they want, one that ignores customers' changing behaviors. More control no longer equals more revenue. In fact, it is just the opposite.

We have also learned that we are all networked—if not today, then very soon. Networked people innovate, create, and invent faster. Consumers are moving from acquiring stuff to having an experience. Leaders are listeners first. This is a not a win-lose world but a win-win world. This is not an end, but another beginning. From Rodney Rumford:

The authors of this book have given you practical and actionable insights and case studies from smart marketing professionals. You would do well to shift your thinking forward and open your mind to new horizons of potential. This is a very exciting time to experiment and test the waters. Metcalfe's law states that the value of the network increases exponentially as more people join it. With over 500 million people on Facebook and close to 180 million on Twitter, the network effect has kicked into overdrive.

Companies have sprung to life and become disruptive by gathering and communicating with millions of users virtually overnight in real-time. Waiting to implement real-time marketing will put you at a huge disadvantage against your competitors.

Welcome to real-time, your new marketing reality. Dive in head first; fail fast, learn lessons, and iterate on lessons. Be nimble.

Get going and do something . . . now!

NOTES

Chapter 1

1. Jessica Guynn, "Facebook Says It Tops 500 Million Users," *Los Angeles Times*, July 22, 2010, p. B1, col. 4.
2. Sam Flemming, detailed report on Chinese social media visit to www.powerrtm .com.
3. Gilles Bouhoyi, Congolese-born entrepreneur. Social media assessment on African continent.
4. Raj Suvarna, complete treatise on social media in India and complete list of social media companies, brands, and celebrities on Twitter, www.powerrtm.com.
5. Larry Page, quotes from transcript Google Zeitgeist 2009 http://www.zeit-geistminds.com/videos/perspective-from-google-2009.

Chapter 2

1. Malcom Gladwell, *The Tipping Point: How Little Things Can Make a Big Difference*. New York: Little, Brown and Company, 2000.
2. Dr. Nicholas Massaro, lecture, "Social Control," Long Beach State University, Long Beach, California, 1975.

Chapter 3

1. IRL stands for "in real life."

Chapter 4

1. Soonhwa Seok, *International Journal on E-Learning 7*, issue 4 (October 2008).

Chapter 5

1. Polly Pearson recommends the 2008 book by Michael Lee Stallard, *Fired Up or Burned Out*, which has great data on the ROI of engaged employees.
2. A social media marketing service designed specifically for the car dealer.
3. From Wikipedia, "The Roxy," "Lou Adler."
4. Among the largest national cable and satellite TV providers, 2010 American Customer Satisfaction Index, www.theacsi.org First Quarter 2009; http://www.theacsi.org/index.php?option=com_content&task=view&id=194&Itemid=20.
5. Forbes.com 2009 Best Branded Mobile Application, http://www.forbes.com/2009/11/23/best-worst-apps-cmo-network-branded-mobile-apps.html. http://www.forbes.com/2009/11/23/best-worst-apps-cmo-network-best-apps_slide_4.html

Chapter 6

1. Nigel Fenwick with Sharyn Leaver, *Use Social Computing to Boost IT Productivity*, Brandy, June 15, 2010, Worthington, executive summary eExcerpt: http://tinyurl.com/24ou3cm.

Chapter 7

1. Extropianism, also referred to as the philosophy of extropy, is an evolving framework of values and standards for continuously improving the human condition. Extropians believe that advances in science and technology someday will let people live indefinitely and that people who are alive today have a good chance of seeing that happen. An Extropian may wish to contribute to this goal by, for example, doing research and development or volunteering to test new technology.
2. Dawn C. Chmielewski, "Disney Plays up Social Networks," *Los Angeles Times*, July 28, 2010, p. B3, col. 5.
3. http://www.reuters.com/article/idUSTRE66I2WW20100719.
4. http://www.zdnet.com/blog/btl/amazon-kindle-sales-accelerating-demand-tipping-point/36891.

INDEX

ABOUT THE AUTHORS

Beverly Macy is CEO and cofounder of Gravity Summit and managing partner of Y&M Partners. She teaches executive marketing courses for the UCLA Business and Management Extension Program. Macy lives in Beverly Hills, California.

Teri Thompson is a creative director at Gravity Summit and the president of Rocky Peak Enterprises, LLC. She served as media director for U2 singer Bono's [RED]™ campaign with Fortune 500 partners and held marketing and production positions at ABC, CBS, and NBC. Thompson lives in Simi Valley, California.